CHAPTER 3 SETTING UP A WIRELESS HOME NETWORK...**28**

Understanding How Wireless Networks Work.......**29**

Setting Up Your Network's Main PC.....................**30**

Connecting Additional PCs to Your Wireless Network **32**

Adding Your Computer to a HomeGroup.............**35**

Accessing Other Computers in Your HomeGroup...**38**

Accessing Other Computers on Your Network **39**

CHAPTER 4 USING WINDOWS 8.1'S NEW INTERFACE...**40**

Exploring the Start Screen.................................**41**

Using Windows with a Mouse..............................**42**

Using Windows with a Touchscreen Display..........**44**

Displaying the Start Screen.................................**46**

Navigating the Start Screen................................**47**

Using the Charms Bar..**48**

Getting Help in Windows.....................................**50**

CHAPTER 5   **PERSONALIZING WINDOWS** 52

Different Windows Lock Screens 53

Customizing the Lock Screen Picture 54

Displaying a Slide Show on the Lock Screen 56

Adding Apps to the Lock Screen 58

Rearranging Tiles on the Start Screen 60

Making Tiles Larger or Smaller 61

Organizing Tiles into Groups 62

Naming Groups of Tiles 63

Removing Tiles 64

Adding New Tiles to the Start Screen 65

Changing Windows Colors 66

Show Your Desktop Background on the
Start Screen 68

Changing Your Profile Picture 70

Configuring Windows Settings 72

Setting Up Additional Users 74

Switching Between Users 77

CHAPTER 6   **WORKING WITH NEW WINDOWS APPS** 78

Apps on the Start Screen 79

Launching an App 80

Closing an App 81

Viewing All Apps 82

Using the Apps Screen (Instead of the
Start Screen) 83

Searching for Apps on Your Computer 84

Pinning an App to the Start Screen 85

Switching Between Open Apps 86

Snapping Two Apps Side by Side 88

Examining Windows' Built-In Apps 90

Finding New Apps in the Windows Store............. 94

CHAPTER 7 **USING THE WINDOWS DESKTOP AND TRADITIONAL APPS**..**96**

Exploring the Windows Desktop 97

Displaying the Traditional Desktop....................... 98

Returning to the Start Screen 99

Pinning Programs to the Taskbar 100

Changing the Desktop Background 101

Changing Desktop Colors.................................... 102

Scrolling a Window 103

Maximizing, Minimizing, and Closing a Window...104

Snapping a Window 105

Using Menus 106

Using Toolbars and Ribbons................................ 107

CHAPTER 8 **USING MICROSOFT WORD**....................... **108**

Comparing Desktop and Web Versions of Word..109

Launching the Word Web App............................. 110

Launching the Word Desktop App....................... 112

Navigating the Word Web App 113

Entering Text 114

Cutting/Copying and Pasting Text....................... 115

Formatting Text.. 116

Formatting Paragraphs.. 117

Saving Your Work 118

Printing a Document... 119

CHAPTER 9   **WORKING WITH FILES AND FOLDERS..... 120**

File Explorer 121

Navigating Folders.................................. 122

Navigating with the Navigation Pane 123

Changing the Way Files Are Displayed 124

Sorting Files and Folders 125

Creating a New Folder.............................. 126

Renaming a File or Folder 127

Copying a File or Folder 128

Moving a File or Folder 129

Searching for a File.................................. 130

Deleting a File or Folder 131

Restoring Deleted Files 132

Emptying the Recycle Bin 133

Compressing a File 134

Extracting Files from a Compressed Folder 135

Working with Files on SkyDrive 136

CHAPTER 10   **USING THE INTERNET................................. 138**

Comparing the Modern and Desktop
Versions of IE.................................... 139

Connecting to an Internet WiFi Hotspot............. 140

Using Internet Explorer (Modern Version).......... 142

Opening Multiple Pages in Tabs.................... 144

Switching Between Tabs 145

Saving Favorite Pages 146

Returning to a Favorite Page 147

Using Internet Explorer (Desktop Version) 148

Opening Multiple Pages in Tabs 150

Switching Between Tabs 151

Saving Favorite Pages 152

Returning to a Favorite Page 153

Searching the Web with Google 154

Searching the Web with Bing 155

Smart Searching from Windows 156

Shopping Online 158

CHAPTER 11   COMMUNICATING WITH EMAIL 160

Windows Mail App 161

Viewing Your Inbox and Reading Messages 162

Moving a Message to Another Folder 164

Replying to an Email Message 165

Composing a New Email Message 166

Adding Other Accounts to the Mail App 168

Managing Your Contacts from the People App ... 170

Using the Yahoo! Mail App 172

CHAPTER 12 SHARING WITH FACEBOOK AND OTHER SOCIAL NETWORKS 176

Comparing Facebook, Pinterest, and Twitter 177

Finding Facebook Friends 178

Reading the News Feed 180

Posting a Status Update 182

Viewing a Friend's Timeline 184

Personalizing Your Timeline Page 185

Viewing a Friend's Photos 186

Sharing Your Photos on Facebook 188

Sharing Interesting Images with Pinterest 190

Finding People to Follow on Pinterest 191

Finding and Repinning Interesting Pins 192

Pinning from a Web Page 194

Tweeting with Twitter 196

Following Other Twitter Users 197

Viewing All Your Social Activity from the Windows People App 198

Posting New Updates from the People App 199

CHAPTER 13 WATCHING TV AND MOVIES ONLINE 200

Playing a Video with the Xbox Video App 201

Watching Movies on Netflix 202

Watching TV Shows on Hulu Plus 206

Watching Videos on YouTube 210

Purchasing and Downloading Movies with the Xbox Video App 212

Viewing Videos with the Xbox Video App 214

CHAPTER 14 PLAYING DIGITAL MUSIC 216

Exploring the Xbox Music App 217

Playing Your Own Music in Windows 218

Purchasing and Downloading New Music 220

Streaming Music Online 222

Downloading Music from the iTunes Store 224

Playing a CD with iTunes 226

Ripping a CD to Your Hard Disk with iTunes 227

Playing Digital Music with iTunes 228

Connecting an iPod to Your PC 229

CHAPTER 15 VIEWING DIGITAL PHOTOS 230

Navigating the Photos App 231

Transferring Pictures from a Memory Card 232

Viewing Your Photos in Windows 234

Editing Your Photos in Windows 236

CHAPTER 16 PROTECTING YOUR COMPUTER 242

PC Settings 243

Using the Windows Action Center 244

Defending Against Malware with Windows
Defender 245

Deleting Unnecessary Files 246

Deleting Unused Programs 247

Backing Up Your Files with File History 248

Restoring Your Computer After a Crash 250

GLOSSARY 252

INDEX 258

EASY COMPUTER BASICS, WINDOWS® 8.1 EDITION

ISBN-13: 978-0-7897-5232-1
ISBN-10: 0-7897-5232-8

Library of Congress Control Number: 2013948171

Printed in the United States of America

First Printing: October 2013

TRADEMARKS

WARNING AND DISCLAIMER

BULK SALES

Que Publishing offers excellent discounts on this book when ordered in quantity for bulk purchases or special sales. For more information, please contact

U.S. Corporate and Government Sales
1-800-382-3419
corpsales@pearsontechgroup.com

For sales outside the United States, please contact

International Sales
international@pearsoned.com

Editor-in-Chief
Greg Wiegand

Acquisitions Editor
Michelle Newcomb

Development Editor
Keith Cline

Managing Editor
Sandra Schroeder

Senior Project Editor
Tonya Simpson

Indexer
Erika Millen

Proofreader
Dan Knott

Technical Editor
Vince Averello

Editorial Assistant
Cindy Teeters

Interior Designer
Anne Jones

Cover Designer
Alan Clements

Compositor
Bronkella Publishing

ABOUT THE AUTHOR

Michael Miller is a successful and prolific author with a reputation for practical advice, technical accuracy, and an unerring empathy for the needs of his readers.

Mr. Miller has written more than 100 best-selling books over the past two decades. His books for Que include *Absolute Beginner's Guide to Computer Basics*, *Easy Facebook*, *Facebook for Grown-Ups*, *My Facebook for Seniors*, *My Windows 8 Computer for Seniors*, and *My Pinterest*.

He is known for his casual, easy-to-read writing style and his practical, real-world advice—as well as his ability to explain a variety of complex topics to an everyday audience.

You can email Mr. Miller directly at easycomputer@molehillgroup.com. His website is located at www.molehillgroup.com.

DEDICATION

*To Sherry—life together **is** easier.*

ACKNOWLEDGMENTS

Thanks to the usual suspects at Que, including but not limited to Greg Wiegand, Michelle Newcomb, Keith Cline, Todd Brakke, and technical editor Vince Averello.

WE WANT TO HEAR FROM YOU!

As the reader of this book, *you* are our most important critic and commentator. We value your opinion and want to know what we're doing right, what we could do better, what areas you'd like to see us publish in, and any other words of wisdom you're willing to pass our way.

We welcome your comments. You can email or write to let us know what you did or didn't like about this book—as well as what we can do to make our books better.

Please note that we cannot help you with technical problems related to the topic of this book.

When you write, please be sure to include this book's title and author as well as your name and email address. We will carefully review your comments and share them with the author and editors who worked on the book.

Email: feedback@quepublishing.com

Mail: Que Publishing
         ATTN: Reader Feedback
         800 East 96th Street
         Indianapolis, IN 46240 USA

READER SERVICES

Visit our website and register this book at quepublishing.com/register for convenient access to any updates, downloads, or errata that might be available for this book.

IT'S AS EASY AS 1-2-3

Each part of this book is made up of a series of short, instructional lessons, designed to help you understand basic information.

1 Each step is fully illustrated to show you how it looks on screen.

2 Each task includes a series of quick, easy steps designed to guide you through the procedure.

3 Items that you select or click in menus, dialog boxes, tabs, and windows are shown in bold.

Tips, notes, and cautions give you a heads-up for any extra information you may need while working through the task.

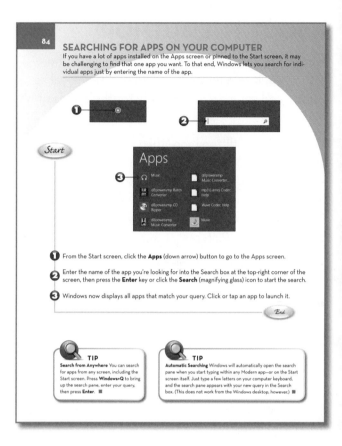

SEARCHING FOR APPS ON YOUR COMPUTER

If you have a lot of apps installed on the Apps screen or pinned to the Start screen, it may be challenging to find that one app you want. To that end, Windows lets you search for individual apps just by entering the name of the app.

1 From the Start screen, click the **Apps** (down arrow) button to go to the Apps screen.

2 Enter the name of the app you're looking for into the Search box at the top-right corner of the screen, then press the **Enter** key or click the **Search** (magnifying glass) icon to start the search.

3 Windows now displays all apps that match your query. Click or tap an app to launch it.

TIP

Search from Anywhere You can search for apps from any screen, including the Start screen. Press **Windows+Q** to bring up the search pane, enter your query, then press **Enter**. ■

TIP

Automatic Searching Windows will automatically open the search pane when you start typing within any Modern app—or on the Start screen itself. Just type a few letters on your computer keyboard, and the search pane appears with your new query in the Search box. (This does not work from the Windows desktop, however.) ■

INTRODUCTION

Computers don't have to be scary or difficult. Computers can be *easy*—if you know what to do.

That's where this book comes in. *Easy Computer Basics, Windows 8.1 Edition* is an illustrated, step-by-step guide to setting up and using your new computer. You'll learn how computers work, how to connect all the pieces and parts, and how to start using them. All you have to do is look at the pictures and follow the instructions. Pretty easy.

After you learn the basics, I show you how to do lots of useful stuff with your new PC. You learn how to use Microsoft Windows to copy and delete files; use Windows' Mail app to send and receive email messages; use Microsoft Word to write letters and memos; use Internet Explorer to search for information on the Internet; and use Facebook, Pinterest, and Twitter to keep up with what your friends are doing. We even cover some fun stuff, including listening to music, viewing digital photographs, and watching movies and TV shows online.

If you're worried about how to keep your PC up and running, we cover some basic system maintenance, too. And, just to be safe, I also show you how to protect your computer when you're online. It's not hard to do.

To help you find the information you need, I've organized *Easy Computer Basics, Windows 8.1 Edition* into 16 chapters.

Chapter 1, "Understanding Personal Computers," discusses all the different types of personal computers out there and describes the pieces and parts of a typical computer system. Read this part to find out all about desktops, all-in-ones, notebooks, and tablets—and the things like hard drives, keyboards, mice, and printers that make them tick.

Chapter 2, "Setting Up Your PC," shows you how to connect all the pieces and parts of a typical PC and get your new computer system up and running.

Chapter 3, "Setting Up a Wireless Home Network," helps you connect all the computers in your house to a wireless network and share a broadband Internet connection.

Chapter 4, "Using Windows 8.1's New Interface," introduces the backbone of your entire system—the Microsoft Windows 8.1 operating system—including how it works and how to use it.

Chapter 5, "Personalizing Windows," shows you how to customize Windows 8.1's lock screen, how to change colors and backgrounds, how to add and delete tiles from the Start screen, and how to add new users to your system.

Chapter 6, "Working with New Windows Apps," walks you through everything you need to know to launch, use, and switch between useful Windows 8.1 apps—and how to find new apps in the Windows Store.

Chapter 7, "Using the Windows Desktop and Traditional Apps," shows you how to use your existing software programs on the Windows desktop—and how to customize the desktop background and colors.

Chapter 8, "Using Microsoft Word," shows you how to use both the desktop and online versions of Microsoft's popular word processor to create letters and other documents.

Chapter 9, "Working with Files and Folders," shows you how to use File Explorer and Microsoft's Sky-Drive to manage all the computer files you create—by moving, copying, renaming, and deleting them.

Chapter 10, "Using the Internet," is all about how to get online and what to do when you're there—including how to use both the desktop and full-screen versions of Internet Explorer to surf the Web, search for information, and shop for items online.

Chapter 11, "Communicating with Email," is all about using email to communicate with friends, family, and co-workers. The focus is on Windows 8.1's Mail app, as well as the Yahoo! Mail app.

Chapter 12, "Sharing with Facebook and Other Social Networks," introduces you to the fascinating world of social networking—and shows you how to share with friends on Facebook, Pinterest, and Twitter.

Chapter 13, "Watching TV and Movies Online," shows you how to use your computer to watch television programming, movies, and other videos from Netflix, Hulu, and YouTube—and with the new Windows Xbox Video app.

Chapter 14, "Playing Digital Music," shows you how to use the Xbox Music app to download and listen to digital music, as well as use iTunes to manage music on your Apple iPod, iPhone, or iPad.

Chapter 15, "Viewing Digital Photos," helps you connect a digital camera to your PC, transfer your photos to your PC, touch up problem pictures, and view photos on your computer screen.

Chapter 16, "Protecting Your Computer," is all about defending against online menaces, keeping your PC running smoothly, backing up your important files, and recovering from serious crashes.

And that's not all. At the back of the book you'll find a glossary of common computer terms—so you can understand what all the techie types are talking about!

(By the way, if something looks a little different on your computer screen than it does in your book, don't dismay. Microsoft is constantly doing little updates and fixes to Windows, so it's possible the looks of some things might have changed a bit between my writing this book and you reading. Nothing to worry about.)

So, is using a computer really this easy? You bet—just follow the simple step-by-step instructions, and you'll be computing like a pro!

UNDERSTANDING PERSONAL COMPUTERS

Chances are you're reading this book because you have a new computer. At this point, you might not be totally sure what it is you've gotten yourself into. Just what is this mess of boxes and cables—how does it all go together, and how does it work?

We start by looking at the physical components of your system—the stuff we call computer *hardware*. A lot of different pieces and parts make up a typical computer system, and the pieces and parts differ depending on the type of computer you have.

You see, no two computer systems are identical. That's because there are several different types of configurations (desktops, notebooks, and such) and because you can always add new components to your system—or disconnect other pieces you don't have any use for.

DIFFERENT TYPES OF COMPUTERS

Traditional desktop PC

All-in-one desktop PC

Notebook PC

Tablet PC

GETTING TO KNOW DESKTOP PCS

A traditional desktop computer is one with a monitor designed to sit on your desktop, along with a separate keyboard and mouse and freestanding stereo speakers. The central component of a traditional desktop system is the *system unit*, which contains the PC's central processing unit (CPU), memory, and motherboard. All the external components connect directly to the system unit.

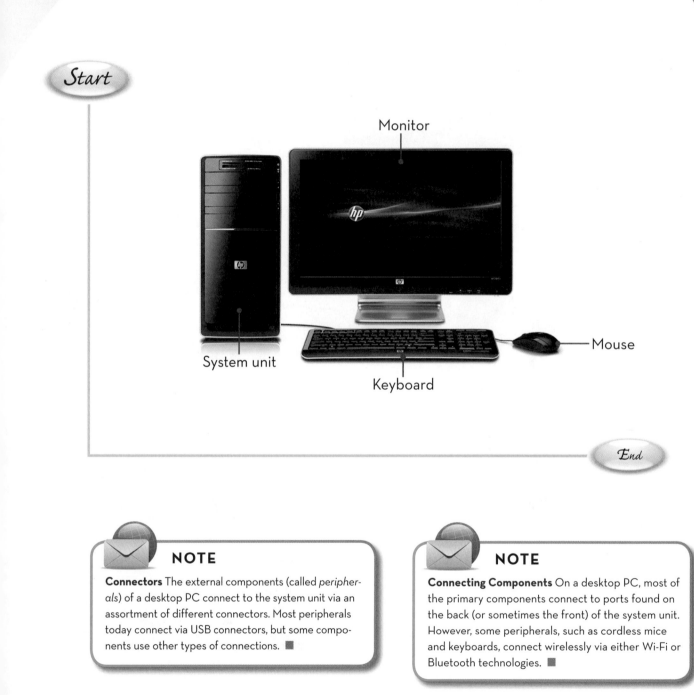

Start

Monitor

Mouse

System unit

Keyboard

End

NOTE

Connectors The external components (called *peripherals*) of a desktop PC connect to the system unit via an assortment of different connectors. Most peripherals today connect via USB connectors, but some components use other types of connections. ■

NOTE

Connecting Components On a desktop PC, most of the primary components connect to ports found on the back (or sometimes the front) of the system unit. However, some peripherals, such as cordless mice and keyboards, connect wirelessly via either Wi-Fi or Bluetooth technologies. ■

GETTING TO KNOW ALL-IN-ONE PCS

An all-in-one computer is a desktop model where the system unit is built in to the monitor. The monitor/system unit also includes built-in speakers, as well as all the ports you need to connect external peripherals. Many people like the easier setup and smaller space requirements of an all-in-one system.

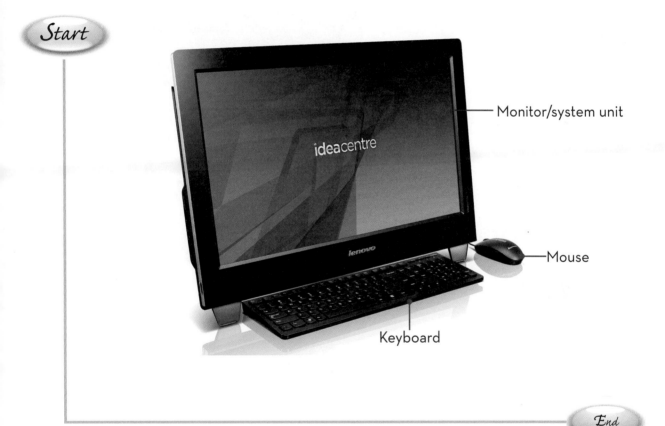

Start

Monitor/system unit

ideacentre

lenovo

Mouse

Keyboard

End

NOTE

Touchscreens Some all-in-one PCs feature touchscreen monitors; you can control them by tapping and swiping the monitor screen with your fingers. ▪

CAUTION

All-in-One Drawbacks The chief drawbacks to all-in-one systems are the price (usually a bit more than traditional desktop PCs) and the fact that if one internal component goes bad, the whole system is out of commission. It's a lot easier to replace a single component than an entire system! ▪

GETTING TO KNOW NOTEBOOK PCS

Most new computers today are notebook models—sometimes called *laptops*. A notebook PC differs from a desktop PC in that all the pieces and parts are combined into a single unit that you can take with you almost anywhere. The built-in battery provides power when you're not near a wall outlet. And some notebook PCs include touchscreen displays, which let you operate Windows with a swipe of your fingertips.

Start

Display ——

Touchpad ——

—— Keyboard

End

NOTE

Different Types of Notebooks There are four different types of notebook computers. *Traditional notebooks* have screens in the 14-inch to 16-inch range, 320GB or larger hard drives, and built-in CD/DVD drives. *Desktop replacement notebooks* have larger 17-inch screens, more powerful processors, but shorter battery life. *Netbooks* have small screens in the 10-inch to 12-inch range, smaller hard drives, no CD/DVD drive, but much longer battery life. *Ultrabooks* have 12-inch to 14-inch screens, are smaller and thinner than traditional notebooks, and use fast solid-state memory rather than hard drives. ■

TIP

External Peripherals Even though a notebook PC has the keyboard, mouse, and monitor built in, you can still connect external keyboards, mice, and monitors to the unit. This is convenient if you want to use a bigger keyboard or monitor or a real mouse (instead of the notebook's trackpad). ■

GETTING TO KNOW TABLET PCS

A tablet PC is a self-contained computer you can hold in one hand. Think of a tablet as the real-world equivalent of one of those communication pads you see on *Star Trek*; it doesn't have a separate keyboard; instead, you operate it by tapping and swiping the screen with your fingers. The Windows 8.1 operating system is optimized for just this sort of touch operation.

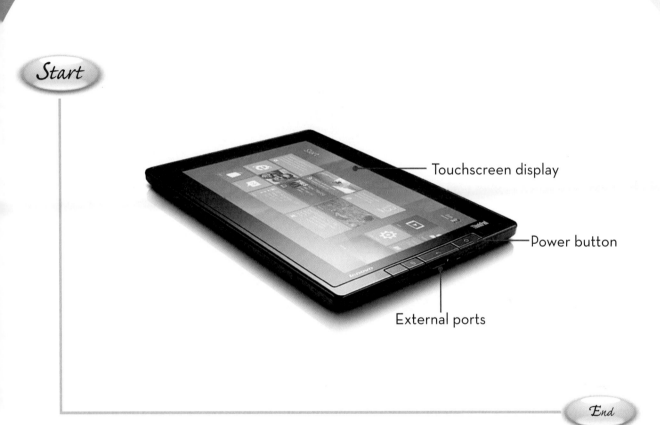

Start

Touchscreen display

Power button

External ports

End

NOTE

Popular Tablets The most popular tablet PC today is the Apple iPad—which doesn't run Windows. (It runs Apple's own portable operating system, dubbed iOS.) There are numerous Windows-based tablets, however, including Microsoft's own Surface and Surface RT. ■

NOTE

Convertible PCs Several manufacturers offer *convertible* or *hybrid* PCs. A convertible PC is a blend of the ultrabook and tablet form factors; think of a convertible PC as an ultrabook that converts into a tablet or as a tablet that converts into an ultrabook. For example, the Asus Vivo Tab looks like an ultrabook but features a screen that detaches from the keyboard—which then functions as a freestanding touchscreen tablet. ■

CONNECTORS

Every external component you plug into your computer has its own connector, and not all connectors are the same. This results in an assortment of jacks—called *ports* in the computer world. The USB port is probably the most common, used to connect all sorts of external peripherals, including printers, keyboards, mice, and disk drives.

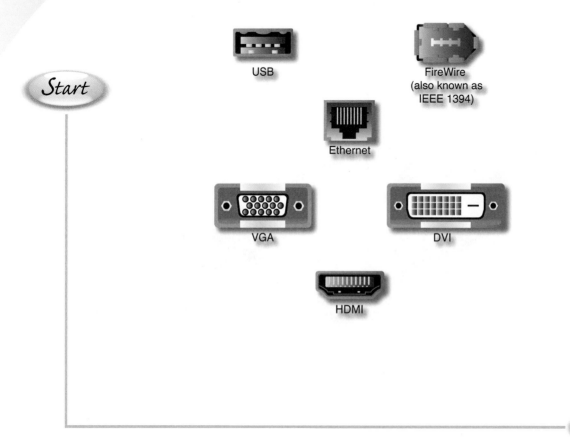

Start

USB

FireWire
(also known as
IEEE 1394)

Ethernet

VGA

DVI

HDMI

End

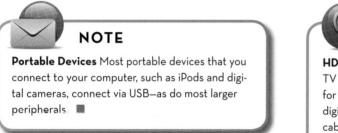

NOTE

Portable Devices Most portable devices that you connect to your computer, such as iPods and digital cameras, connect via USB—as do most larger peripherals. ■

TIP

HDMI If you want to connect your computer to your TV to watch Internet videos on the TV screen, look for a computer with an HDMI port. HDMI carries digital audio and high-definition video in a single cable. Most of today's flat-screen TVs have multiple HDMI inputs. ■

HARD DISK DRIVES: LONG-TERM STORAGE

The hard disk drive inside your computer stores all your important data—up to 2 terabytes (TB) or more, depending on your computer. A hard disk consists of metallic platters that store data magnetically. Special read/write heads realign magnetic particles on the platters, much like a recording head records data onto magnetic recording tape.

Start

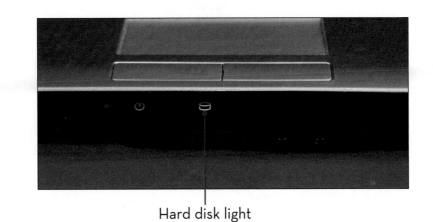

Hard disk light

End

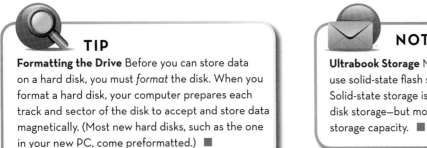

TIP

Formatting the Drive Before you can store data on a hard disk, you must *format* the disk. When you format a hard disk, your computer prepares each track and sector of the disk to accept and store data magnetically. (Most new hard disks, such as the one in your new PC, come preformatted.) ■

NOTE

Ultrabook Storage Most ultrabook and tablet PCs use solid-state flash storage rather than hard disks. Solid-state storage is lighter and faster than hard disk storage—but more expensive and with a smaller storage capacity. ■

KEYBOARDS

A computer keyboard looks and functions just like a typewriter keyboard, except that computer keyboards have a few more keys (for navigation and special program functions). When you press a key on your keyboard, it sends an electronic signal to your system unit that tells your machine what you want it to do.

Function keys

Alpha/
numeric keys

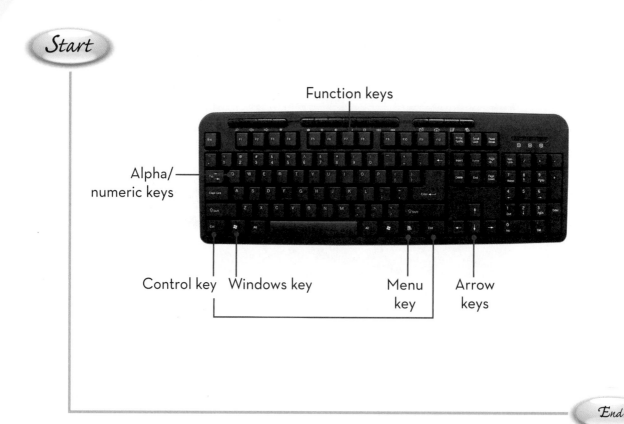

Control key   Windows key

Menu
key

Arrow
keys

NOTE

Windows Key Many essential operations are triggered by use of the special Windows key on the computer keyboard. (For example, you open the Windows Start screen by pressing the **Windows** key.) This key is indicated by the Windows logo. ■

TIP

Wireless Keyboards If you want to cut the cord, consider a wireless keyboard or mouse. These wireless devices operate via radio frequency signals and let you work several feet away from your computer, with no cables necessary. ■

TOUCHPADS

On a desktop PC, you control your computer's onscreen pointer (called a *cursor*) with an external device called a *mouse*. On a notebook PC, you use a small *touchpad* instead. Move your finger around the touchpad to move the cursor, and then click the left and right buttons below the touchpad to initiate actions in your program.

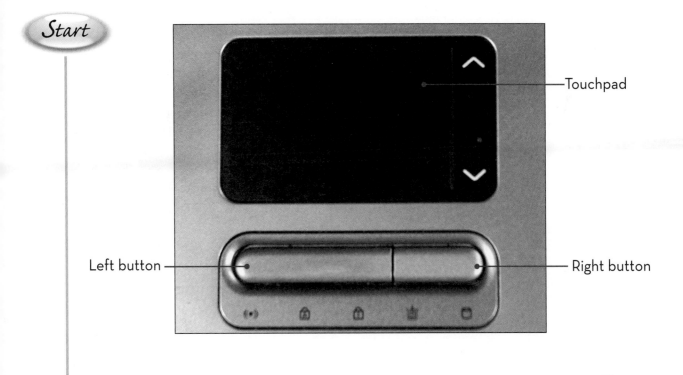

Touchpad

Left button

Right button

End

TIP

External Mice If you'd rather use a mouse than a touchpad, you can connect any external mouse to your notebook PC via the USB port. Some manufacturers sell so-called notebook mice that are smaller and more portable than normal models. ■

NOTE

Mouse Options Most external mice offer more control options than built-in touchpads. For example, some mice include a *scrollwheel* you can use to quickly scroll through a web page or word processing document. ■

MEMORY CARD READERS

Many computers today include a set of memory card readers, usually grouped on the front or side of the unit. Memory cards store photos and movies recorded on digital cameras and camcorders. To read the contents of a memory card, simply insert the card into the proper slot of the memory card reader.

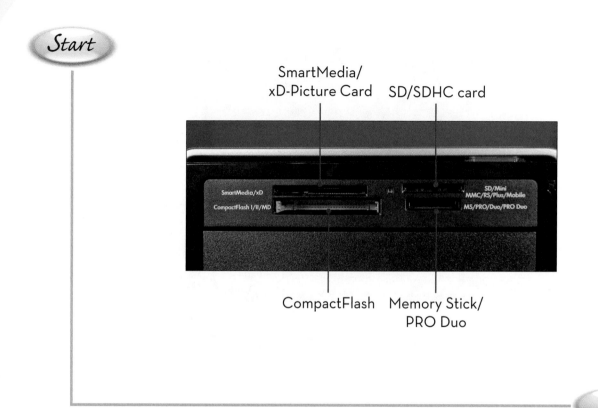

Start

SmartMedia/
xD-Picture Card   SD/SDHC card

CompactFlash   Memory Stick/
PRO Duo

End

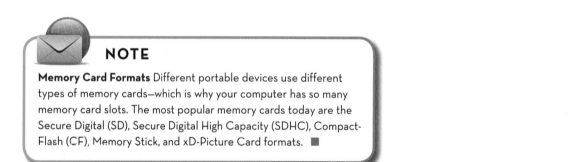

NOTE

Memory Card Formats Different portable devices use different types of memory cards—which is why your computer has so many memory card slots. The most popular memory cards today are the Secure Digital (SD), Secure Digital High Capacity (SDHC), Compact-Flash (CF), Memory Stick, and xD-Picture Card formats. ■

CD AND DVD DRIVES

Computer or data CDs, DVDs, and Blu-ray discs look just like the compact discs and movies you play on your home audio/video system. Data is encoded in microscopic pits below the disc's surface and is read from the disc via a drive that uses a consumer-grade laser. The laser beam follows the tracks of the disc and reads the pits, translating the data into a form your computer can understand.

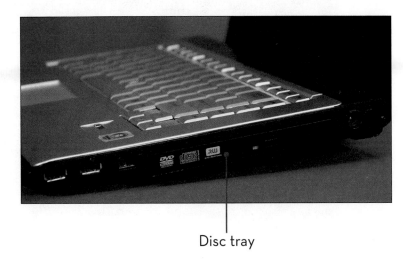

Disc tray

End

NOTE

CD, DVD, and Blu-ray Many new PCs come with combination CD/DVD drives that can read and write both CDs and DVDs. Some models include Blu-ray drives for high-definition video. But most ultrabooks and tablets don't come with a CD/DVD drive, helping to decrease weight and increase battery life. ■

NOTE

Music and Movies A computer CD drive can play back both data and commercial music CDs. A computer DVD drive can play back both data and commercial movie DVDs. ■

COMPUTER SCREENS

Your computer electronically transmits words and pictures to the computer screen built in to your notebook or to a separate video monitor on a desktop system. These images are created by a *video card* or chip installed inside the computer. Settings in Windows tell the video card or chip how to display the images you see on the screen.

Start

LCD screen —

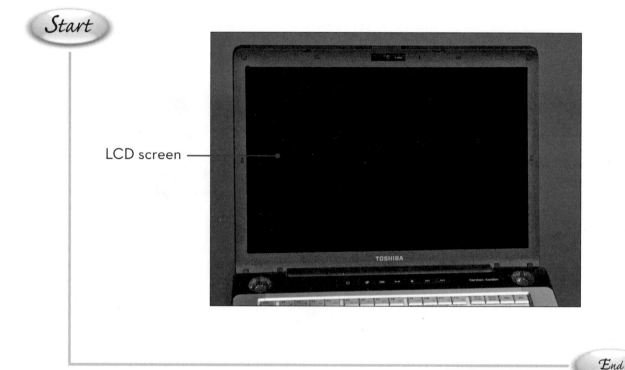

End

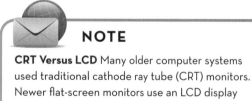

NOTE

CRT Versus LCD Many older computer systems used traditional cathode ray tube (CRT) monitors. Newer flat-screen monitors use an LCD display instead, which takes up less desk space. ■

NOTE

Touchscreen Displays Tablet PCs, along with some all-in-one and hybrid models, feature touchscreen displays. These displays function just like traditional displays but are also touch sensitive, which means that you can control your system by tapping and swiping the screen with your fingers. ■

PRINTERS

To create a hard copy of your work, you must add a printer to your system. The two most common types are *laser* printers and *inkjet* printers. Laser printers work much like copy machines, applying toner (powdered ink) to paper by using a small laser. Inkjet printers shoot jets of ink onto the paper's surface to create the printed image.

Start

Operating buttons

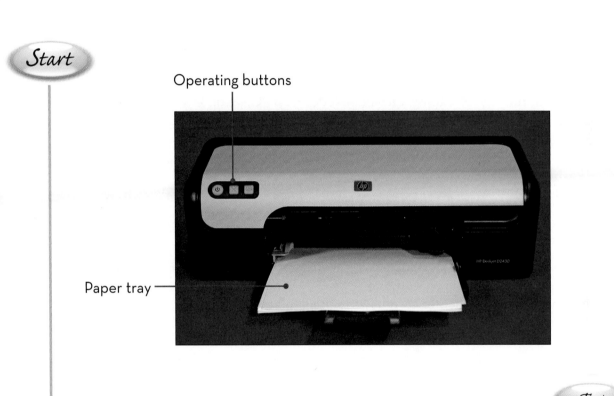

Paper tray

End

TIP

Black and White Versus Color Black-and-white printers are faster than color printers and better if you're printing memos, letters, and other single-color documents. Color printers are essential if you want to print pictures taken with a digital camera. ■

NOTE

Multifunction Printers So-called multifunction printers offer copy, scan, and fax functionality, in addition to traditional printing. ■

SETTING UP YOUR PC

When you first get a new PC, you have to get everything set up, connected, and ready to run. If you're using a traditional desktop PC, setup involves plugging in all the external devices—your monitor, speakers, keyboard, and such. If you're using an all-in-one desktop, the task is a bit easier because the system unit, monitor, and speakers are all in a single unit; all you have to connect are the keyboard and mouse.

Setup is even easier if you have a notebook PC, as all the major components are built in to the computer itself. Same thing with a tablet; there's really nothing to connect.

If you're connecting a desktop PC, or even a notebook with external peripherals, start by positioning it so that you easily can access all the connections on the unit. You'll need to carefully run the cables from each of the external peripherals to the main unit, without stretching the cables or pulling anything out of place. And remember, when you plug in a cable, make sure that it's *firmly* connected—both to the computer and to the specific piece of hardware. Loose cables can cause all sorts of weird problems, so be sure they're plugged in really well.

THE WINDOWS LOCK SCREEN

Time —

Connectivity status —

Power status

Date

Real-time data

SETTING UP A TRADITIONAL DESKTOP PC

If you have a traditional desktop computer, you need to connect all the pieces and parts to your computer's system unit before powering it on. After connecting all your peripherals, you can then connect your system unit to a power source. Just ensure that the power source is turned off before you connect!

Start

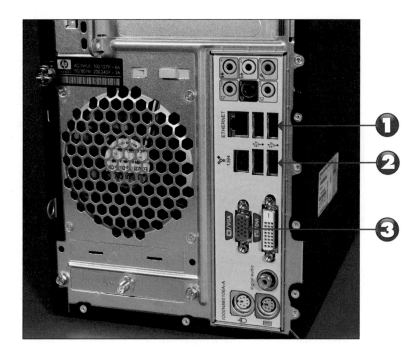

1 Connect the mouse cable to a USB port on your system unit.

2 Connect the keyboard cable to a USB port on your system unit.

3 Connect the blue monitor cable to the blue monitor port on your system unit; make sure the other end is connected to your video monitor.

Continued

NOTE

Mice and Keyboards Most newer mice and keyboards connect via USB. Some older models, however, connect to dedicated mouse and keyboard ports on your system unit. You should use whatever connection is appropriate. ■

TIP

Digital Connections Some newer computer monitors use a Digital Video Interface (DVI) or HDMI connection instead of the older Video Graphics Array (VGA) type of connection. If you have a choice, a DVI or HDMI connection delivers a crisper picture than the older analog connection. HDMI is preferred if you're connecting to a flat-screen TV or home theater system because it transmits both video and audio. ■

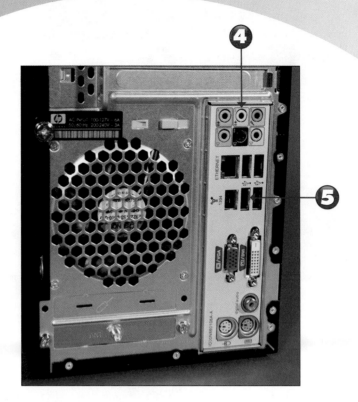

④ Connect the green phono cable from your main external speaker to the audio out or sound out connector on your system unit; connect the other end of the cable to the speaker.

⑤ Connect one end of your printer's USB cable to a USB port on the back of your system unit; connect the other end of the cable to your printer.

Continued

TIP

Your Connection Might Vary Not all speaker systems connect the same way. For example, some systems run the main cable to one speaker (such as the subwoofer) and then connect that speaker to the other speakers in the systems. Other systems connect via USB. Make sure to read the manufacturer's instructions before you connect your speaker system. ■

NOTE

Connect by Color Most PC manufacturers color-code the cables and connectors to make the connection even easier. Just plug the blue cable into the blue connector and so on. ■

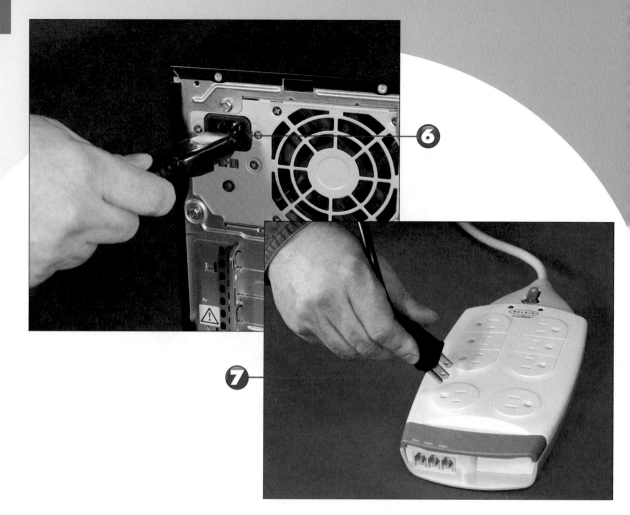

6 Connect one end of your computer's power cable to the power connector on the back of your system unit; connect the other end of the power cable to a power source.

7 Connect your printer, speakers, and other powered external peripherals to an appropriate power source.

End

TIP

Use a Surge Suppressor For extra protection, connect the power cable on your system unit to a surge suppressor rather than directly into an electrical outlet. This protects your PC from power-line surges that can damage its delicate internal parts. ■

CAUTION

Power Surges A power surge, whether from a lightning strike or an issue with your electric company, can do significant damage to a computer system. Too much power, even for just a second, can destroy your computer's microprocessor, memory chips, and other delicate components. In many instances, recovery from a power surge is either costly or impossible. ■

SETTING UP A NOTEBOOK PC

Setting up a notebook PC is much simpler than setting up a desktop model. That's because almost everything is built in to the notebook—except external peripherals, such as a printer. Just connect the printer, plug your notebook into a power outlet, and you're ready to go.

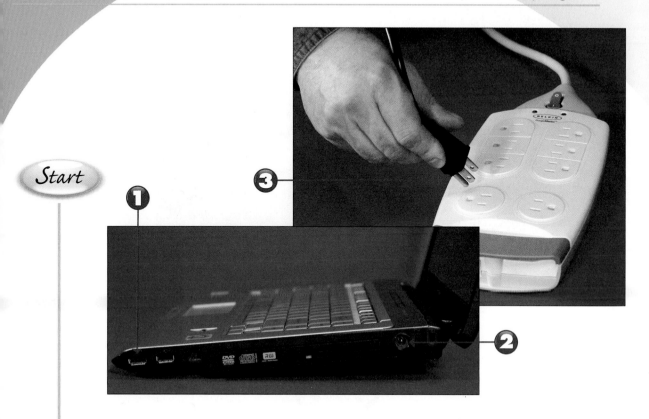

Start

End

1. Connect one end of your printer's USB cable to a USB port on your notebook; connect the other end of the cable to your printer.

2. Connect one end of your computer's power cable to the power connector on the side or back of your notebook; connect the other end of the power cable to a power source.

3. Connect your printer, speakers, and other powered external peripherals to an appropriate power source.

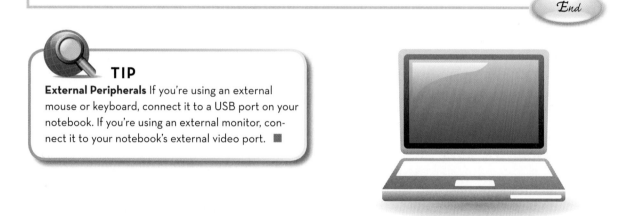

TIP

External Peripherals If you're using an external mouse or keyboard, connect it to a USB port on your notebook. If you're using an external monitor, connect it to your notebook's external video port. ■

SETTING UP AN ALL-IN-ONE DESKTOP PC

In an all-in-one desktop PC, the speakers and system unit are built in to the monitor, so you have fewer things to connect—just the mouse, keyboard, and any external peripherals, such as a printer. This makes for a much quicker and easier setup.

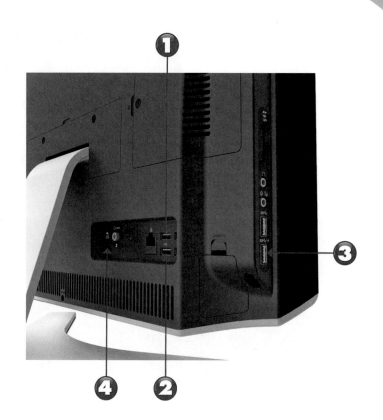

Start

1 Connect the mouse cable to a USB port on the back of the monitor.

2 Connect the keyboard cable to a USB port on the back of the monitor.

3 Connect one end of your printer's USB cable to a USB port on the back or side of your system unit; connect the other end of the cable to your printer.

4 Connect one end of your computer's power cable to the power connector on the back of your system unit.

Continued

TIP

Back and Side Connections Most all-in-one PCs have USB ports on both the back and side of the unit. It doesn't matter which of these ports you use, although connecting to the back ports is usually a little cleaner looking—it does a better job of hiding the cables from view. ■

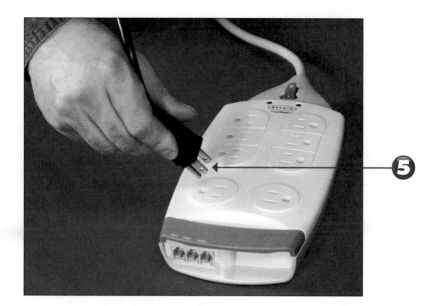

5 Connect the other end of the power cable to a power source, and then connect your printer and other powered external peripherals to the same power source.

End

NOTE

External Speakers Some all-in-one PCs feature a speaker output you can use to add additional external speakers or perhaps a subwoofer (for better-sounding bass). ■

POWERING ON

Now that you have everything connected, sit back and rest for a minute. Next up is the big step: turning it all on!

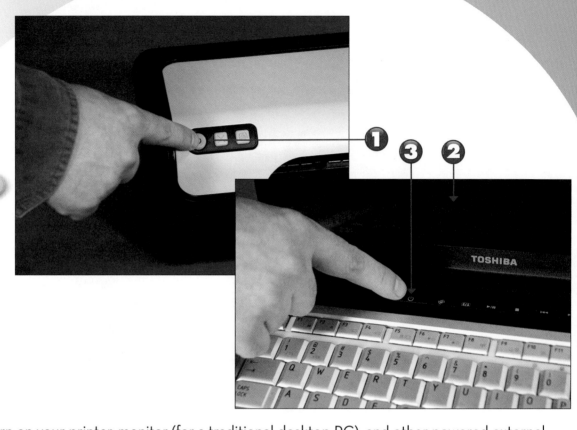

Start

1 Turn on your printer, monitor (for a traditional desktop PC), and other powered external peripherals.

2 If you're using a notebook PC, open the notebook's case so that you can see the screen and access the keyboard.

3 Press the power or "on" button on your computer.

End

NOTE

Booting Up Technical types call the procedure of starting up a computer *booting* or *booting up* the system. Restarting a system (turning it off and then back on) is called *rebooting*. ■

CAUTION

Go in Order Your computer is the *last* thing you turn on in your system. That's because when it powers on it has to sense all the other components—which it can do only if the other components are plugged in and turned on. ■

LOGGING ON TO WINDOWS

Windows launches automatically as your computer starts up. After you get past the Windows lock screen, you're taken directly to the Windows Start screen, and your system is ready to run.

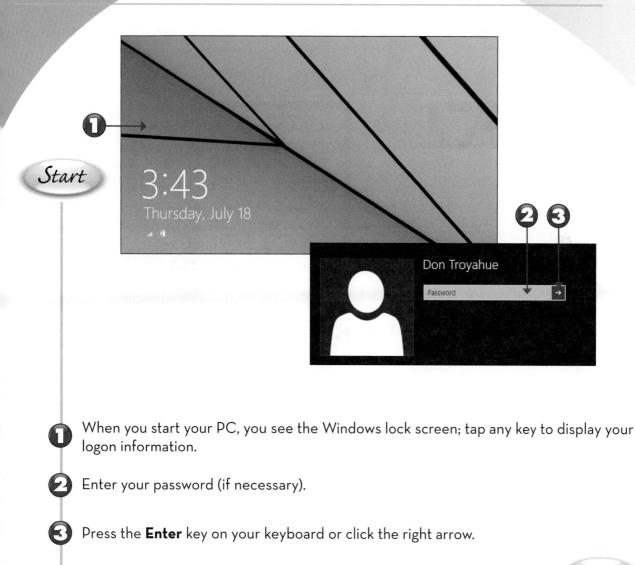

Start

3:43
Thursday, July 18

Don Troyahue

Password

End

① When you start your PC, you see the Windows lock screen; tap any key to display your logon information.

② Enter your password (if necessary).

③ Press the **Enter** key on your keyboard or click the right arrow.

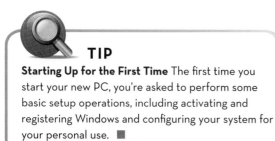

TIP
Starting Up for the First Time The first time you start your new PC, you're asked to perform some basic setup operations, including activating and registering Windows and configuring your system for your personal use. ■

NOTE
Lock Screen Information The Windows lock screen displays a photographic background with some useful information on top—including the date and time, power status, and WiFi (connectivity) status. ■

SHUTTING DOWN

When you want to turn off your computer, you do it through Windows. In fact, you don't want to turn off your computer any other way. You *always* want to turn things off through the official Windows procedure.

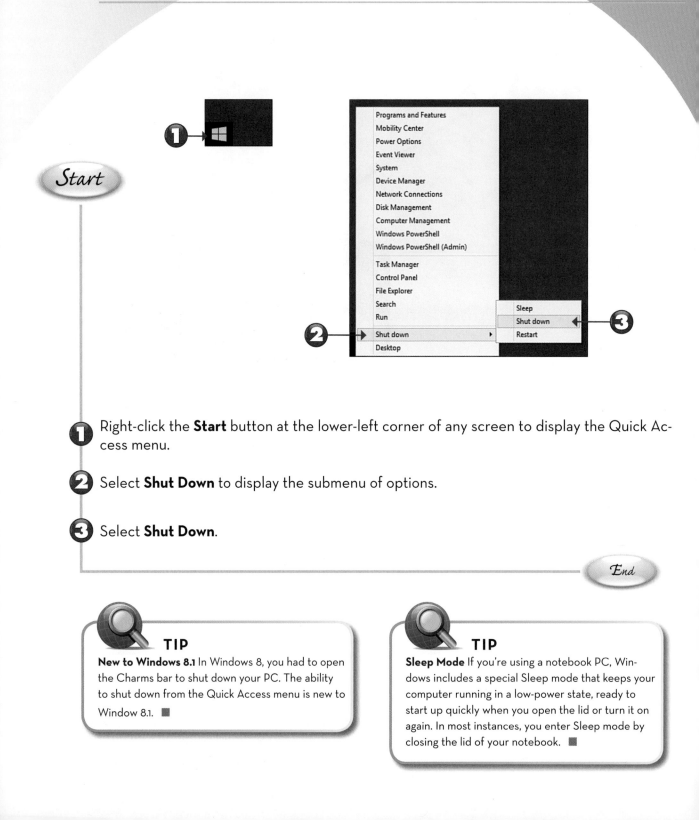

1 Right-click the **Start** button at the lower-left corner of any screen to display the Quick Access menu.

2 Select **Shut Down** to display the submenu of options.

3 Select **Shut Down**.

TIP

New to Windows 8.1 In Windows 8, you had to open the Charms bar to shut down your PC. The ability to shut down from the Quick Access menu is new to Window 8.1. ■

TIP

Sleep Mode If you're using a notebook PC, Windows includes a special Sleep mode that keeps your computer running in a low-power state, ready to start up quickly when you open the lid or turn it on again. In most instances, you enter Sleep mode by closing the lid of your notebook. ■

ADDING NEW DEVICES TO YOUR SYSTEM

At some point in the future, you might want to expand your system—by adding a second printer, a scanner, a webcam, or something equally new and exciting. Most of these peripherals are external and connect to your PC using a USB cable. When you're connecting a USB device, not only do you not have to open your PC's case, but you also don't even have to turn off your system when you add the new device.

Start

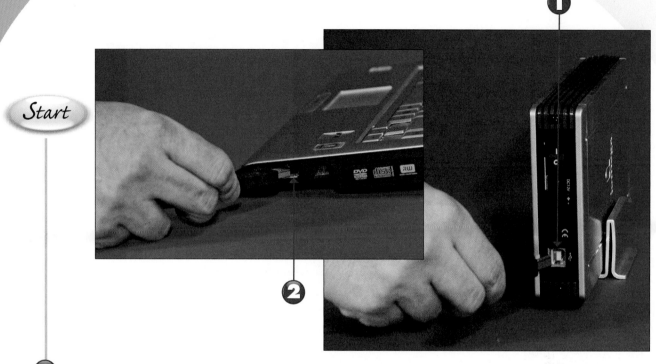

End

① Connect one end of the USB cable to your new device.

② Connect the other end of the cable to a free USB port on your PC.

TIP

USB Hubs If you connect too many USB devices, you can run out of USB connectors on your PC. If that happens, buy an add-on USB hub, which lets you plug in multiple USB peripherals to a single USB port. ■

TIP

First Connection The first time you connect a device to your PC, Windows might ask you what you want to do with this device. Make a selection, and Windows will automatically perform that action every time you connect that device. ■

Chapter 3

SETTING UP A WIRELESS HOME NETWORK

When you want to connect two or more computers in your home, you need to create a computer *network*. A network is all about sharing; you can use your network to share files, peripherals (such as printers), and even a broadband Internet connection.

There are two ways to connect your network: wired or wireless. A wireless network is more convenient (no wires to run), which makes it the network of choice for most home users. Wireless networks use radio frequency (RF) signals to connect one computer to another. The most popular type of wireless network uses the WiFi standard and can transfer data at 11Mbps (802.11b), 54Mbps (802.11g), or 600Mbps (802.11n).

UNDERSTANDING HOW WIRELESS NETWORKS WORK

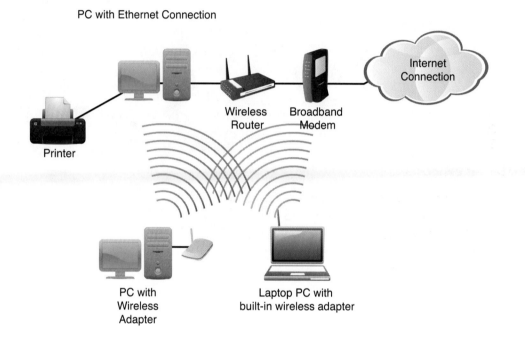

PC with Ethernet Connection

Internet Connection

Wireless Router

Broadband Modem

Printer

PC with Wireless Adapter

Laptop PC with built-in wireless adapter

SETTING UP YOUR NETWORK'S MAIN PC

The focal point of your wireless network is the *wireless router*. The wireless PCs on your network must be connected to or contain *wireless adapters*, which function as mini-transmitters/receivers to communicate with the base station.

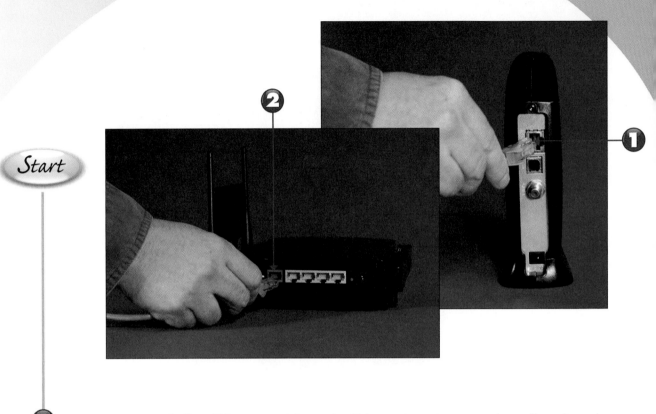

Start

 Connect one end of an Ethernet cable to the Ethernet port on your broadband modem.

 Connect the other end of the Ethernet cable to one of the Ethernet ports on your wireless router—preferably the one labeled Internet or WAN.

Continued

TIP
Internet Port Most routers have a dedicated input for your broadband modem, sometimes labeled Internet—although the modem can be connected to any open Ethernet input on the router. ■

NOTE
Broadband Routers Some Internet service providers (ISPs) provide broadband modems that include built-in wireless routers. If you have one of these, you don't need to buy a separate router. ■

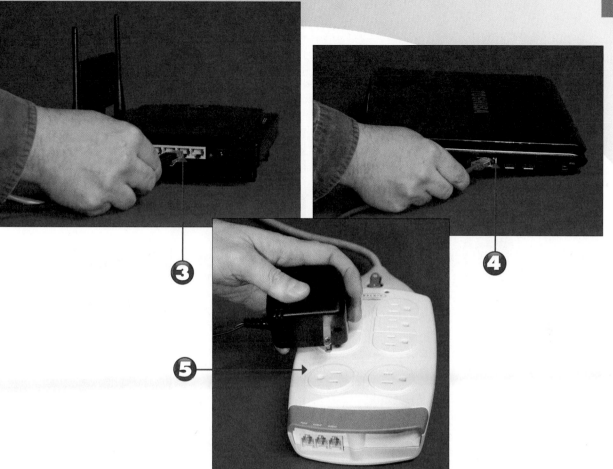

3 Connect one end of an Ethernet cable to another Ethernet port on your wireless router.

4 Connect the other end of the Ethernet cable to the Ethernet port on your main PC.

5 Connect your wireless router to a power source and, if it has a power switch, turn it on. Your computer should now be connected to the router and your network.

End

TIP

Router Configuration Some wireless routers require you to connect your main computer via Ethernet for initial configuration, as described here. Other routers will connect wirelessly to your main computer for the entire configuration process. When in doubt, follow the instructions that came with your router. ■

TIP

Wireless Security To keep outsiders from tapping into your wireless network, you need to enable wireless security for the network. This adds an encrypted key to your wireless connection; no other computer can access your network without this key. ■

CONNECTING ADDITIONAL PCS TO YOUR WIRELESS NETWORK

Each additional PC on your network requires its own wireless adapter. Most notebook and tablet PCs come with a wireless adapter built in. Some desktop PCs come with built-in wireless adapters; others may require you to connect an external adapter.

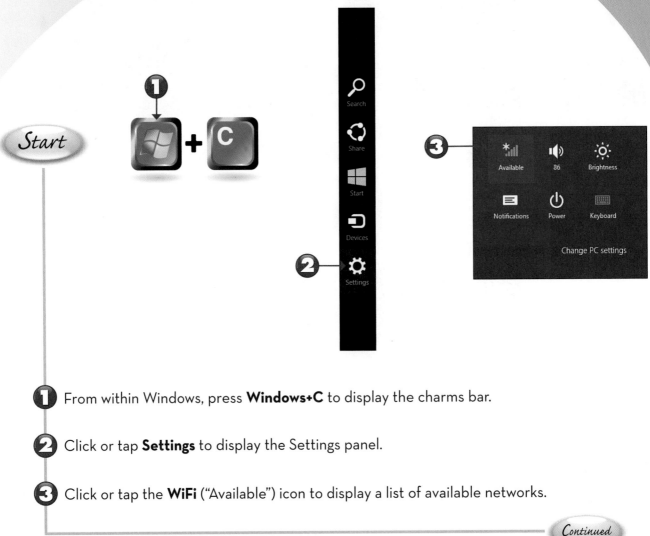

Start

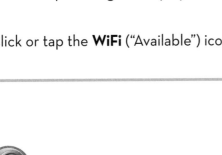

1 From within Windows, press **Windows+C** to display the charms bar.

2 Click or tap **Settings** to display the Settings panel.

3 Click or tap the **WiFi** ("Available") icon to display a list of available networks.

Continued

TIP

Wireless Adapters A wireless adapter can be a small external device that connects to the PC via USB, an expansion card that installs inside your system unit, or a PC card that inserts into a laptop PC's card slot. ■

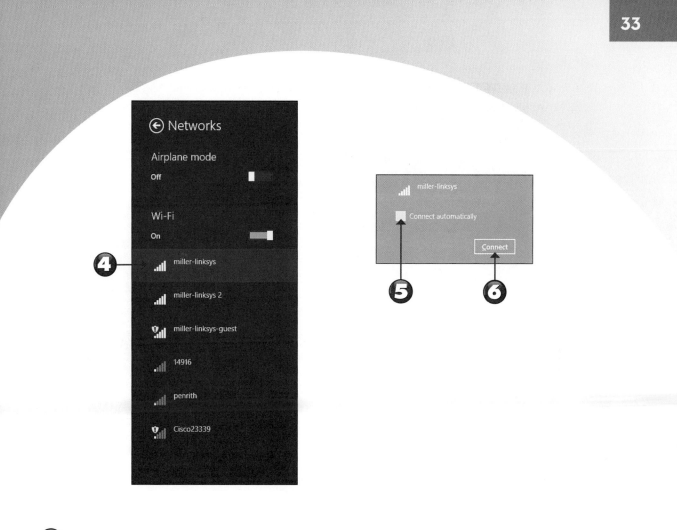

④ Click or tap your wireless network; this expands the panel for this network.

⑤ To connect automatically to this network in the future, check the **Connect Automatically** box.

⑥ Click **Connect**.

Continued

TIP

Connect Automatically When you're connecting to your home network, it's a good idea to enable the Connect Automatically feature. This lets your computer connect to your network without additional prompting or interaction on your part. ■

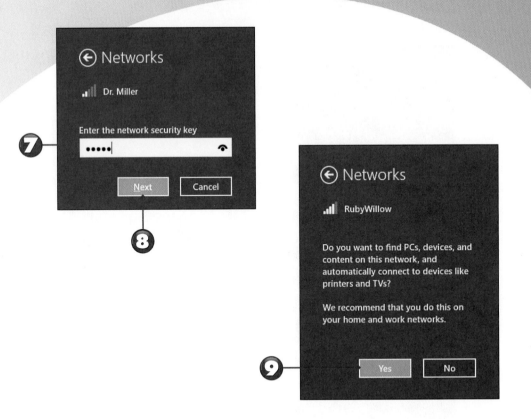

7 When prompted, enter the password (called the *network security key*) for your network.

8 Click **Next.**

9 When the next screen appears, click **Yes** to connect with other PCs and devices on your home network.

End

TIP

Connecting Securely If you've enabled wireless security on your wireless router, you will be prompted to enter the passphrase or security key assigned during the router setup, as noted in steps 7 and 8. If you haven't enabled wireless security, you should. ■

TIP

One-Button Connect If your router supports "one-button wireless setup" (based on the Wi-Fi Protected Setup technology), you'll be prompted to press the "connect" button on the router to connect. You can connect via this button or by entering the network password as normal. ■

ADDING YOUR COMPUTER TO A HOMEGROUP

The easiest way to connect multiple home computers is to create a HomeGroup for your network. A *HomeGroup* is kind of a simplified network that lets you automatically share files and printers between connected computers.

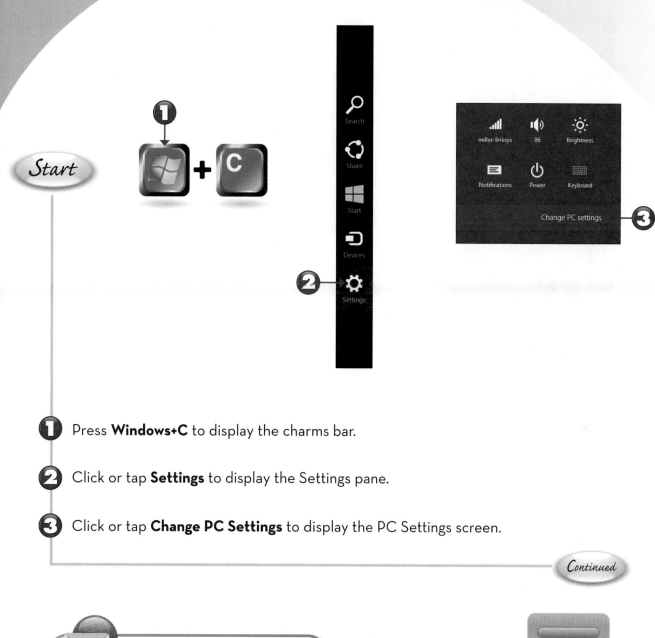

1 Press **Windows+C** to display the charms bar.

2 Click or tap **Settings** to display the Settings pane.

3 Click or tap **Change PC Settings** to display the PC Settings screen.

Continued

NOTE

For Newer Windows Only PCs running Windows 7 or above can be part of a HomeGroup. PCs running older versions of Windows do not have the Home-Group feature and must use the normal Windows networking functions instead. ■

4 Scroll down the list on the left and select **Network**.

5 From the Network list, select **HomeGroup**.

6 Click or tap the **Create** button.

Continued

TIP
File/Printer Sharing When configuring your Home-Group, you can choose to share your Documents, Music, Pictures, Videos, or Printers and Devices. ■

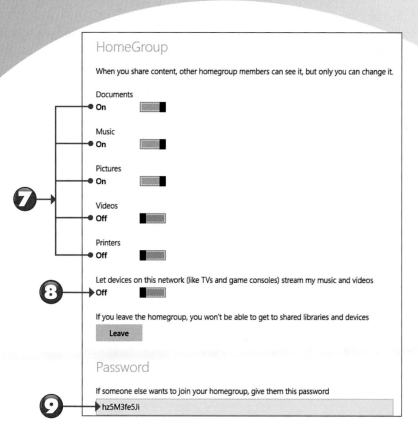

From the next screen, switch "on" those items you want to share with other computers— Documents, Music, Pictures, Videos, and Printers.

7

If you want noncomputer devices, such as network connected TVs or videogame consoles, to be able to access the content on this computer, click or tap "on" the **Let Devices on This Network (Like TVs and Game Consoles) Stream My Music and Videos** option.

8

Go to the Password section and write down the password that Windows generated. You'll need to provide this to users of other computers on your network who want to join your HomeGroup.

9

End

NOTE

Configuring Other PCs You'll need to configure each computer on your network to join your new HomeGroup. Enter the original HomeGroup password as instructed. ■

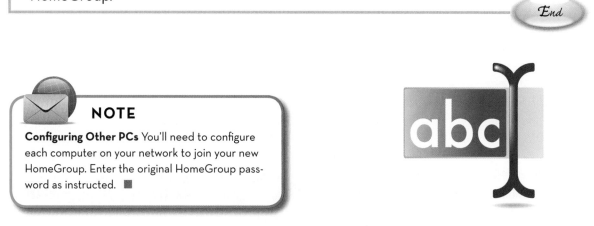

ACCESSING OTHER COMPUTERS IN YOUR HOMEGROUP

Once you have your home network set up, you can access shared content stored on other computers on your network. How you do so depends on whether the other computer is part of your HomeGroup. We'll look at HomeGroup access first.

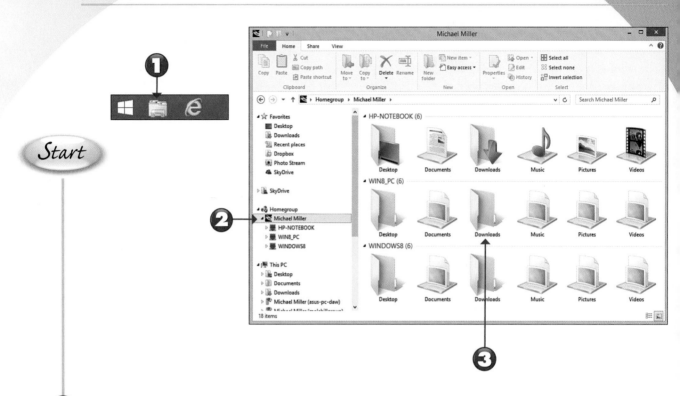

Start

1 From the Windows desktop, click the **File Explorer** icon on the taskbar.

2 When File Explorer opens, go to the HomeGroup section of the navigation pane and click the HomeGroup you want to access.

3 Windows now displays the shared folders on all the computers in your HomeGroup. Double-click a folder to access that particular content.

End

A computer doesn't have to be connected to your HomeGroup for you to access its content. Windows lets you access any computer connected to your home network—although you can only share content the computer's owner has configured as sharable.

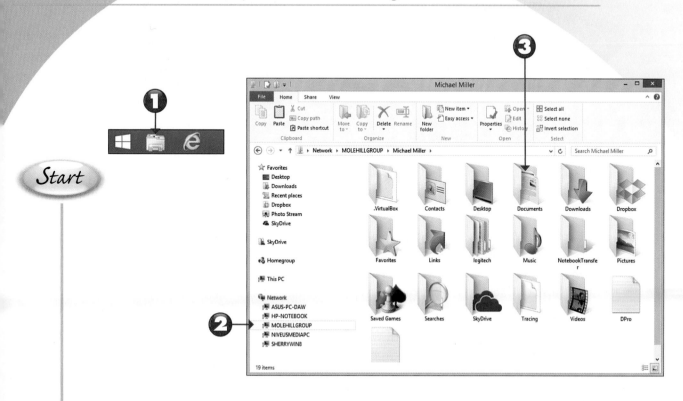

Start

1 From the Windows desktop, click the **File Explorer** icon on the taskbar.

2 When File Explorer opens, go to the Network section of the navigation pane and click the computer you want to access.

3 Windows now displays the shared folders on the selected computer. Double-click a folder to view that folder's content.

End

TIP
Look for the Public Folder On most older computers, shared files are stored in the Public folder. Look in this folder first for the files you want. ■

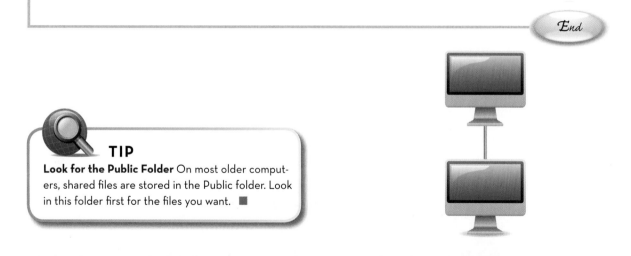

Chapter 4

USING WINDOWS 8.1'S NEW INTERFACE

Microsoft Windows is a piece of software called an *operating system*. An operating system does what its name implies: It operates your computer system, working in the background every time you turn on your PC. The *desktop* that fills your screen is part of Windows, as is the taskbar at the bottom of the screen and the big menu that pops up when you click the Start button.

If you've used a version of Windows prior to Windows 8, or seen someone else using Windows in the past, you might think that this new version of Windows looks a lot different—and you'd be right. Windows 8 introduced a completely different *user interface* to the operating system, and Windows 8.1 builds on that. The Windows 8/8.1 user interface is called the *Modern* interface, and it differs from the traditional Windows desktop.

In Windows 8.1, everything starts on the Start screen (the home screen full of tiles for different apps) and goes from there. The traditional desktop is still there (as an app, and used to run older software programs), but you'll be spending most of your time with the new Modern interface and its tiled Start screen.

EXPLORING THE START SCREEN

Large tile   Medium tile   Profile picture/
username

Wide tile

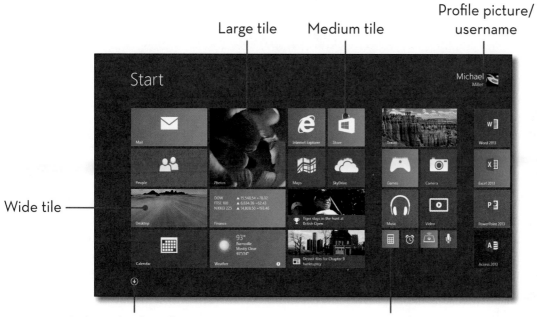

Click to display all apps   Small tile

USING WINDOWS WITH A MOUSE

To use Windows efficiently, you must master a few simple operations, all of which you perform with your mouse. Most mouse operations include *pointing* and *clicking*. Normal clicking uses the left mouse button; however, some operations require that you click the right mouse button instead.

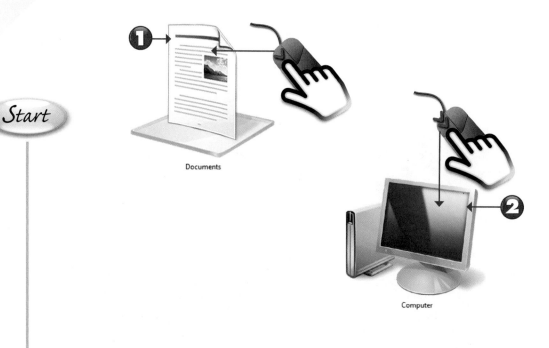

Documents

Computer

1 To single-click, position the cursor over the onscreen item and click the left mouse or touchpad button.

2 To double-click, position the cursor over the onscreen item and click the left mouse or touchpad button twice in rapid succession.

Continued

 TIP

Click to Select Pointing and clicking is an effective way to select icons, menu items, directories, and files. ■

 NOTE

Mouse Over Another common mouse operation is called the *mouse over*, or *hovering*, where you hold the cursor over an onscreen item without pressing either of the mouse buttons. For example, when you mouse over an icon or menu item, Windows displays a *ToolTip* that tells you a little about the selected item. ■

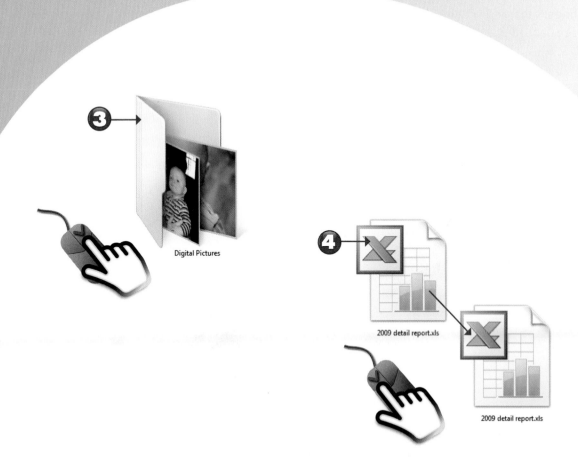

Digital Pictures

2009 detail report.xls

2009 detail report.xls

3 To right-click, position the cursor over the onscreen item, and then click the *right* mouse button.

4 To drag and drop an item from one location to another, position the cursor over the item, click and hold the left mouse button, drag the item to a new position, and then release the mouse button.

End

TIP
Pop-Up Menus Many items in Windows feature a context-sensitive pop-up menu. You access this menu or list by right-clicking the item. (When in doubt, right-click the item and see what pops up!) ■

TIP
Moving Files You can drag and drop to move files from one folder to another. You also can delete files by dragging and dropping them onto the Recycle Bin icon. ■

USING WINDOWS WITH A TOUCHSCREEN DISPLAY

If you're using Windows on a computer or tablet with a touchscreen display, you use your fingers instead of a mouse to do what you need to do. So, it's important to learn some essential touchscreen operations.

Start

1. Tapping is the equivalent of clicking with your mouse. Tap an item with the tip of your finger and release.

2. To display additional information about any item, press and hold the item with the tip of your finger.

Continued

TIP

Right-Click = Press and Hold Pressing and holding is the touchscreen equivalent of right-clicking an item with your mouse. ■

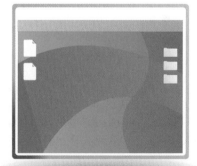

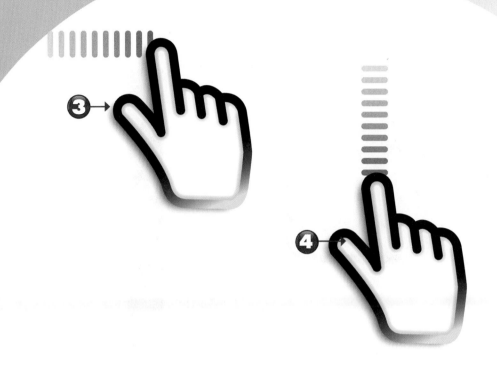

3 To scroll down a page or perform many edge-centric operations, swipe the screen in the desired direction with your finger.

4 You can also scroll up, down, or sideways by touching and dragging the page with one or more fingers.

End

TIP

Zooming In To zoom in on a given screen (that is, to make a selection larger), use two fingers to touch two points on the item, and then move your fingers apart. ■

TIP

Zooming Out To zoom out of a given screen (that is, to make a selection smaller and see more of the surrounding page), use two fingers—or your thumb and first finger—to touch two points on the item, and then pinch your fingers in toward each other. ■

DISPLAYING THE START SCREEN

You can easily return to the Start screen from any other screen in Windows, even the desktop, using either the keyboard or the mouse. For many users, clicking the Start button (which appears at the lower-left corner of every screen) is the quickest way to display the Start screen.

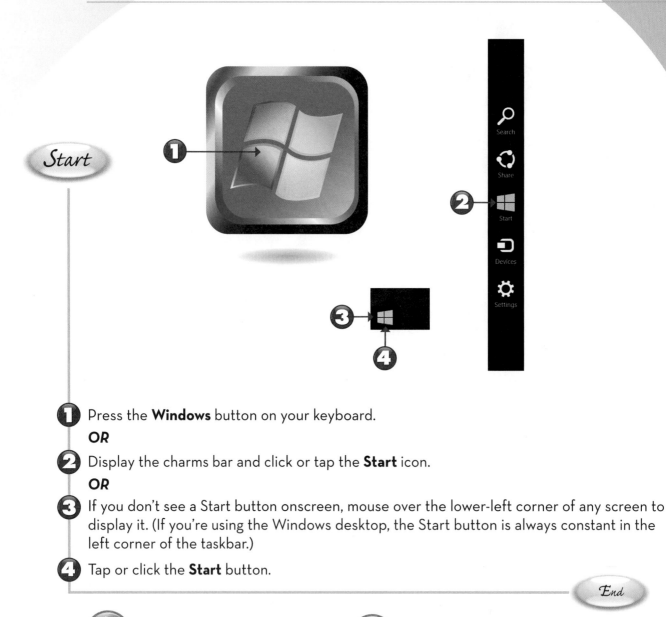

1 Press the **Windows** button on your keyboard.

OR

2 Display the charms bar and click or tap the **Start** icon.

OR

3 If you don't see a Start button onscreen, mouse over the lower-left corner of any screen to display it. (If you're using the Windows desktop, the Start button is always constant in the left corner of the taskbar.)

4 Tap or click the **Start** button.

End

TIP

New to Windows 8.1 The Start button was not present in Windows 8. The ability to return to the Start screen by clicking the Start button is new to Windows 8.1. ■

NOTE

Start Menu The Windows 8.1 Start button does not function like the Start button in older versions of Windows. Prior to Windows 8, clicking the Start button brought up a Start menu of all the apps installed on your system. The new Windows 8.1 Start button takes you to the Start screen, instead; there is no Start menu in Windows 8 or 8.1. ■

NAVIGATING THE START SCREEN

Everything in Windows 8 revolves around the Start screen. The Start screen is where you start out and where you launch new apps and software programs.

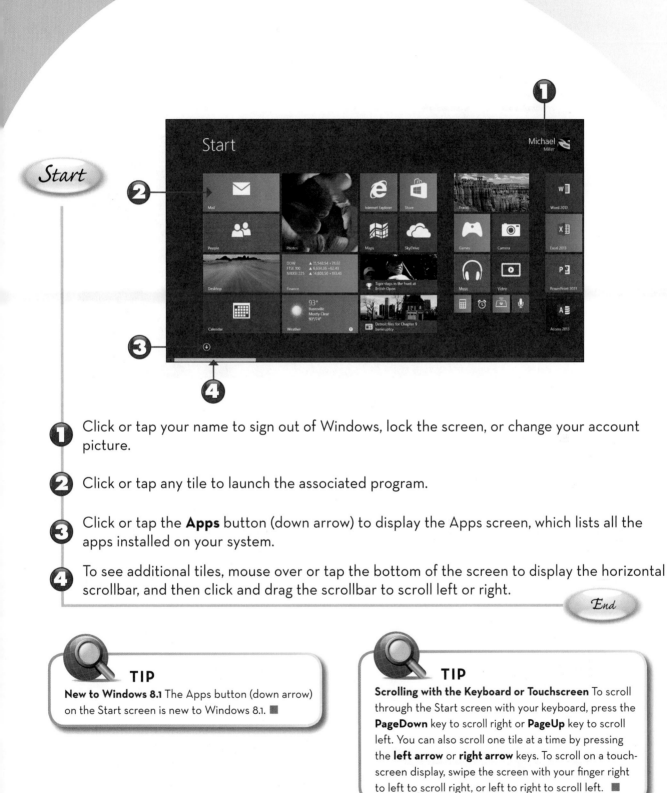

1. Click or tap your name to sign out of Windows, lock the screen, or change your account picture.

2. Click or tap any tile to launch the associated program.

3. Click or tap the **Apps** button (down arrow) to display the Apps screen, which lists all the apps installed on your system.

4. To see additional tiles, mouse over or tap the bottom of the screen to display the horizontal scrollbar, and then click and drag the scrollbar to scroll left or right.

End

TIP

New to Windows 8.1 The Apps button (down arrow) on the Start screen is new to Windows 8.1. ■

TIP

Scrolling with the Keyboard or Touchscreen To scroll through the Start screen with your keyboard, press the **PageDown** key to scroll right or **PageUp** key to scroll left. You can also scroll one tile at a time by pressing the **left arrow** or **right arrow** keys. To scroll on a touchscreen display, swipe the screen with your finger right to left to scroll right, or left to right to scroll left. ■

USING THE CHARMS BAR

Windows 8 has more functions up its sleeve, although they're not obvious during normal use. These are a series of system functions, called *charms*, which are accessed from a charms bar that appears on the right side of the screen.

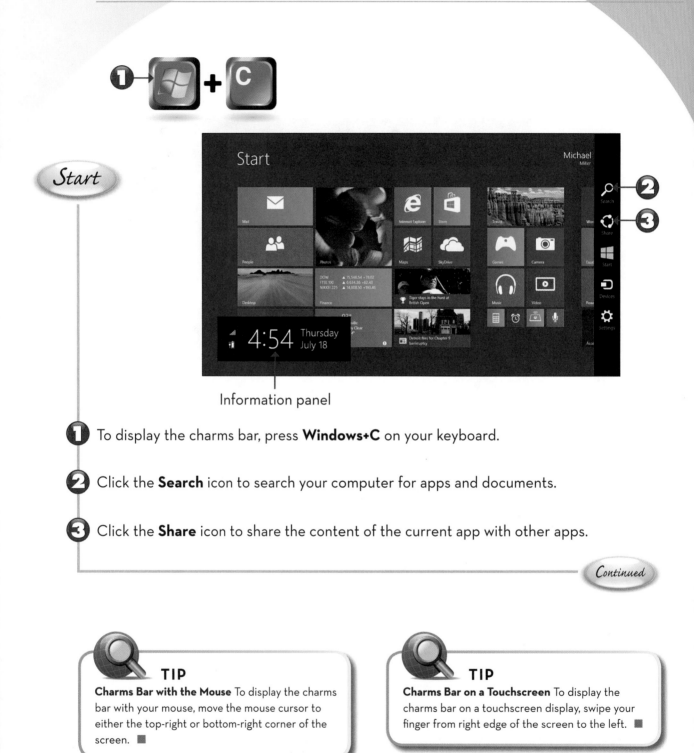

Start

Information panel

1 To display the charms bar, press **Windows+C** on your keyboard.

2 Click the **Search** icon to search your computer for apps and documents.

3 Click the **Share** icon to share the content of the current app with other apps.

Continued

TIP

Charms Bar with the Mouse To display the charms bar with your mouse, move the mouse cursor to either the top-right or bottom-right corner of the screen. ■

TIP

Charms Bar on a Touchscreen To display the charms bar on a touchscreen display, swipe your finger from right edge of the screen to the left. ■

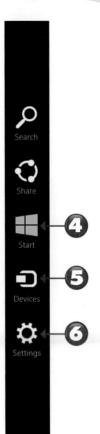

4 Click the **Start** icon to return to the Start screen from any other location in Windows.

5 Click the **Devices** icon to configure the settings of any external devices connected to your PC.

6 Click the **Settings** icon to access and configure various Windows settings.

TIP
Charms Bar from Any Screen You can access the charms bar from any Windows screen, even if you have an app displayed full screen. Each app has its own customized charms bar, with options specific to that app. ■

NOTE
Notification Panel Whenever the charms bar is displayed, Windows also displays a notification panel at the bottom left of the screen. This panel duplicates the information shown on the Windows Lock screen: current date and time, Internet connection status, and power status. ■

GETTING HELP IN WINDOWS

When you can't figure out how to perform a particular task, ask for help. In Windows 8, you can ask for help through the Windows Help and Support Center.

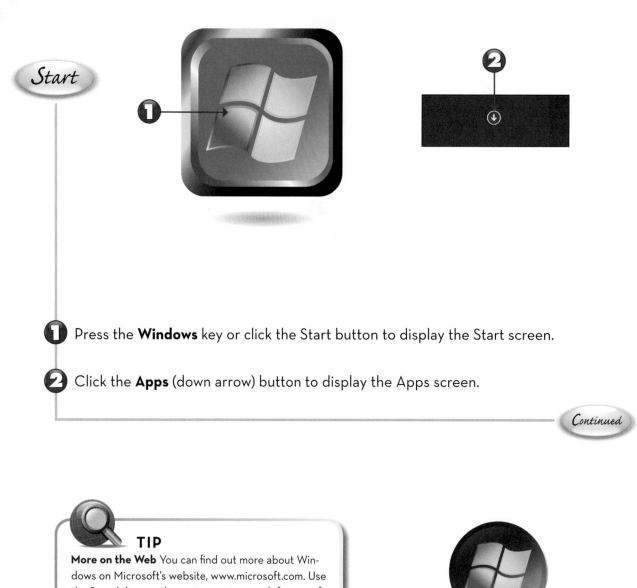

1 Press the **Windows** key or click the Start button to display the Start screen.

2 Click the **Apps** (down arrow) button to display the Apps screen.

Continued

TIP

More on the Web You can find out more about Windows on Microsoft's website, www.microsoft.com. Use the Search box on the main page to search for specific information. ■

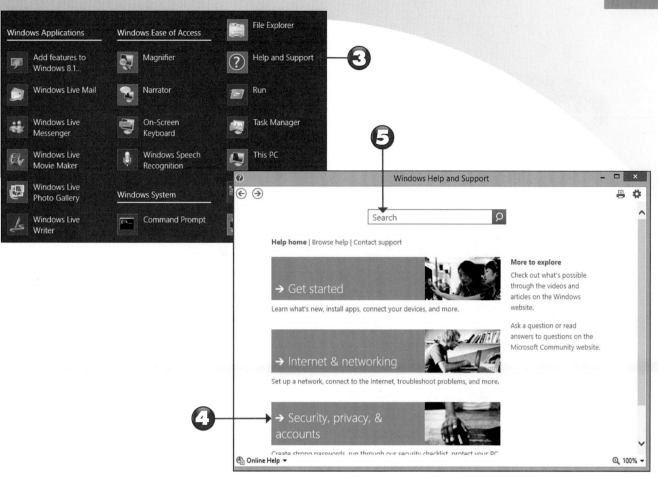

③ Scroll to the Windows System section and tap or click **Help and Support**. This opens a Help and Support window on the Windows desktop.

④ Click one of the suggested help topics on the main screen.
OR

⑤ Enter a description of your issue into the Search box, and then press **Enter**.

End

TIP
Browse for Help You can also browse the topics in the Windows Help system. Click **Browse Help** at the top of the Help window, and then click the appropriate topic below. ■

CAUTION
Less Than Helpful The Windows Help system doesn't have all the answers. If you can't find what you need in the Help system, you can go online to the Microsoft Support website (support.microsoft.com), or access the technical support offered by your computer's manufacturer. Also useful are the other books and articles offered by this book's publisher, available online at www.quepublishing.com. ■

PERSONALIZING WINDOWS

When you first turn on your new computer system, you see the Windows lock screen, and then the Start screen, as Microsoft (or your computer manufacturer) set them up for you. If you like the way these screens look, great. If not, you can change them.

Windows presents a lot of different ways to personalize the look and feel of your system. In fact, one of the great things about Windows is how quickly you can make Windows look like *your* version of Windows, different from anybody else's.

DIFFERENT WINDOWS LOCK SCREENS

CUSTOMIZING THE LOCK SCREEN PICTURE

The lock screen is what you see when you first power on your computer or begin to log on to Windows. You can easily change the background picture of the lock screen to something you like better and add information from up to seven apps to the screen.

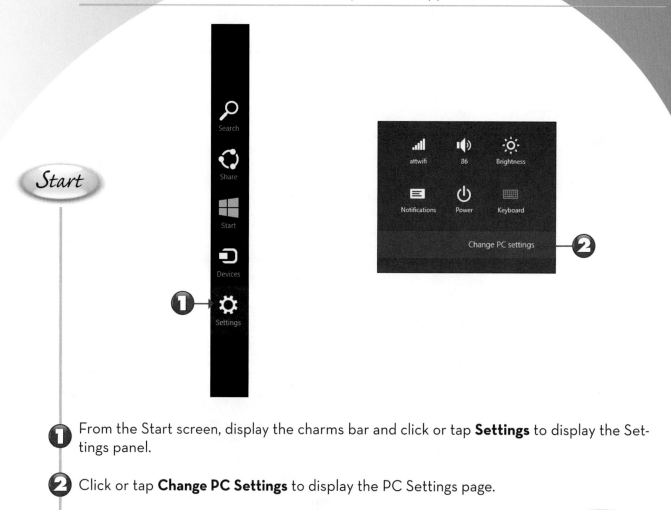

Start

1. From the Start screen, display the charms bar and click or tap **Settings** to display the Settings panel.

2. Click or tap **Change PC Settings** to display the PC Settings page.

Continued

TIP

Lock Screen The lock screen appears when you first power on your PC and any time you log off from your personal account or switch users. It also appears when you awaken your computer from Sleep mode. ■

NOTE

Smartphone Lock Screens The Windows lock screen is similar to the lock screens you see on various smartphones, such as the Apple iPhone, whenever you "wake up" the phone. ■

3 Click or tap **PC & Devices** in the left column.

4 Click or tap **Lock Screen**.

5 Go to the Background section, and click or tap the thumbnail for the picture you want to use.

End

TIP

Personalize Your Picture To use your own picture as the background, click the **Browse** button. When the Files screen appears, navigate to and click or tap the picture you want to use, and then click or tap the **Choose Picture** button. ■

DISPLAYING A SLIDE SHOW ON THE LOCK SCREEN

Windows 8.1 lets you turn your computer into a kind of digital picture frame by displaying a slide show of your photos on the lock screen.

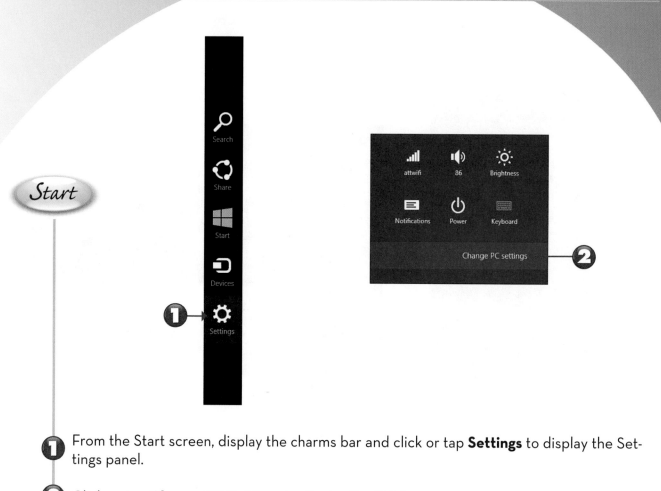

Start

① From the Start screen, display the charms bar and click or tap **Settings** to display the Settings panel.

② Click or tap **Change PC Settings** to display the PC Settings page.

Continued

TIP
New to Windows 8.1 The ability to display a picture slide show on the lock screen is new to Windows 8.1. ∎

TIP
Display the Lock Screen You can display the lock screen (and your photo slide show) at any time by going to the Start screen, clicking your profile picture at the top right, and selecting **Lock**. You also can have Windows display the lock screen after 15 minutes of inactivity by selecting that option on the lock screen customization screen. ∎

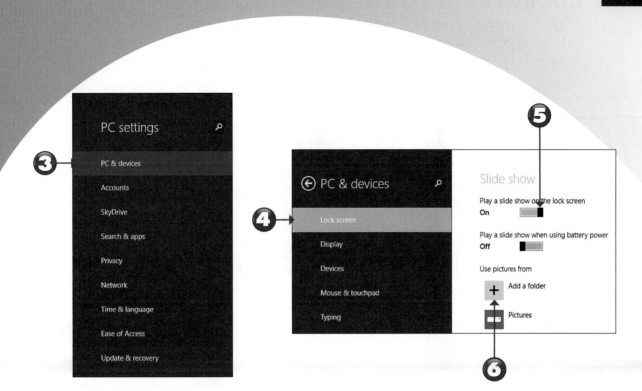

③ Click or tap **PC & Devices** in the left column.

④ Click or tap **Lock Screen**.

⑤ Click "on" the **Play a Slide Show on the Lock Screen** switch.

⑥ Click **Add a Folder** to select the picture folder you want to display in your slide show.

End

TIP

Let Windows Pick If you'd rather let Windows pick your slide show pictures, click "on" the **Let Windows Choose Pictures for My Slide Show** switch. ■

TIP

Turn Off the Slide Show You can instruct Windows to turn off the slide show (and dim the screen) after a set period of time. Go to the Turn Off Screen After Slide Show Has Played For control and select a time period—30 minutes, 1 hour, or 3 hours. To keep the slide show playing indefinitely, select **Don't Turn Off**. ■

ADDING APPS TO THE LOCK SCREEN

The lock screen can display a number of apps that run in the background and display useful or interesting information, even while your computer is locked. By default, you see the date/time, power status, and connection status, but it's easy to add other apps to the lock screen.

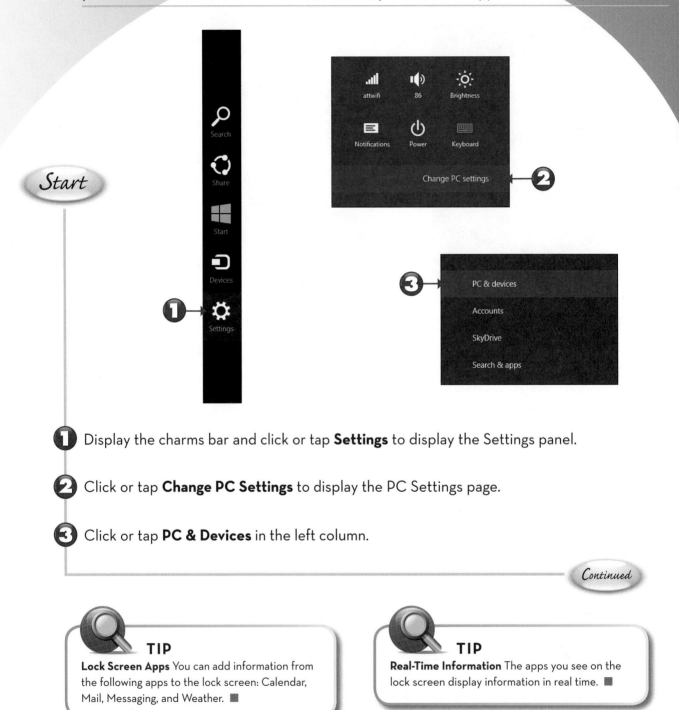

1 Display the charms bar and click or tap **Settings** to display the Settings panel.

2 Click or tap **Change PC Settings** to display the PC Settings page.

3 Click or tap **PC & Devices** in the left column.

Continued

TIP

Lock Screen Apps You can add information from the following apps to the lock screen: Calendar, Mail, Messaging, and Weather. ■

TIP

Real-Time Information The apps you see on the lock screen display information in real time. ■

⊖ PC & devices   ⌕

Lock screen ← **4**

Display

Devices

Lock screen apps

Choose apps to run in the background and show quick status and notifications, even when your screen is locked

✉ 🗓 ⏰ ☀ **+** **+** **+**
              5

Choose an app

6 → ⏰ Alarms

🗓 Calendar

Comics

✉ Mail

MedicineCabinet

4 Click or tap **Lock Screen** in the left panel.

5 Scroll down the Lock Screen panel to the Lock Screen Apps section and click a + button to display the Choose an App panel.

6 Click or tap the app you want to add.

End

TIP

Displaying Live Information You can also opt for one of the lock screen apps to display detailed live information, such as unread messages or current weather conditions. To select which app displays detailed information, click or tap the app button in the Choose an App to Display Detailed Status section. ■

TIP

Displaying Alarms In addition, you can display timer alarms on the lock screen. Go to the Choose an App to Show Alarms option, click the + button, and click **Alarms**. You can then set wake-up alarms in the Alarms app and have them displayed on your PC's lock screen. ■

REARRANGING TILES ON THE START SCREEN

As you know, the Start screen is your own personal home base in Windows. The Start screen is composed of dozens of individual tiles, each representing an app, program, operation, or file. If you don't like where a given tile appears on the Start screen, you can rearrange the order of your tiles.

Start

1 Click and drag the selected tile to a new position. You can also move tiles from one group to another.

End

TIP

Using a Touchscreen Display To move a tile on a touchscreen display, use your finger to press and drag the tile to a new position. ■

TIP

Tile Groups Tiles on the Start screen are organized into groups. To move a tile to a different group, click and drag the tile from one group to another. ■

MAKING TILES LARGER OR SMALLER

Tiles on the Start screen can be displayed in one of four different sizes. Select the size that best suits your personal needs. (For example, you might want to display the Weather tile at the Large size to see more forecast information.)

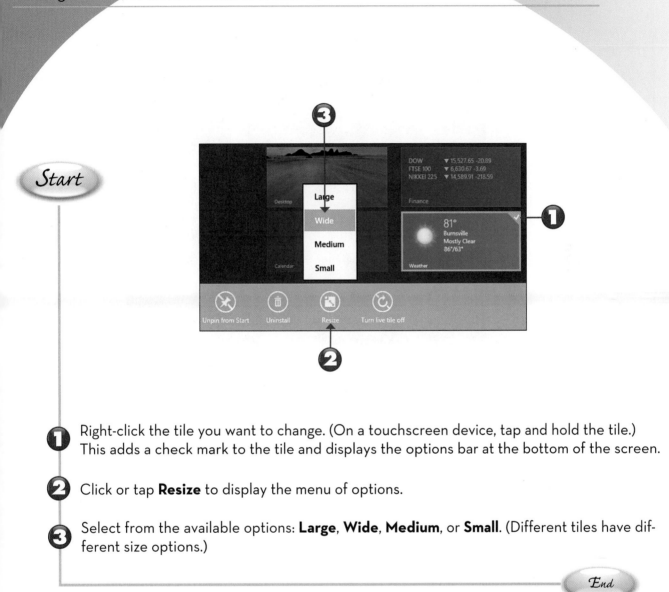

Start

End

1. Right-click the tile you want to change. (On a touchscreen device, tap and hold the tile.) This adds a check mark to the tile and displays the options bar at the bottom of the screen.

2. Click or tap **Resize** to display the menu of options.

3. Select from the available options: **Large**, **Wide**, **Medium**, or **Small**. (Different tiles have different size options.)

TIP
Live Tiles Many tiles are "live," in that they display the current operation or information. For example, the Weather tile displays the current weather conditions, and the Photos tile displays a slide show of pictures on your computer. ■

TIP
Turning Off Live Tiles To turn off a live tile (to display the default tile icon), right-click the tile to change; this adds a check mark to the tile and displays the options bar at the bottom of the screen. Click or tap **Turn Live Tile Off**. ■

ORGANIZING TILES INTO GROUPS

The tiles on the Start screen are organized into multiple groups of like tiles. You can create new tile groups at any time.

① Click and drag an existing tile to the right of its current group until you see a shaded vertical bar.

② Drop the tile onto that bar. This creates a new group with that tile as the first tile.

TIP

Shrink the Start Screen You can shrink the Start screen in order to see more tiles and complete groups. Move your cursor to the bottom right corner of the Start screen and click the **Zoom** (-) button. (Or, on a touchscreen device, pinch the screen to shrink it.) Click an open area of the screen to return to the full-size view. ■

TIP

Rearrange Tile Groups When you shrink the Start screen, you can easily rearrange your tile groups. Just click and drag a complete tile group from one position to another. ■

NAMING GROUPS OF TILES

You can give each tile group a name so that you know what's where. For example, you might want to organize all your media-related (photos, music, and video) tiles into one group and call it Media.

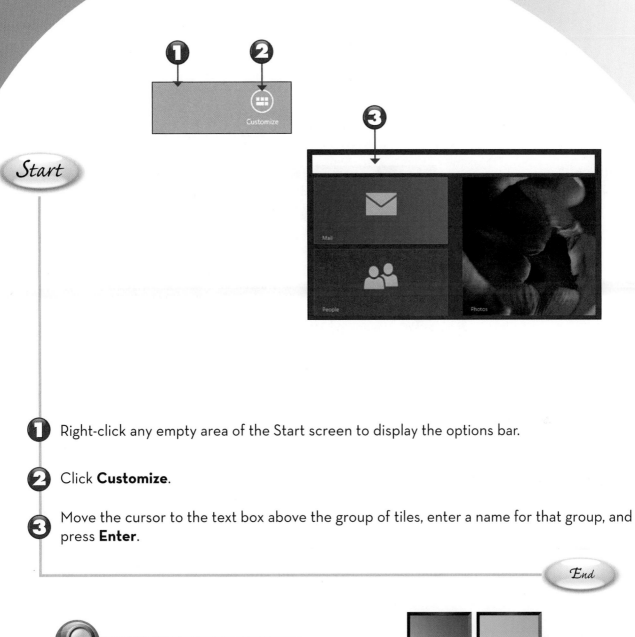

Start

End

1 Right-click any empty area of the Start screen to display the options bar.

2 Click **Customize**.

3 Move the cursor to the text box above the group of tiles, enter a name for that group, and press **Enter**.

TIP

Remove a Name To remove the name from a tile group, display the options bar, click **Customize**, and then click the **X** next to the current name. ■

REMOVING TILES

You might find that there are one or more tiles on your Start screen that you never use. You can remove unused tiles to get them out of your way and make room for additional titles.

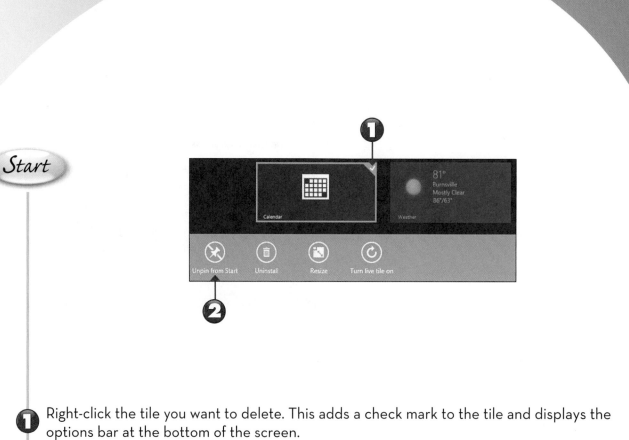

Start

1 Right-click the tile you want to delete. This adds a check mark to the tile and displays the options bar at the bottom of the screen.

2 Click or tap **Unpin from Start**.

End

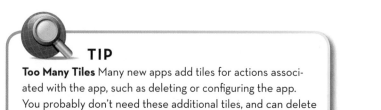

TIP

Too Many Tiles Many new apps add tiles for actions associated with the app, such as deleting or configuring the app. You probably don't need these additional tiles, and can delete them—leaving only the main tile to launch the app itself. ■

ADDING NEW TILES TO THE START SCREEN

Windows 8.1 does not automatically add new apps to the Start screen. (Windows 8 did; Windows 8.1 doesn't.) You can, however, add (or pin) a tile for any app or utility to the Start screen at any time.

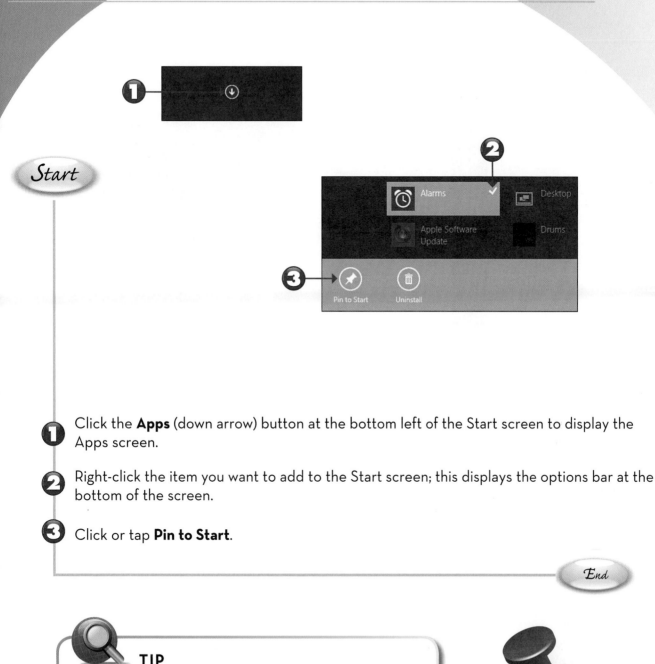

Start

1 Click the **Apps** (down arrow) button at the bottom left of the Start screen to display the Apps screen.

2 Right-click the item you want to add to the Start screen; this displays the options bar at the bottom of the screen.

3 Click or tap **Pin to Start**.

End

TIP

Display the Apps Button If you do not see the Apps (down arrow) button on the Start screen, just move your mouse or, on a touchscreen device, swipe up from the bottom of the screen with your finger. ■

CHANGING WINDOWS COLORS

When you configured Windows when you first turned on your new computer, you were asked to choose a color scheme. Fortunately, you're not locked into your initial choice. You can change the color scheme for your Start screen (and subsidiary screens) at any time.

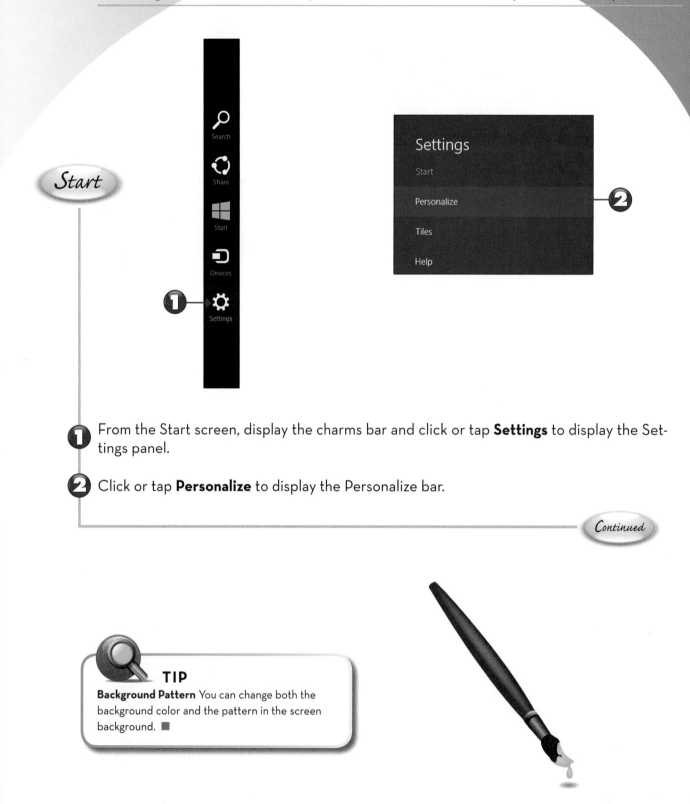

1 From the Start screen, display the charms bar and click or tap **Settings** to display the Settings panel.

2 Click or tap **Personalize** to display the Personalize bar.

Continued

TIP

Background Pattern You can change both the background color and the pattern in the screen background. ■

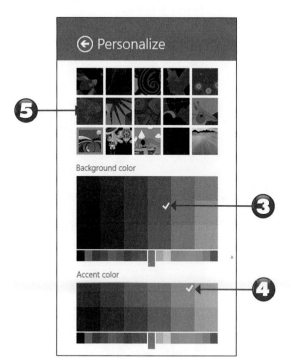

3 Select a background color from the Background Color chooser.

4 Select an accent color from the Accent Color chooser.
OR

5 Select a background theme from the selection at the top of the bar. (This option preselects background and accent colors to match the selected pattern.)

End

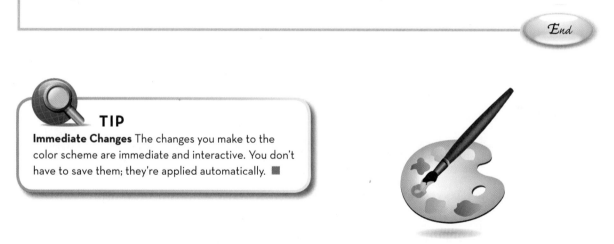

TIP

Immediate Changes The changes you make to the color scheme are immediate and interactive. You don't have to save them; they're applied automatically. ■

SHOW YOUR DESKTOP BACKGROUND ON THE START SCREEN

In Windows 8.1, you can display the same background picture on the Start screen as you do on the Windows desktop. This makes the transition from the desktop environment to the Modern Start screen less visually jarring.

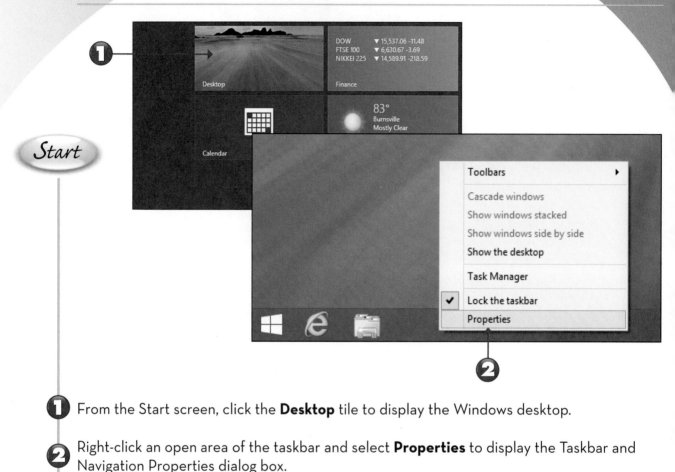

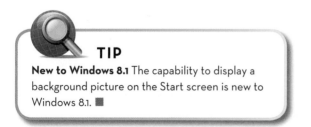

1. From the Start screen, click the **Desktop** tile to display the Windows desktop.

2. Right-click an open area of the taskbar and select **Properties** to display the Taskbar and Navigation Properties dialog box.

Continued

TIP

New to Windows 8.1 The capability to display a background picture on the Start screen is new to Windows 8.1. ■

TIP

Change the Desktop Background To change the background picture on the desktop (and the Start screen, if you have them linked), right-click the desktop and select **Personalize**. ■

③ Click the **Navigation** tab.

④ Go to the Start Screen section and check the **Show My Desktop Background on Start** option.

⑤ Click the **OK** button.

End

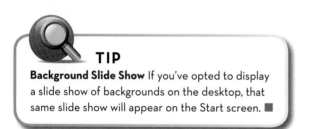

TIP

Background Slide Show If you've opted to display a slide show of backgrounds on the desktop, that same slide show will appear on the Start screen. ■

CHANGING YOUR PROFILE PICTURE

When you first configured Windows, you picked a default image to use as your profile picture. You can, at any time, change this picture to something more to your liking.

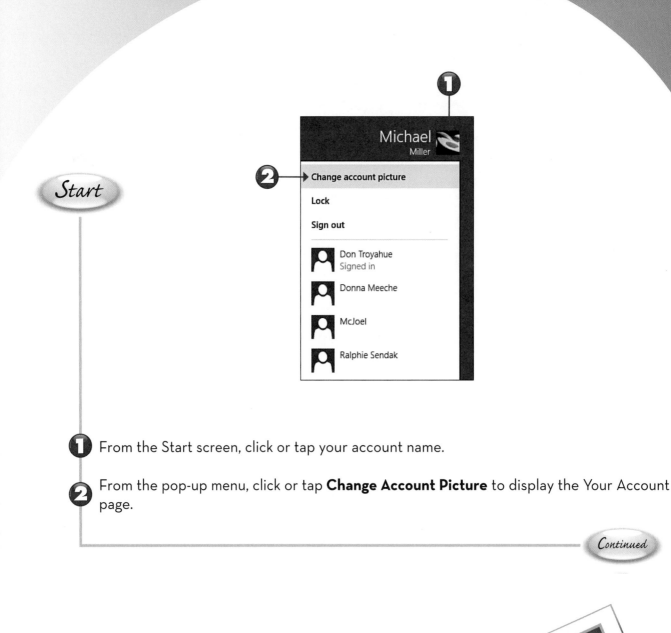

Start

① From the Start screen, click or tap your account name.

② From the pop-up menu, click or tap **Change Account Picture** to display the Your Account page.

Continued

TIP

Webcam Picture If your computer has a webcam, you can take a picture with your webcam to use for your account picture. From the Your Account page, click or tap the **Camera** button and follow the onscreen directions from there. ■

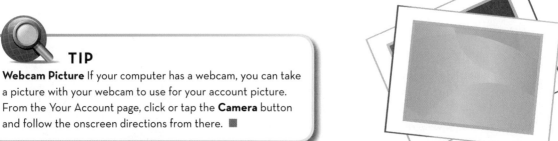

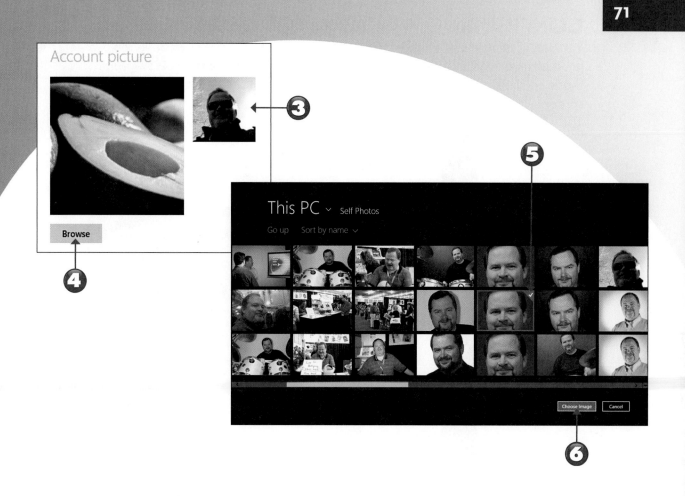

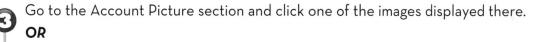

Go to the Account Picture section and click one of the images displayed there.
OR

Click the **Browse** button to browse for pictures from the Files screen.

Navigate to and click or tap the picture you want.

Tap or click the **Choose Image** button.

End

TIP

SkyDrive Photos By default, the Files screen displays photos stored on your PC (This PC). To browse photos stored online in your SkyDrive account, click the down arrow next to This PC and select **SkyDrive**. ■

CONFIGURING WINDOWS SETTINGS

You can configure many other Windows system settings if you want. In most cases, the default settings work just find and you don't need to change a thing. However, you can change these settings if you so desire. You configure most of these settings from the PC Settings screen.

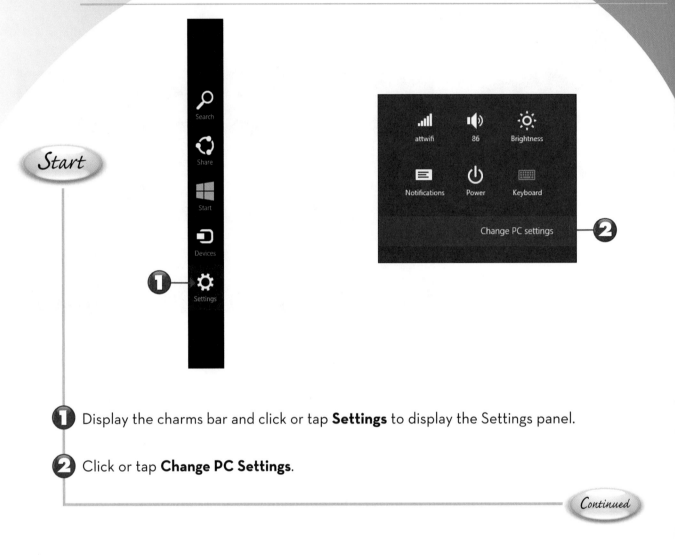

Start

① Display the charms bar and click or tap **Settings** to display the Settings panel.

② Click or tap **Change PC Settings**.

Continued

TIP

Windows Settings The following tabs are available on the PC Settings page: PC & Devices, Accounts, SkyDrive, Search & Apps, Privacy, Network, Time & Language, Ease of Access, and Update & Recovery. ■

TIP

New to Windows 8.1 Windows 8.1 lets you configure many more settings from the PC Settings screen than you could in Windows 8. In that version of Windows, you were forced to use the Control Panel (on the desktop) to configure most system settings. ■

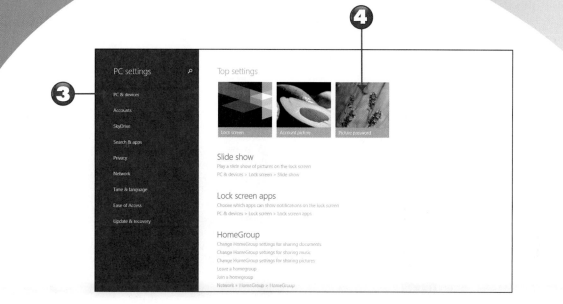

3 Select a tab on the left to display the associated settings on the right.

4 Configure the settings as necessary.

End

TIP

Control Panel You can also configure most system settings from the Windows Control Panel, which is a holdover from older versions of Windows. To open the Control Panel, right-click the lower-left corner of any screen to display the Quick Access menu, then select **Control Panel**. ■

SETTING UP ADDITIONAL USERS

Chances are you're not the only person using your computer; it's likely that you'll be sharing your PC with your spouse and kids, at least to some degree. Fortunately, you can configure Windows so that different people using your computer sign on with their own custom settings—and access to their own personal files. You do this by assigning each user in your household his own password-protected user account.

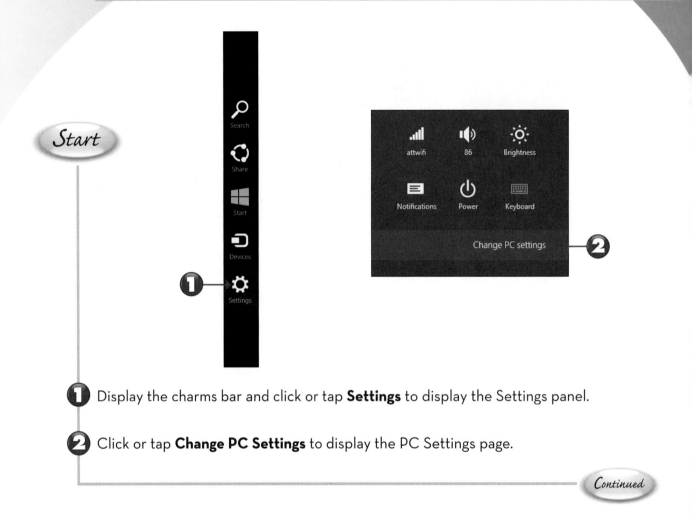

1 Display the charms bar and click or tap **Settings** to display the Settings panel.

2 Click or tap **Change PC Settings** to display the PC Settings page.

Continued

TIP
Two Types of Accounts Windows lets you create two different types of user accounts: online and local. An *online account* is linked to a new or existing Microsoft account and lets you synchronize your account settings between multiple computers. A *local account* is exclusive to your current computer and doesn't link to any online services. ■

NOTE
Microsoft Account By default, Windows creates new user accounts using existing or new Microsoft accounts. You need a Microsoft Account login to use many of the interactive features of Windows 8, such as linking your account to Facebook or Microsoft's SkyDrive; a Microsoft account is also necessary to access features with live updates, such as the Weather and News apps. ■

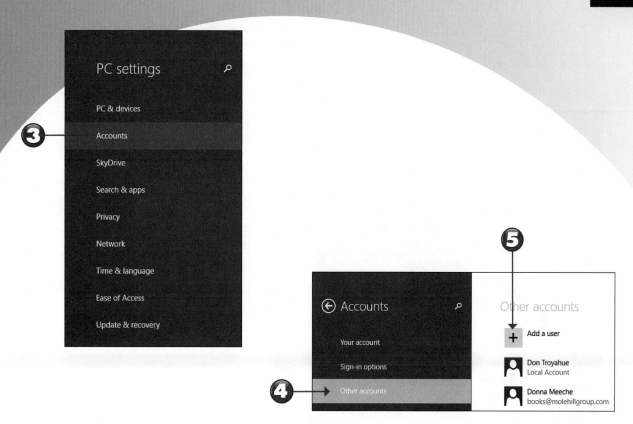

 Click or tap **Accounts** in the left column to display the Accounts page.

Click or tap **Other Accounts** in the left column.

Click or tap the **Add a User** button to display the Add a User page.

Continued

TIP
Creating a New Microsoft Account If you have an existing Microsoft account, such as for Hotmail or Xbox Live, you can use that as your Windows account. If you don't yet have a Microsoft account, you can create one at any time—it's free. ■

TIP
Three Ways to Log On When you set up an account, you can choose from three different ways to log on. You can log on to an account with a traditional password, a PIN code, or a picture password. ■

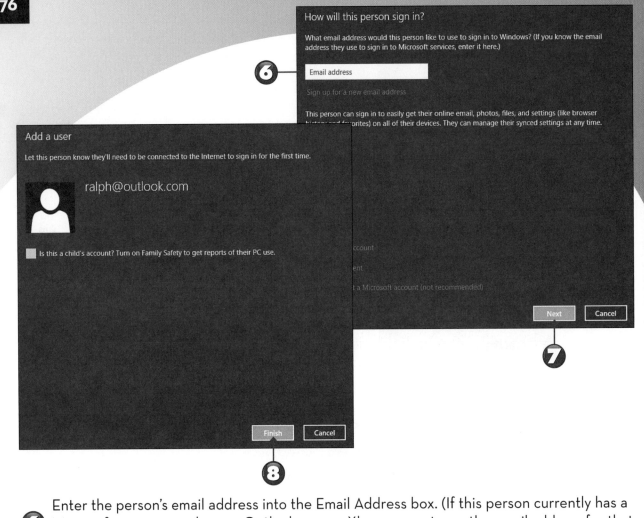

How will this person sign in?

What email address would this person like to use to sign in to Windows? (If you know the email address they use to sign in to Microsoft services, enter it here.)

Email address

Sign up for a new email address

This person can sign in to easily get their online email, photos, files, and settings (like browser history and favorites) on all of their devices. They can manage their synced settings at any time.

Add a user

Let this person know they'll need to be connected to the Internet to sign in for the first time.

ralph@outlook.com

Is this a child's account? Turn on Family Safety to get reports of their PC use.

Finish Cancel

Next Cancel

6 Enter the person's email address into the Email Address box. (If this person currently has a Microsoft account, such as an Outlook.com or Xbox account, use the email address for that account.)

7 Click or tap the **Next** button.

8 When the next screen appears, click the **Finish** button.

End

TIP

Link to a Microsoft Account If you created your initial Windows user account as a local account, you can later link your account to a new or existing Microsoft account. This way, you can take full advantage of Microsoft's various web services. To do this, go to your Accounts page, select **Your Account**, and then click **Connect to a Microsoft Account**. ■

SWITCHING BETWEEN USERS

If other people are using your computer, they might want to log on with their own accounts. To do this, you'll need to change users—which you can do without shutting off your PC.

Start

1 Press the **Windows** key or click the **Start** button to return to the Start screen.

2 Click or tap your username and picture in the top-right corner.

3 From the pop-up menu, click or tap the next user's name.

4 When prompted, enter the new user's password, and then press **Enter** or click or tap the **right arrow**.

End

TIP

Signing Out When you switch users, both accounts remain active; the original user account is just suspended in the background. If you would rather log off completely from a given account, and return to the Windows lock screen, click your username or picture on the Start screen, and then click **Sign Out**. ■

Chapter 6

WORKING WITH NEW WINDOWS APPS

Most of the productive and fun things you do on your computer are done with *applications*, sometimes called *apps*. An app is a software program that performs one or more functions.

Some apps are work related, others provide useful information, and still others are more entertaining in nature. For example, the Weather app lets you check current weather conditions and forecasts; the Mail app lets you send and receive email messages over the Internet.

There are actually two kinds of apps in Windows 8.1. Newer Modern-style apps, developed specifically for Windows 8/8.1, run full screen from the Windows Start screen. Older software apps run in individual windows on the traditional Windows desktop. Most people will use a mix of traditional and Modern-style apps in their day-to-day use.

APPS ON THE START SCREEN

LAUNCHING AN APP

You can launch an app wherever you find it. Many apps are "pinned" to the Start screen, in the form of tiles. Clicking the tile launches the app.

Start

1 Click or tap a tile to launch the associated app.

End

TIP

Other Places to Find Apps Not all apps are pinned to the Start screen. You can find additional apps on the Apps page, or you can search for apps—both of which are discussed later in this chapter. ■

CLOSING AN APP

In earlier versions of Windows, you needed to close open apps when you were done with them. That's not the case with Modern apps, which you can keep running as long as you like without using valuable system resources. That said, you can still close open apps, if you want.

 Start

1 From the open app, move the mouse cursor to the top of the screen until it changes to a hand shape.

2 Click and drag the top of the screen downward to the middle until it shrinks and disappears.

End

NOTE

Paused An open but unused app is essentially paused until you return to it and consumes minimal system resources. ■

TIP

Swipe to Close On a touchscreen display, use your finger to swipe the top of the open app downward to close. ■

VIEWING ALL APPS

All the apps and utilities installed on your computer system are displayed on the Apps screen. This screen essentially replaces the Start menu found on older versions of Windows.

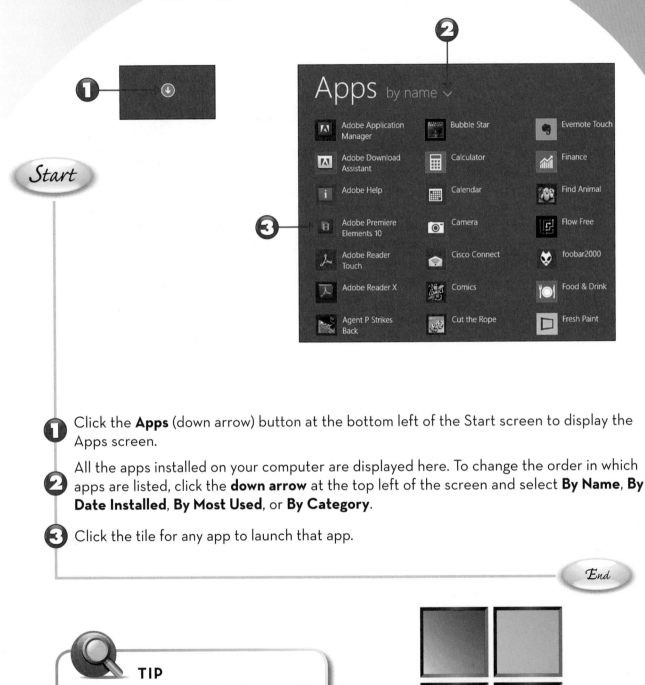

1 Click the **Apps** (down arrow) button at the bottom left of the Start screen to display the Apps screen.

2 All the apps installed on your computer are displayed here. To change the order in which apps are listed, click the **down arrow** at the top left of the screen and select **By Name**, **By Date Installed**, **By Most Used**, or **By Category**.

3 Click the tile for any app to launch that app.

TIP

Return to Start To return to the Start screen, click or tap the **up arrow** at the bottom left of the Apps screen—or just press the Windows key. ■

USING THE APPS SCREEN (INSTEAD OF THE START SCREEN)

Because all your apps are displayed on the Apps screen, you might want to display the Apps screen instead of the normal Windows Start screen. Windows 8.1 lets you swap the two screens, which means that when you click or tap the Start button, you go to the Apps screen instead.

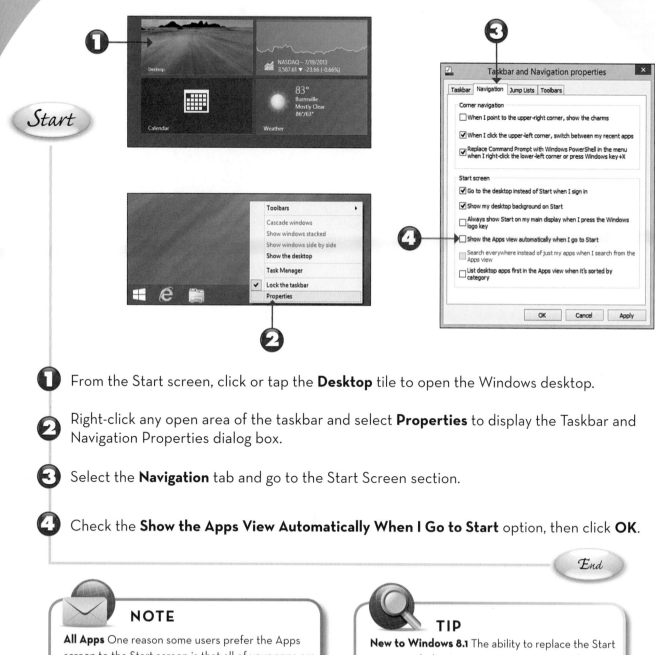

1 From the Start screen, click or tap the **Desktop** tile to open the Windows desktop.

2 Right-click any open area of the taskbar and select **Properties** to display the Taskbar and Navigation Properties dialog box.

3 Select the **Navigation** tab and go to the Start Screen section.

4 Check the **Show the Apps View Automatically When I Go to Start** option, then click **OK**.

End

NOTE

All Apps One reason some users prefer the Apps screen to the Start screen is that all of your apps are displayed on the Apps screen. In Windows 8.1, newly installed apps are not automatically added to the Start screen. ■

TIP

New to Windows 8.1 The ability to replace the Start screen with the Apps screen is new to Windows 8.1. ■

SEARCHING FOR APPS ON YOUR COMPUTER

If you have a lot of apps installed on the Apps screen or pinned to the Start screen, it may be challenging to find that one app you want. To that end, Windows lets you search for individual apps just by entering the name of the app.

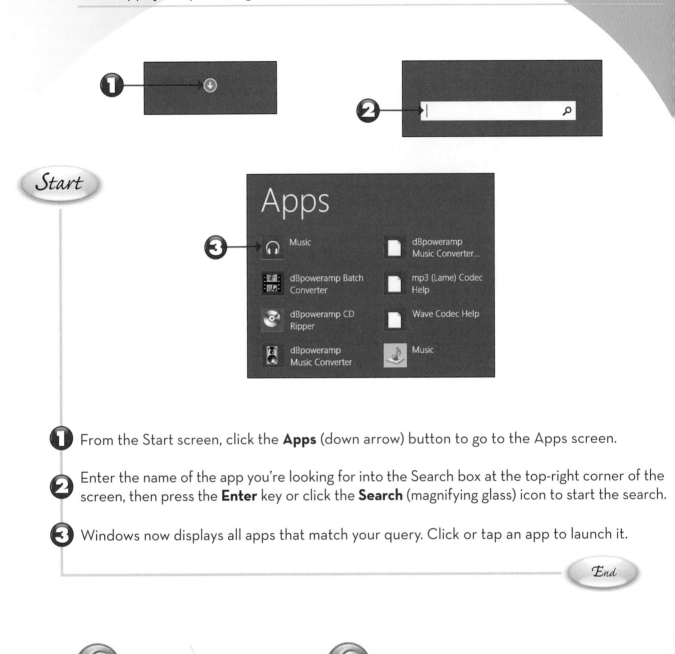

① From the Start screen, click the **Apps** (down arrow) button to go to the Apps screen.

② Enter the name of the app you're looking for into the Search box at the top-right corner of the screen, then press the **Enter** key or click the **Search** (magnifying glass) icon to start the search.

③ Windows now displays all apps that match your query. Click or tap an app to launch it.

End

TIP

Search from Anywhere You can search for apps from any screen, including the Start screen. Press **Windows+Q** to bring up the search pane, enter your query, then press **Enter**. ■

TIP

Automatic Searching Windows will automatically open the search pane when you start typing within any Modern app—or on the Start screen itself. Just type a few letters on your computer keyboard, and the search pane appears with your new query in the Search box. (This does not work from the Windows desktop, however.) ■

PINNING AN APP TO THE START SCREEN

You might find that it's easier to launch a frequently used app by adding it to the Windows Start screen. This is called *pinning* the app, and creates a tile for the app; click or tap the tile to launch the app.

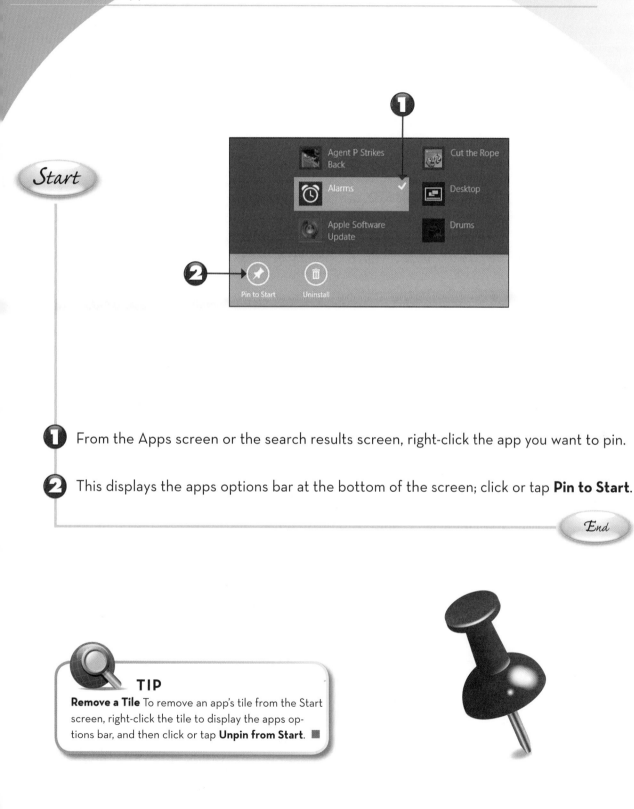

From the Apps screen or the search results screen, right-click the app you want to pin.

This displays the apps options bar at the bottom of the screen; click or tap **Pin to Start**.

TIP

Remove a Tile To remove an app's tile from the Start screen, right-click the tile to display the apps options bar, and then click or tap **Unpin from Start**. ■

SWITCHING BETWEEN OPEN APPS

If you have more than one open app, it's easy to switch between them. In fact, there are several ways to do this.

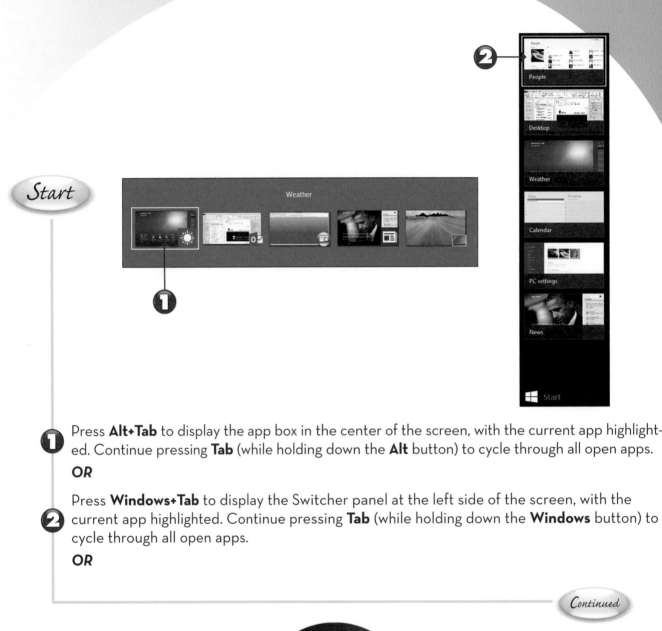

Start

Weather

1 Press **Alt+Tab** to display the app box in the center of the screen, with the current app highlighted. Continue pressing **Tab** (while holding down the **Alt** button) to cycle through all open apps.

OR

2 Press **Windows+Tab** to display the Switcher panel at the left side of the screen, with the current app highlighted. Continue pressing **Tab** (while holding down the **Windows** button) to cycle through all open apps.

OR

Continued

3 "Bump" the mouse cursor against the top-left corner of the screen to display the Switcher panel.

4 Click or tap the thumbnail of the app you want to switch to.

End

TIP
Touchscreen Switching If you have a touchscreen computer or tablet, press and drag your finger from the left edge of the screen inward toward the center. The next open app appears on top of the previous app. ∎

SNAPPING TWO APPS SIDE BY SIDE

Modern Windows apps don't always have to display full screen. You can "snap" multiple apps onto a single screen—and then resize them to any width you want.

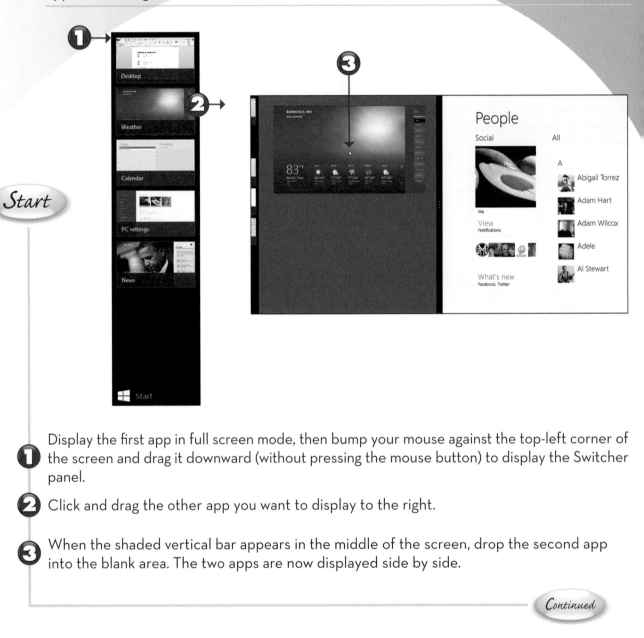

Start

1 Display the first app in full screen mode, then bump your mouse against the top-left corner of the screen and drag it downward (without pressing the mouse button) to display the Switcher panel.

2 Click and drag the other app you want to display to the right.

3 When the shaded vertical bar appears in the middle of the screen, drop the second app into the blank area. The two apps are now displayed side by side.

Continued

TIP

New to Windows 8.1 The ability to resize snapped apps is new to Windows 8.1. In Windows 8, the two snapped apps were positioned at a fixed 70/30 ratio. ■

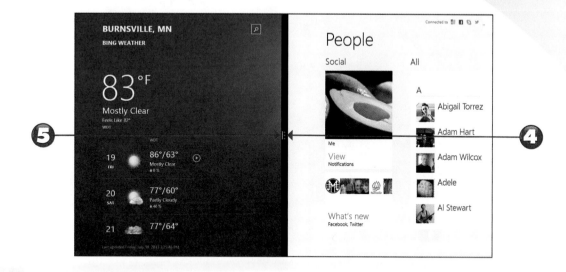

4 To change the width of the displayed apps, click and drag the vertical bar to one side or another.

5 To revert to a single app onscreen, click and drag the vertical bar all the way to the other side of the screen from that app.

End

NOTE

Eight Apps Onscreen Windows 8.1 lets you have up to eight apps onscreen at a single time, depending on the size (resolution) of your PC display. The larger your display, the more apps you can snap. ◼

EXAMINING WINDOWS' BUILT-IN APPS

Windows 8.1 ships with a number of useful apps built in to the operating system. You launch all these apps from the Windows Start or Apps screens.

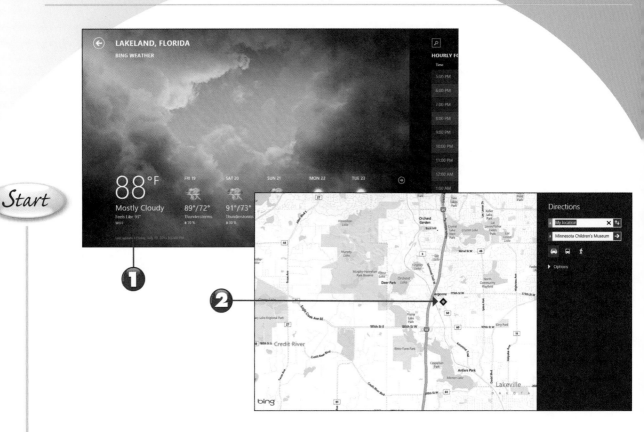

The Weather app displays current weather conditions as well as a 5-day forecast and radar maps.

The Maps app displays a map of your current location, as well as step-by-step directions to any location you want to visit.

Continued

TIP

More to the Right Scroll right through the Weather app to view additional weather information, including an hourly forecast, various weather maps, and a graph for historical weather in your location. Click any item to view more detail. ■

NOTE

Bing Maps The Maps app is based on Bing Maps, which is Microsoft's web-based mapping service. ■

3 The Calendar app displays upcoming appointments in daily, weekly, or monthly views.

4 The Alarms app turns your computer into a digital alarm clock, and also includes timer and stopwatch functions.

Continued

TIP

Calculator App Windows 8.1 also includes a Calculator app that functions as a standard or scientific calculator. It also lets you convert various measurements from one format to another (such as liters to teaspoons). ■

⑤ The News app displays the latest news headlines; click a headline to read the full story.

⑥ The Sports app displays the latest sports headlines, as well as scores from your favorite teams.

Continued

TIP

Finance App Windows 8.1 also includes a Finance app that lets you track stock performance in real time on your computer. ▪

7 The Bing Food & Drink app lets you search for recipes online, as well as create shopping lists based on the recipes you choose.

8 The Bing Health & Fitness app includes numerous tools to help you lead a healthier life, including a Diet Tracker, Exercise Tracker, and Health Tracker.

End

TIP

More Healthy Options The Health & Fitness app also includes online workouts and useful information about medical conditions and prescription drugs. ■

TIP

Travel App Windows 8.1 also includes a Travel app that provides information about popular travel destinations worldwide. ■

FINDING NEW APPS IN THE WINDOWS STORE

When you're in need of a new app to perform a particular task, the first place to look is in the Microsoft Windows Store. This is an online store for Modern-style full-screen apps, both free and paid. You shop the Windows Store by clicking or tapping the **Store** tile on the Windows Start screen.

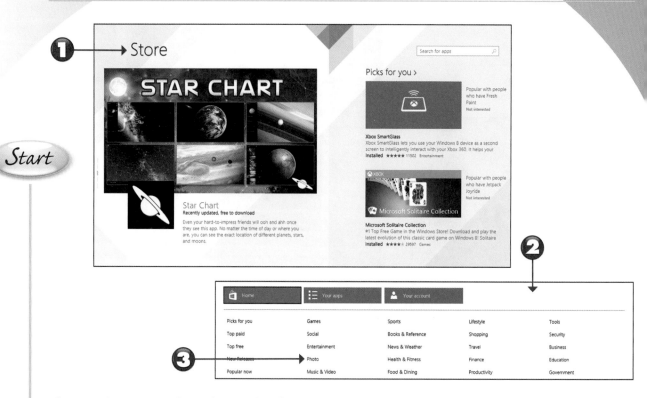

1 The Windows Store launches with a featured app. Scroll right to view Picks for You, Popular Now, New Releases, and Top Paid and Free apps.

2 To view apps by category, right-click to display the top options bar.

3 Click a category to view all apps in that category.

Continued

NOTE

App Store Microsoft's Windows Store is similar in concept to Apple's App Store for iPhones and iPads, as well as the Google Play store for Android devices. ■

TIP

Updating Apps In Windows 8.1, you no longer have to manually update apps when they've been updated. All app updates now happen automatically, without any manual intervention required. ■

4 To search for apps, enter an app's name into the Search box at the top-right corner of the screen, and then press **Enter**.

5 Click **Buy** to purchase and install a paid app, or click **Install** to download and install a free app.

End

NOTE

Pricing Whereas a traditional computer software program can cost hundreds of dollars, most apps in the Windows Store cost $10 or less—and many are available for free. ■

TIP

Try Before You Buy Most paid apps let you try them before you buy them. Click the Try button to install a trial version of that app on your PC. ■

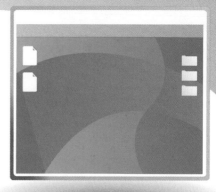

USING THE WINDOWS DESKTOP AND TRADITIONAL APPS

As you learned in Chapter 6, "Working with New Windows Apps," Modern-style apps are newer apps designed specifically for Windows 8 and 8.1. But lots of older software programs that you might find useful are still available, such as Microsoft Word, Adobe Photoshop Elements, and even Apple's iTunes. You need to learn how these traditional software programs work.

You launch traditional software apps from the Start or Apps screens, the same as Modern-style apps. These older apps, however, run on the traditional Windows desktop, within their own windows. Therefore, you can have multiple open apps onscreen at the same time, with the windows stacked on top of or tiled next to each other.

EXPLORING THE WINDOWS DESKTOP

Open window

Recycle
Bin

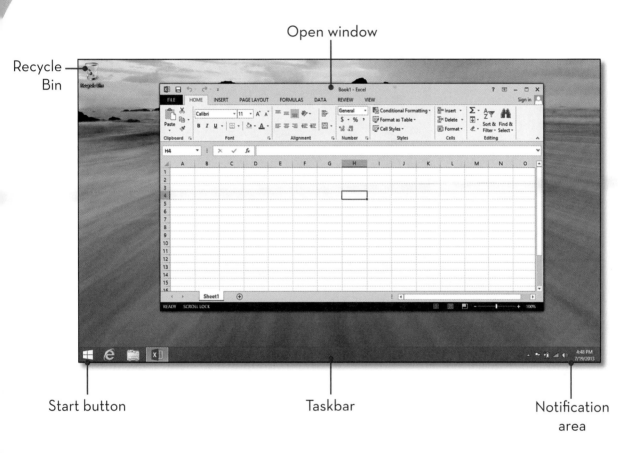

Start button

Taskbar

Notification
area

DISPLAYING THE TRADITIONAL DESKTOP

To display the traditional Windows desktop, all you have to do is tap or click the **Desktop** tile on the Start screen. This opens the desktop operating environment, from which you can use traditional software apps.

Start

1 Click or tap the **Desktop** tile on the Start screen.

End

NOTE

Launching Automatically The traditional desktop launches automatically when you open a traditional (non-Modern) app. ■

TIP

The New Desktop In versions of Windows prior to Windows 8, all you had was the desktop; there wasn't a tiled Start screen. The older desktop featured a Start menu where all apps were listed. In Windows 8/8.1, you use the Start screen, not the Start menu, to open new programs. ■

RETURNING TO THE START SCREEN

The Start menu found in older versions of Windows is no longer present in Windows 8 and 8.1. Instead, you launch programs from the Modern-style Start screen, which you access by clicking the Start button on the desktop taskbar.

Start

1 Click or tap the **Start** button at the left end of the taskbar.

End

TIP

New to Windows 8.1 Windows 8 removed both the Start menu and the Start button from the desktop. Windows 8.1 returns the Start button to the desktop, although clicking it now displays the Start screen (not the Start menu—which is still missing in action). ■

TIP

Keyboard Shortcut You can also return to the Start screen by pressing the **Windows** key on your computer keyboard. ■

PINNING PROGRAMS TO THE TASKBAR

Instead of exiting from the desktop environment to the Start screen whenever you want to launch a new program, you can instead "pin" shortcuts to your favorite programs to the desktop taskbar. You can then launch one of these programs by clicking the shortcut on the taskbar.

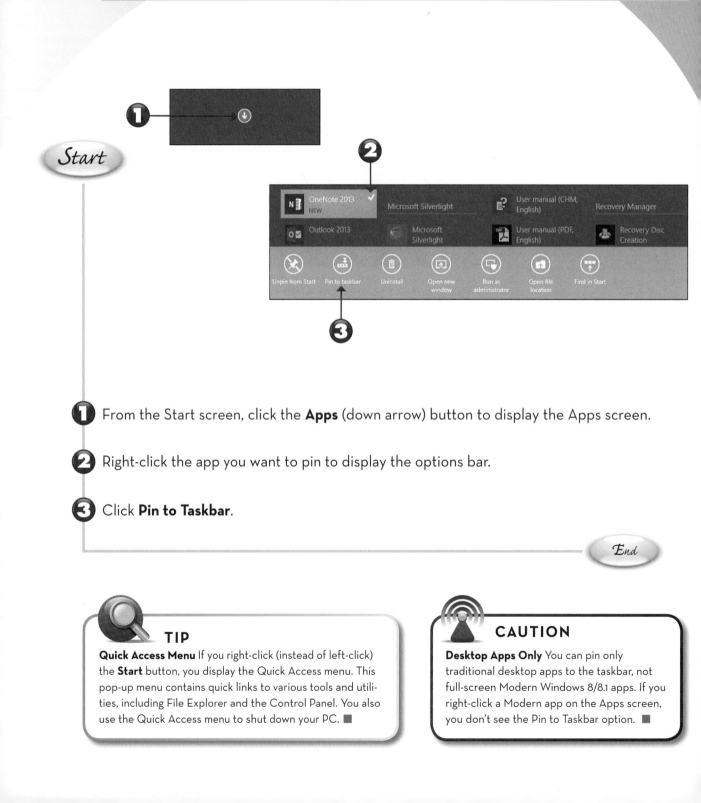

① From the Start screen, click the **Apps** (down arrow) button to display the Apps screen.

② Right-click the app you want to pin to display the options bar.

③ Click **Pin to Taskbar**.

End

TIP

Quick Access Menu If you right-click (instead of left-click) the **Start** button, you display the Quick Access menu. This pop-up menu contains quick links to various tools and utilities, including File Explorer and the Control Panel. You also use the Quick Access menu to shut down your PC. ■

CAUTION

Desktop Apps Only You can pin only traditional desktop apps to the taskbar, not full-screen Modern Windows 8/8.1 apps. If you right-click a Modern app on the Apps screen, you don't see the Pin to Taskbar option. ■

CHANGING THE DESKTOP BACKGROUND

Many users like to personalize their Windows desktop by choosing their own picture for the desktop background. You can even select a slide show of different desktop pictures that change over time.

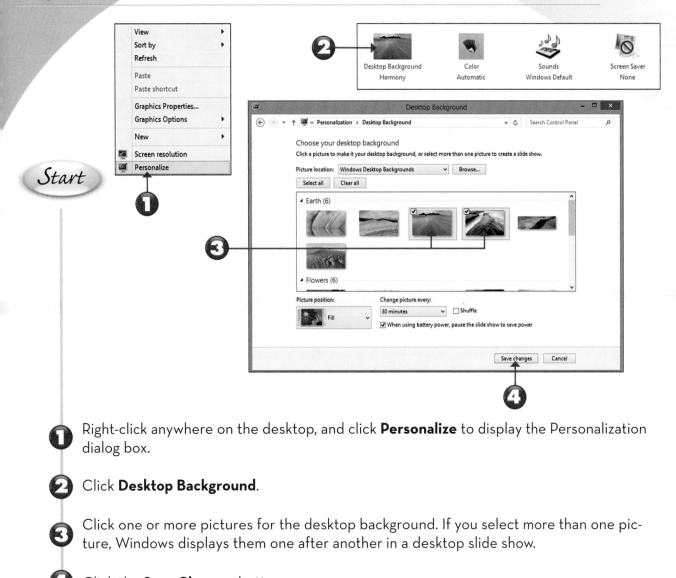

Start

Right-click anywhere on the desktop, and click **Personalize** to display the Personalization dialog box.

Click **Desktop Background**.

Click one or more pictures for the desktop background. If you select more than one picture, Windows displays them one after another in a desktop slide show.

Click the **Save Changes** button.

End

TIP

Different Locations By default, Windows displays pictures stored in the Windows Desktop Backgrounds folder. To select pictures in another location, pull down the **Picture Location** list or click the **Browse** button and make a different selection. ■

CHANGING DESKTOP COLORS

Windows also lets you change the colors of the taskbar and windows borders.

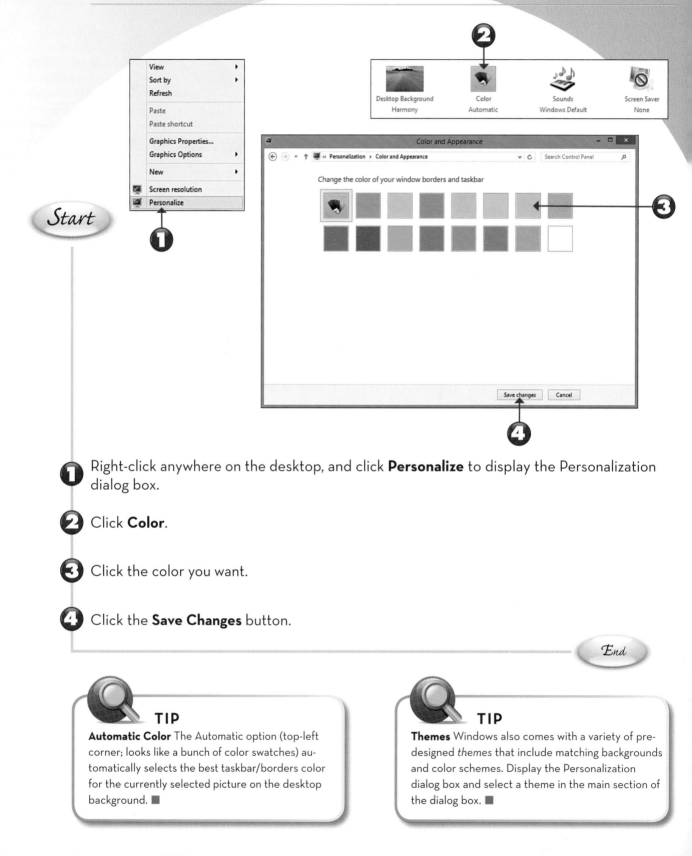

① Right-click anywhere on the desktop, and click **Personalize** to display the Personalization dialog box.

② Click **Color**.

③ Click the color you want.

④ Click the **Save Changes** button.

TIP

Automatic Color The Automatic option (top-left corner; looks like a bunch of color swatches) automatically selects the best taskbar/borders color for the currently selected picture on the desktop background. ■

TIP

Themes Windows also comes with a variety of pre-designed *themes* that include matching backgrounds and color schemes. Display the Personalization dialog box and select a theme in the main section of the dialog box. ■

SCROLLING A WINDOW

Many windows contain more information than can be displayed in the window at once. When you have a long document or web page, for example, only the first part of the document or page is displayed in the window. To view the rest of the document or page, you have to scroll down through the window, using the various parts of the scrollbar.

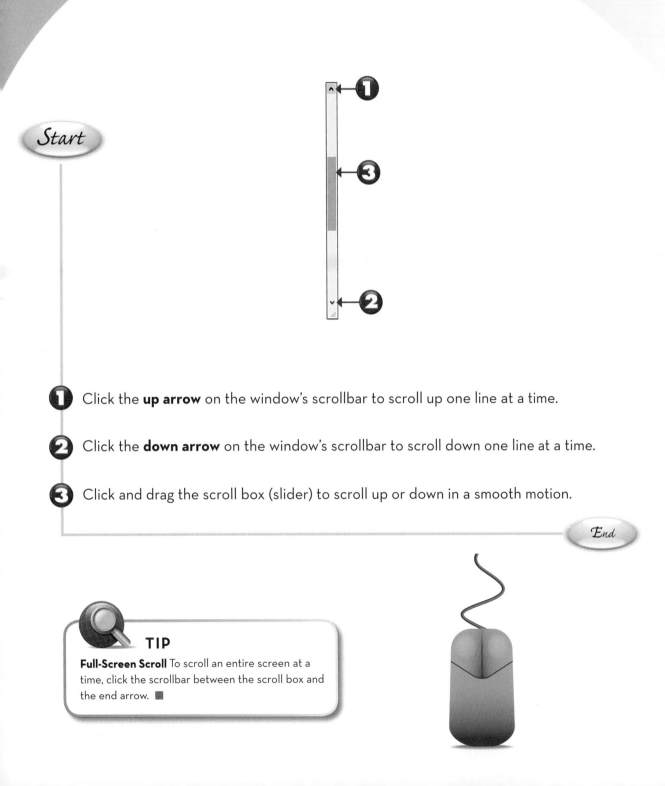

Start

1 Click the **up arrow** on the window's scrollbar to scroll up one line at a time.

2 Click the **down arrow** on the window's scrollbar to scroll down one line at a time.

3 Click and drag the scroll box (slider) to scroll up or down in a smooth motion.

End

TIP

Full-Screen Scroll To scroll an entire screen at a time, click the scrollbar between the scroll box and the end arrow. ■

MAXIMIZING, MINIMIZING, AND CLOSING A WINDOW

After you've opened a window, you can maximize it to display full screen. You can also minimize it so that it disappears from the desktop and resides as a button on the Windows taskbar, and you can close it completely.

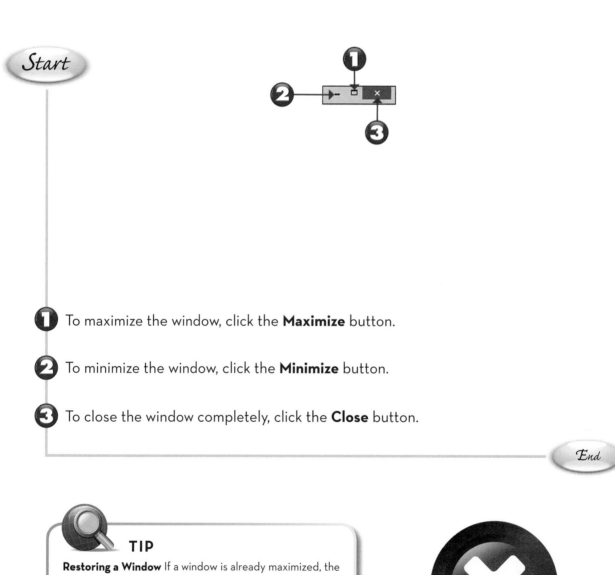

Start

1 To maximize the window, click the **Maximize** button.

2 To minimize the window, click the **Minimize** button.

3 To close the window completely, click the **Close** button.

End

TIP

Restoring a Window If a window is already maximized, the Maximize button changes to a Restore Down button. When you click the **Restore Down** button, the window resumes its previous (pre-maximized) dimensions. ■

SNAPPING A WINDOW

You can automatically organize the open windows on the desktop in several ways. You can easily maximize windows and stack multiple windows side by side with just a few drags of the mouse.

Start

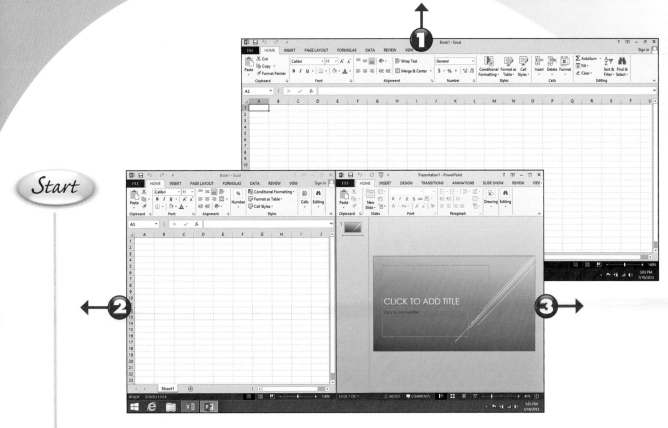

1 To maximize a window, click the window's title bar and drag it to the top edge of the screen, or press **Windows + up arrow**.

2 To snap a window to the left side of the screen, click the window's title bar and drag it to the left edge of the screen, or press **Windows + left arrow**.

3 To snap a window to the right side of the screen, click the window's title bar and drag it to the right edge of the screen, or press **Windows + right arrow**.

End

TIP

Restoring a Maximized Window To restore a maximized window, click the window's title bar and drag it down from the top of the screen, or press **Windows + down arrow**. ■

USING MENUS

Many older Windows programs use a set of pull-down menus to store all the commands and operations you can perform. The menus are aligned across the top of the window, just below the title bar, in what is called a *menu bar*. You open (or pull down) a menu by clicking the menu's name; you select a menu item by clicking it with your mouse.

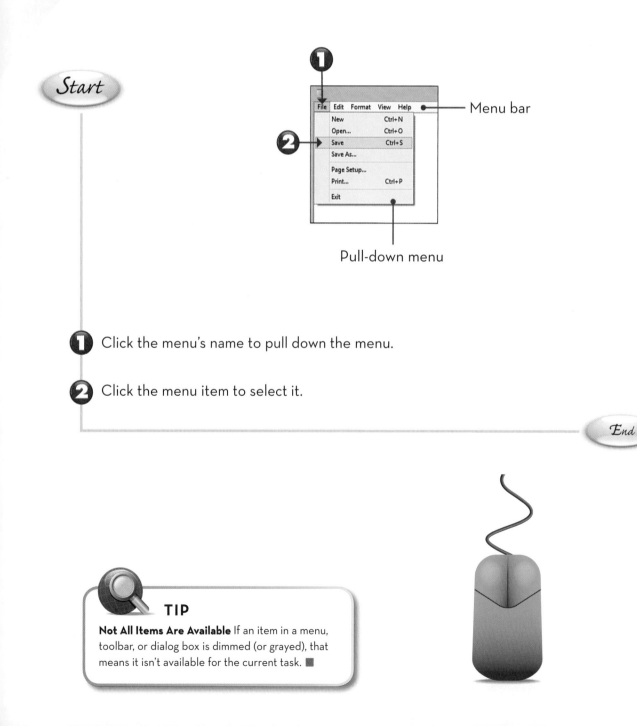

Menu bar

Pull-down menu

1 Click the menu's name to pull down the menu.

2 Click the menu item to select it.

TIP

Not All Items Are Available If an item in a menu, toolbar, or dialog box is dimmed (or grayed), that means it isn't available for the current task. ■

USING TOOLBARS AND RIBBONS

Some Windows programs put the most frequently used operations on one or more *toolbars* or *ribbons*, usually located just below the menu bar. A toolbar looks like a row of buttons, each with a small picture (called an *icon*) and maybe a bit of text. You activate the associated command or operation by clicking the button with your mouse.

Start

Tab

Ribbon

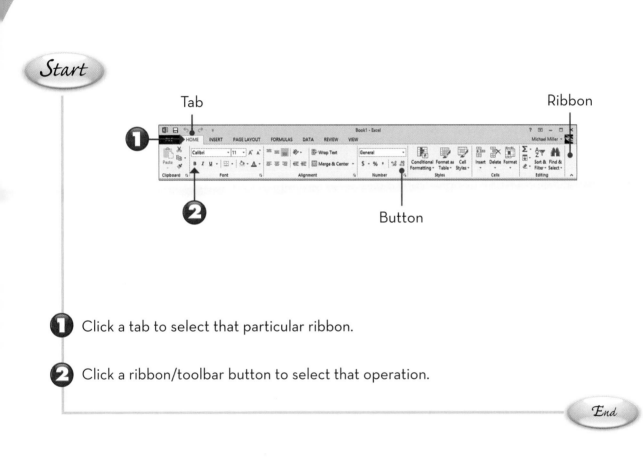

Button

1 Click a tab to select that particular ribbon.

2 Click a ribbon/toolbar button to select that operation.

End

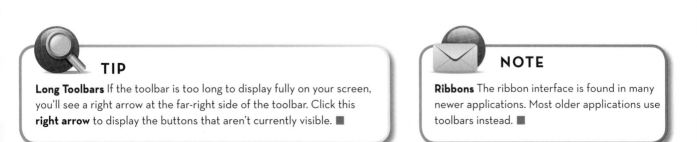

TIP

Long Toolbars If the toolbar is too long to display fully on your screen, you'll see a right arrow at the far-right side of the toolbar. Click this **right arrow** to display the buttons that aren't currently visible. ■

NOTE

Ribbons The ribbon interface is found in many newer applications. Most older applications use toolbars instead. ■

USING MICROSOFT WORD

When you want to write a letter, fire off a quick memo, create a fancy report, or publish a newsletter, you use a type of software program called a *word processor*. For most computer users, Microsoft Word is the word processing program of choice. Word is a full-featured word processor, and it's included on many new PCs and as part of the Microsoft Office software suite. You can use Word for all your writing needs—from basic letters to fancy newsletters and for everything in between.

Two versions of Word are available. Microsoft Word Web App is a free web-based version you access using Internet Explorer or another web browser. There's also the traditional desktop software version of Word, which you can purchase from any consumer electronics store or download from Microsoft or various Internet retailers.

For many users, the Word Web App is sufficient, even though it lacks some of the advanced features of the more expensive desktop version. If you want to do sophisticated page layouts, mail merges, and similar functions, you'll need to purchase the desktop software version of Word. Otherwise, use the free online version—it's fine for writing memos, letters, and the like.

COMPARING DESKTOP AND WEB VERSIONS OF WORD

Microsoft
Word desktop
software

Microsoft
Word Web
App

LAUNCHING THE WORD WEB APP

If you don't want to go to all the trouble of purchasing and installing an expensive piece of software, you can use the free Microsoft Word Web App from your web browser. You access Word Web App (and all the free Office Web Apps) from Microsoft's SkyDrive web-based storage system.

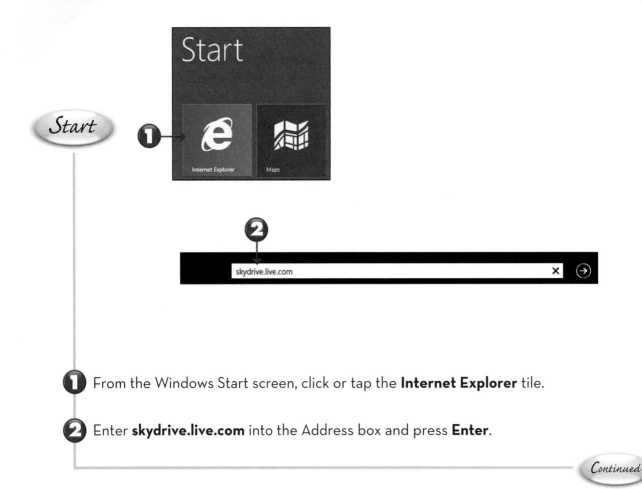

Start

1 From the Windows Start screen, click or tap the **Internet Explorer** tile.

2 Enter **skydrive.live.com** into the Address box and press **Enter**.

Continued

NOTE

SkyDrive App You can also open and edit existing Word documents using the SkyDrive app found on the Windows Start screen. However, you can't use the SkyDrive app to create new documents; you have to do this from within Internet Explorer. ■

NOTE

Office Web Apps Microsoft's Office Web Apps include Word (word processing), Excel (spreadsheets), Power-Point (presentations), and OneNote (notes and planning). Learn more about Office Web Apps—and the desktop version of Office—online at office.microsoft.com. ■

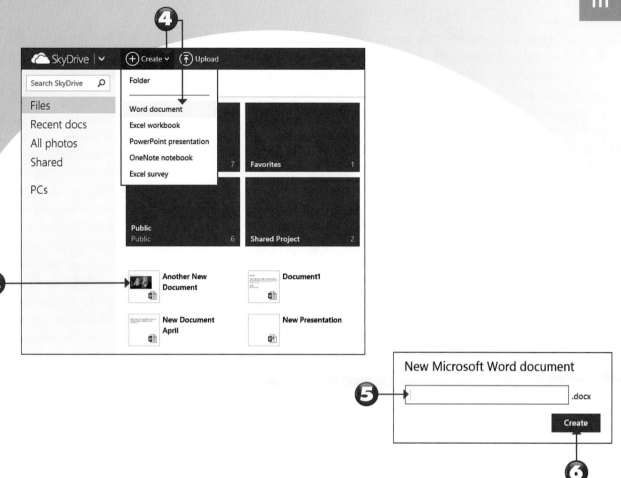

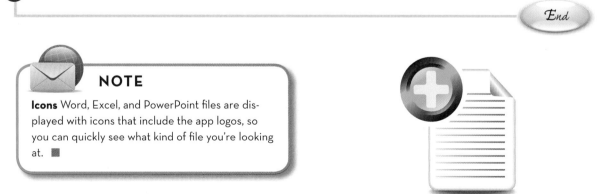

3️⃣ You now see all the files you've previously uploaded to SkyDrive, organized in the folders you created. To open an existing document, double-click it.

4️⃣ To open a new Word document, click the **Create** icon on the toolbar at the top of the screen, then click **Word Document**.

5️⃣ Enter a name for this new document into the New Microsoft Word Document dialog box.

6️⃣ Click the **Create** button.

End

NOTE

Icons Word, Excel, and PowerPoint files are displayed with icons that include the app logos, so you can quickly see what kind of file you're looking at. ■

LAUNCHING THE WORD DESKTOP APP

When you need to create more sophisticated documents, use the full-featured desktop version of Microsoft Word. It works similarly to the web version, but with more formatting options.

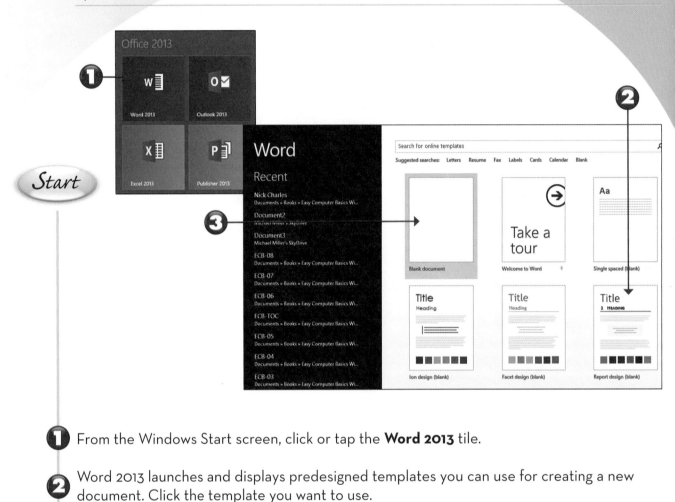

From the Windows Start screen, click or tap the **Word 2013** tile.

Word 2013 launches and displays predesigned templates you can use for creating a new document. Click the template you want to use.

OR

Click **Blank Document** to start your new document without a template.

NOTE

Word 2013 The latest version of Microsoft Word is Word 2013. Older versions look and operate slightly differently from what is described in this chapter. ■

NOTE

Office 365 Home Premium You usually purchase Microsoft Word as part of the Microsoft Office suite of programs; the latest version is called Office 365. Microsoft offers several editions of Office, but most home users will find the Home Premium edition the best fit because it includes the Word, Excel, PowerPoint, Outlook, Publisher, Access, and OneNote apps. A 1-year subscription, good for up to five PCs, runs $99.99. ■

NAVIGATING THE WORD WEB APP

The Word Web App, like the desktop version of Word, uses a ribbon-based interface with different ribbons for different types of operations. Each ribbon contains buttons and controls for specific operations. For example, the Home ribbon contains controls for formatting fonts, paragraphs, and the like; the Insert ribbon includes controls for inserting tables, pictures, clip art, and such.

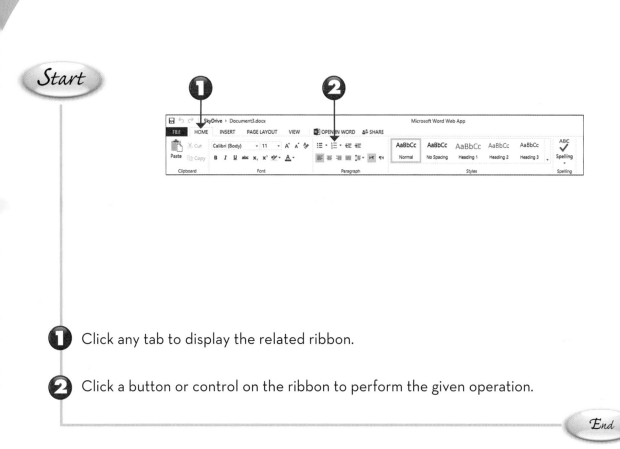

① Click any tab to display the related ribbon.

② Click a button or control on the ribbon to perform the given operation.

TIP

Context-Sensitive Ribbons Some ribbons appear automatically when you perform a specific task. For example, if you insert a picture and then select that picture, a new Format ribbon tab (not otherwise visible) will appear, with controls for formatting the selected picture. ■

TIP

Different Ribbons The desktop software version of Microsoft Word contains additional ribbons (such as Page Layout, References, and Mailings) not found in the Word Web App. ■

ENTERING TEXT

You enter text in a Word document at the *insertion point*, which appears onscreen as a blinking cursor. When you start typing on your keyboard, the new text is added at the insertion point.

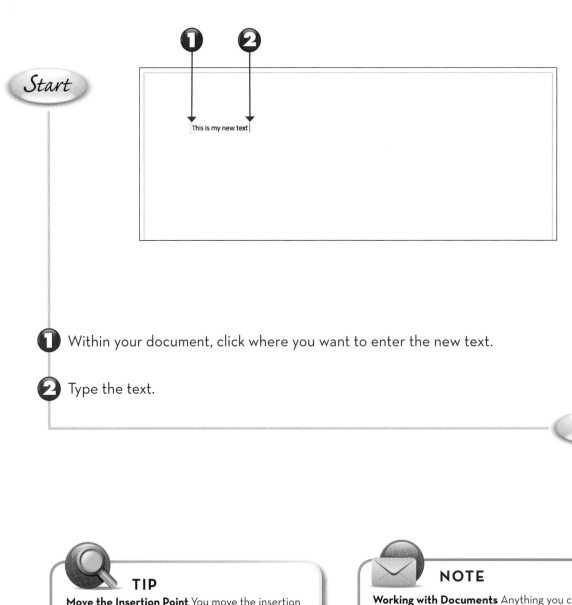

Start

This is my new text

1 Within your document, click where you want to enter the new text.

2 Type the text.

End

CUTTING/COPYING AND PASTING TEXT

Word lets you cut, copy, and paste text—or graphics—to and from anywhere in your document or between documents. Use your mouse to select the text you want to edit, and then select the appropriate command from the Home ribbon.

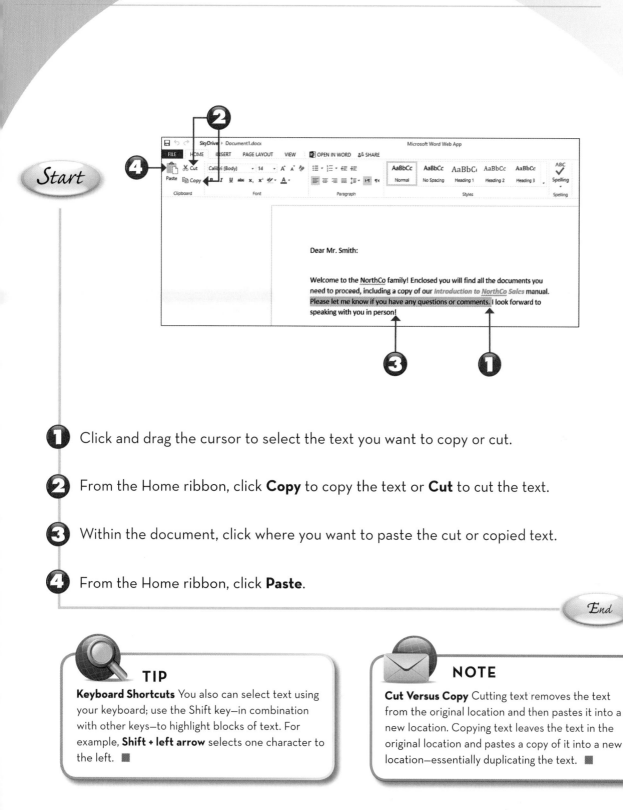

1 Click and drag the cursor to select the text you want to copy or cut.

2 From the Home ribbon, click **Copy** to copy the text or **Cut** to cut the text.

3 Within the document, click where you want to paste the cut or copied text.

4 From the Home ribbon, click **Paste**.

TIP

Keyboard Shortcuts You also can select text using your keyboard; use the Shift key—in combination with other keys—to highlight blocks of text. For example, **Shift + left arrow** selects one character to the left. ■

NOTE

Cut Versus Copy Cutting text removes the text from the original location and then pastes it into a new location. Copying text leaves the text in the original location and pastes a copy of it into a new location—essentially duplicating the text. ■

FORMATTING TEXT

After your text is entered and edited, you can use Word's numerous formatting options to add some pizzazz to your document.

Font

Font size

Font color

Bold

Italic

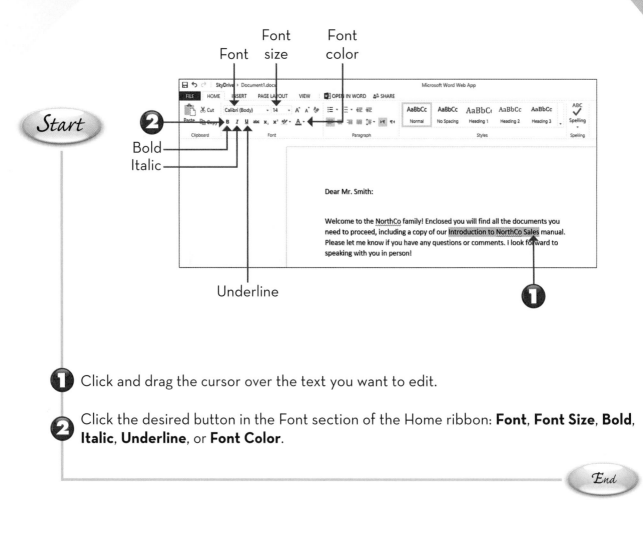

Underline

Start

① Click and drag the cursor over the text you want to edit.

② Click the desired button in the Font section of the Home ribbon: **Font**, **Font Size**, **Bold**, **Italic**, **Underline**, or **Font Color**.

End

FORMATTING PARAGRAPHS

When you're creating a more complex document, you need to format more than just a few words here and there. To format complete paragraphs, use Word's Paragraph formatting options on the Home ribbon.

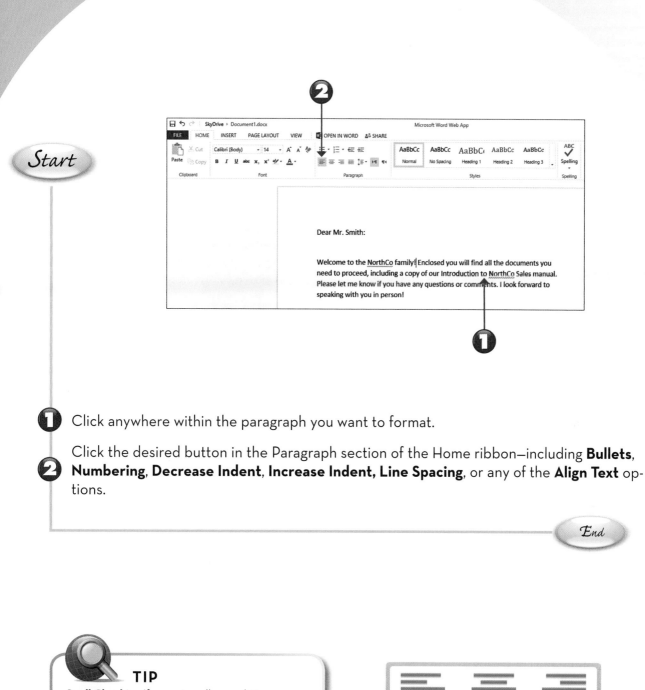

Start

1 Click anywhere within the paragraph you want to format.

2 Click the desired button in the Paragraph section of the Home ribbon—including **Bullets**, **Numbering**, **Decrease Indent**, **Increase Indent**, **Line Spacing**, or any of the **Align Text** options.

End

TIP

Spell Checking If you misspell a word, it appears onscreen with a squiggly red underline. Right-click the misspelled word and select the correct spelling from the list. ■

SAVING YOUR WORK

As you work on a file, you need to save your edits periodically. This is an easy process.

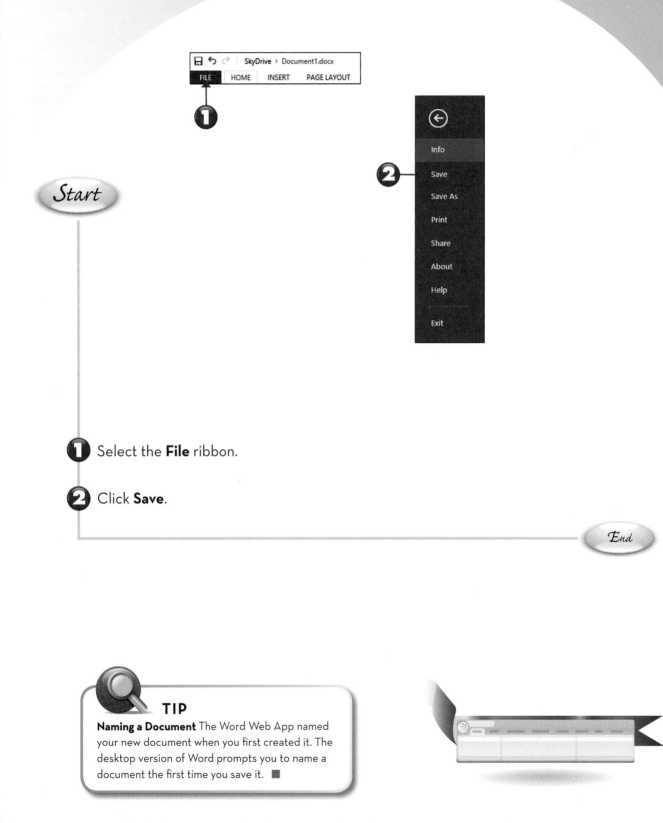

Start

1 Select the **File** ribbon.

2 Click **Save**.

End

TIP

Naming a Document The Word Web App named your new document when you first created it. The desktop version of Word prompts you to name a document the first time you save it. ■

PRINTING A DOCUMENT

When you've finished editing your document, you can instruct Word to send a copy to your printer. With the Word Web App, this involves creating a PDF-format copy of your document, opening that document with a PDF viewer app (such as Adobe Reader), and then using that app's print function to print the document.

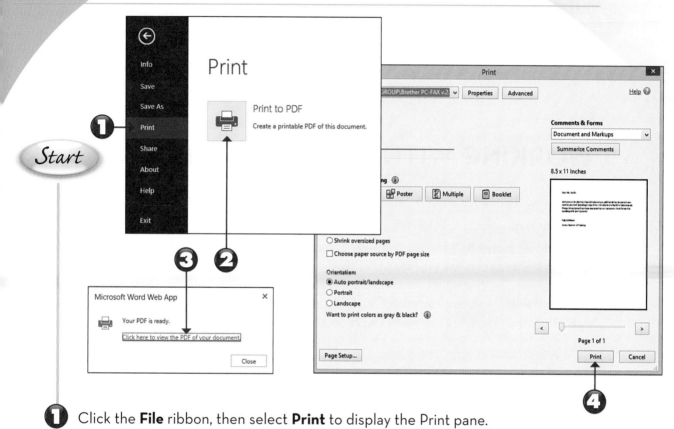

Start

1 Click the **File** ribbon, then select **Print** to display the Print pane.

2 Click **Print to PDF**.

3 When the document is converted to PDF format, click **Click Here to View the PDF of Your Document**.

4 This opens the Print dialog box for your PDF viewer app. Configure any necessary options, then click the **Print** button to print the document.

End

TIP

PDF Printing The Word Web App uses your computer's default PDF viewer to print your documents. If you don't have a PDF viewer installed on your system, you can download Adobe Reader for free from get.adobe.com/reader/. ■

TIP

Open or Save? If you're prompted to open or save the PDF document when printing from the Word Web App, select **Open**. This should open the Print dialog box for your PDF viewer app. ■

Chapter 9

WORKING WITH FILES AND FOLDERS

All the data for documents and programs on your computer is stored in electronic files. These files are then arranged into a series of folders and subfolders—just as you'd arrange paper files in a series of file folders in a filing cabinet.

In Windows 8 and 8.1, you use the File Explorer app on the traditional desktop to view and manage your folders and files. You open File Explorer by opening the desktop and then clicking the **File Explorer** icon on the taskbar. (You also can open File Explorer from the Quick Access menu that displays when you right-click the **Start** button on any screen.)

FILE EXPLORER

Tabs

Expand/contract ribbon

Move up one folder level

Return to the last-viewed folder

Ribbon

Search box

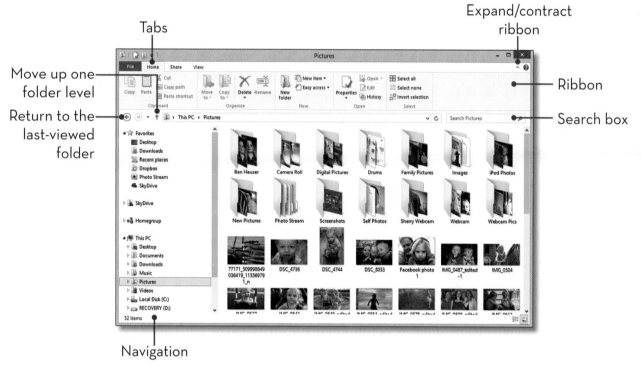

Navigation pane

NAVIGATING FOLDERS

You can navigate through the folders and subfolders in File Explorer in several ways.

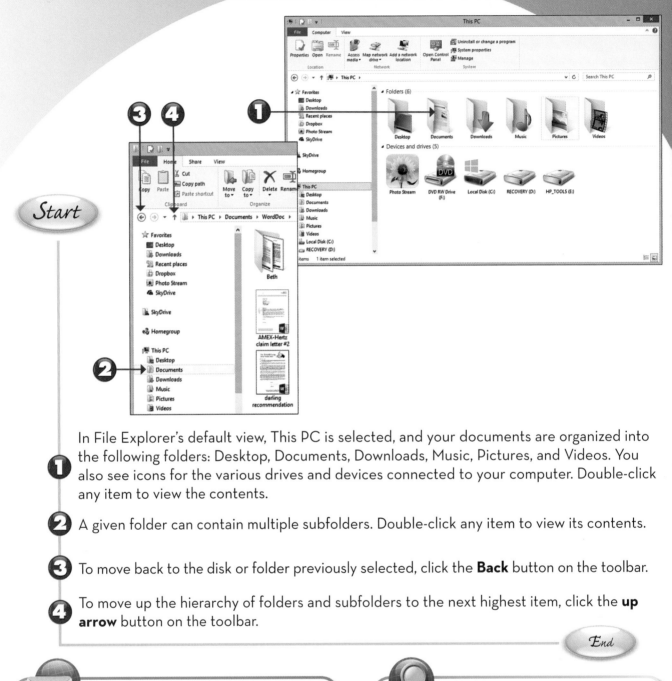

Start

In File Explorer's default view, This PC is selected, and your documents are organized into the following folders: Desktop, Documents, Downloads, Music, Pictures, and Videos. You also see icons for the various drives and devices connected to your computer. Double-click any item to view the contents.

A given folder can contain multiple subfolders. Double-click any item to view its contents.

To move back to the disk or folder previously selected, click the **Back** button on the toolbar.

To move up the hierarchy of folders and subfolders to the next highest item, click the **up arrow** button on the toolbar.

End

NOTE

Major Folders The Documents, Music, Pictures, and other folders displayed in File Explorer are not the only folders on your PC, but they are the ones most likely to contain data files. Other folders, which can be displayed if you click **Local Disk** in the navigation pane, are more likely to contain programs and apps rather than documents and data. ■

TIP

Breadcrumbs The list of folders and subfolders in File Explorer's Address box presents a "breadcrumb" approach to navigation. You can view additional items by clicking the separator arrow next to the folder icon in the Address box; this displays a pull-down menu of the contents of the item to the left of the arrow. ■

NAVIGATING WITH THE NAVIGATION PANE

Another way to navigate your files and folders is to use the navigation pane. This pane, on the left side of the File Explorer window, displays both favorite links and hierarchical folder trees for your computer, network, and SkyDrive online storage.

Start

1. Click the **arrow** icon next to any folder to display all the subfolders it contains.

2. Click a folder to display its contents in the main File Explorer window.

End

NOTE

Favorites By default, Windows Favorites include Desktop, Downloads, Recent Places, and SkyDrive. Other Favorites may be added, depending on your own individual usage. ■

TIP

This PC To navigate all the drives and folders on your computer, click the **This PC** folder in the navigation pane. (In previous versions of Windows, This PC was labeled either Computer or My Computer.) ■

CHANGING THE WAY FILES ARE DISPLAYED

You can choose to view the contents of a folder in a variety of ways. The icon views are nice in that they show a small thumbnail preview of any selected file.

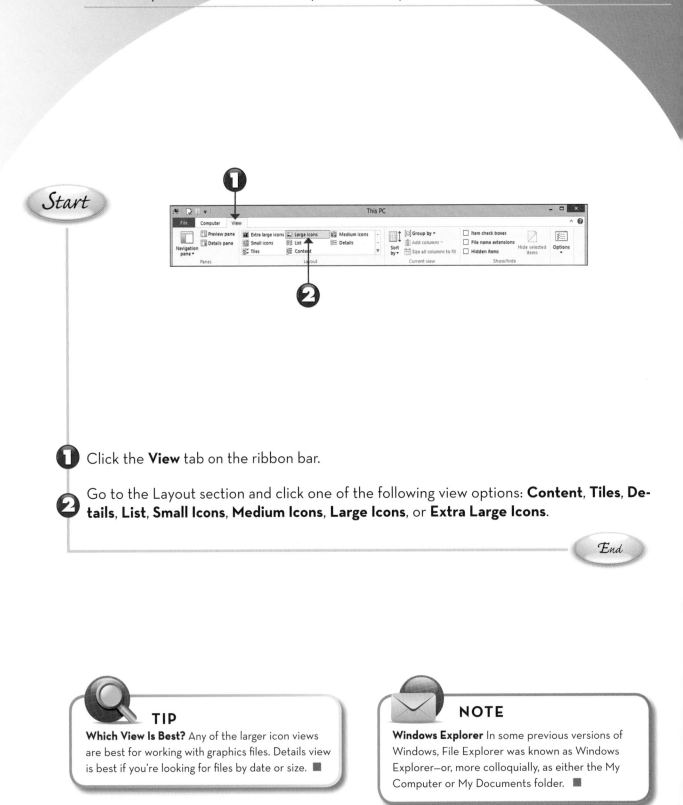

Start

① Click the **View** tab on the ribbon bar.

② Go to the Layout section and click one of the following view options: **Content**, **Tiles**, **Details**, **List**, **Small Icons**, **Medium Icons**, **Large Icons**, or **Extra Large Icons**.

End

TIP

Which View Is Best? Any of the larger icon views are best for working with graphics files. Details view is best if you're looking for files by date or size. ■

NOTE

Windows Explorer In some previous versions of Windows, File Explorer was known as Windows Explorer—or, more colloquially, as either the My Computer or My Documents folder. ■

SORTING FILES AND FOLDERS

When viewing files in File Explorer, you can sort your files and folders in a number of ways. To view your files in alphabetic order, choose to sort by **Name**. To see all similar files grouped together, choose to sort by **Type**. To sort your files by the date and time they were last edited, select **Date Modified**.

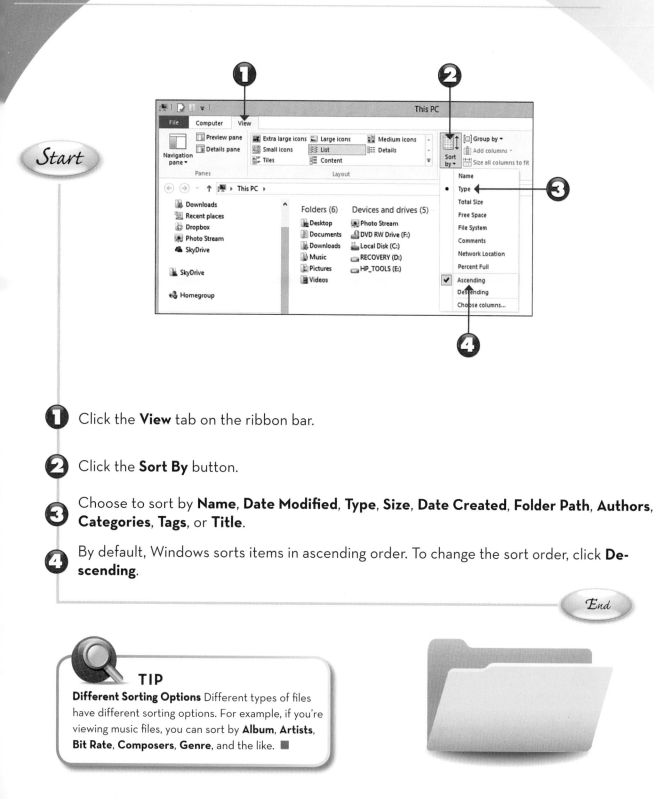

Start

① Click the **View** tab on the ribbon bar.

② Click the **Sort By** button.

③ Choose to sort by **Name**, **Date Modified**, **Type**, **Size**, **Date Created**, **Folder Path**, **Authors**, **Categories**, **Tags**, or **Title**.

④ By default, Windows sorts items in ascending order. To change the sort order, click **Descending**.

End

TIP

Different Sorting Options Different types of files have different sorting options. For example, if you're viewing music files, you can sort by **Album**, **Artists**, **Bit Rate**, **Composers**, **Genre**, and the like. ■

CREATING A NEW FOLDER

The more files you create, the harder it is to organize and find things on your hard disk. When the number of files you have becomes unmanageable, you need to create more folders—and subfolders—to better categorize your files.

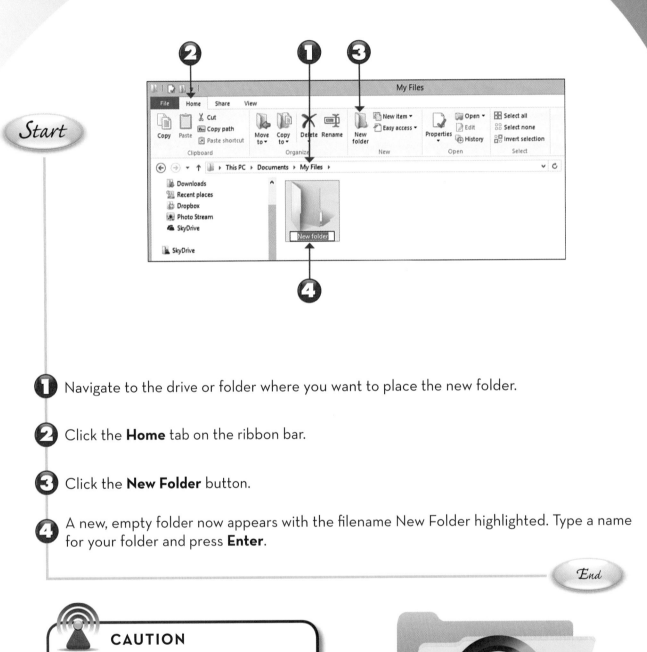

Start

1 Navigate to the drive or folder where you want to place the new folder.

2 Click the **Home** tab on the ribbon bar.

3 Click the **New Folder** button.

4 A new, empty folder now appears with the filename New Folder highlighted. Type a name for your folder and press **Enter**.

End

CAUTION

Illegal Characters Folder names and filenames can include up to 255 characters—including many special characters. You *can't*, however, use the following "illegal" characters: \ / : * ? " < > |. ▪

RENAMING A FILE OR FOLDER

When you create a new file or folder, it helps to give it a name that describes its contents. Sometimes, however, you might need to change a file's name. Fortunately, Windows makes renaming an item relatively easy.

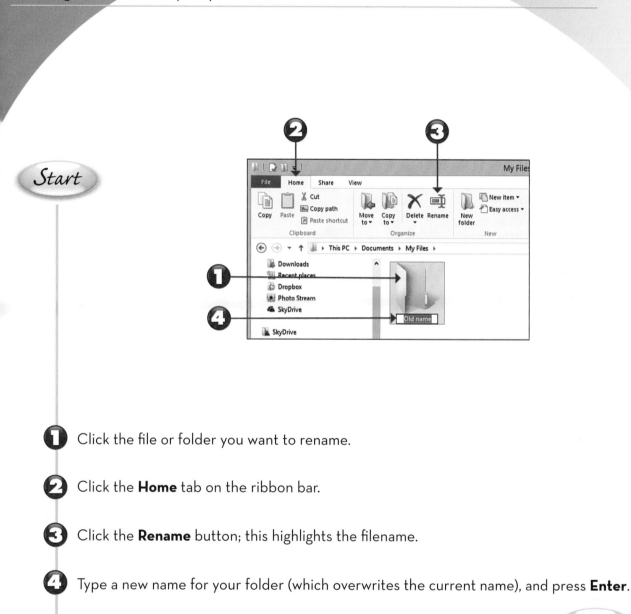

Start

① Click the file or folder you want to rename.

② Click the **Home** tab on the ribbon bar.

③ Click the **Rename** button; this highlights the filename.

④ Type a new name for your folder (which overwrites the current name), and press **Enter**.

End

CAUTION

Don't Change the Extension The one part of the filename you should never change is the extension—the part that comes after the final "dot" if you choose to show file extensions. Try to change the extension, and Windows will warn you that you're doing something wrong. ■

TIP

Keyboard Shortcut You can also rename a file by selecting the file and pressing **F2** on your computer keyboard. This highlights the filename and readies it for editing. ■

COPYING A FILE OR FOLDER

There are many ways to copy a file in Windows 8. The easiest method is to use the **Copy To** button on the Home ribbon.

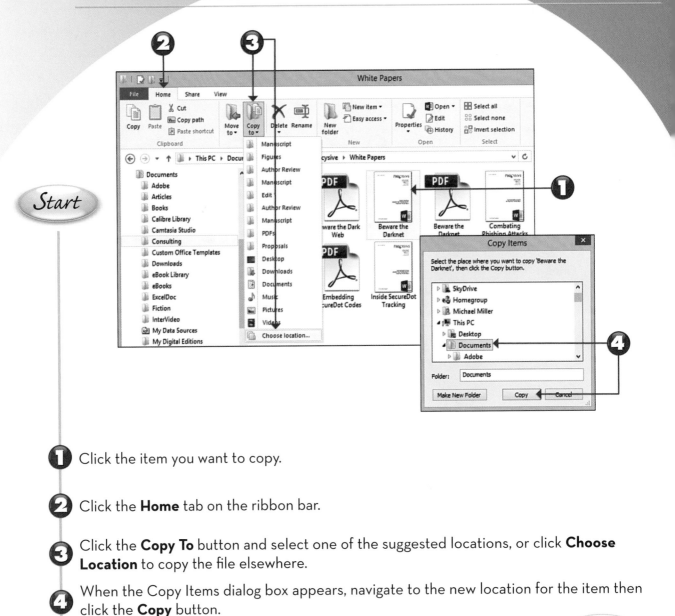

① Click the item you want to copy.

② Click the **Home** tab on the ribbon bar.

③ Click the **Copy To** button and select one of the suggested locations, or click **Choose Location** to copy the file elsewhere.

④ When the Copy Items dialog box appears, navigate to the new location for the item then click the **Copy** button.

MOVING A FILE OR FOLDER

Moving a file or folder is different from copying it. Moving cuts the item from its previous location and pastes it into a new location. Copying leaves the original item where it was *and* creates a copy of the item elsewhere.

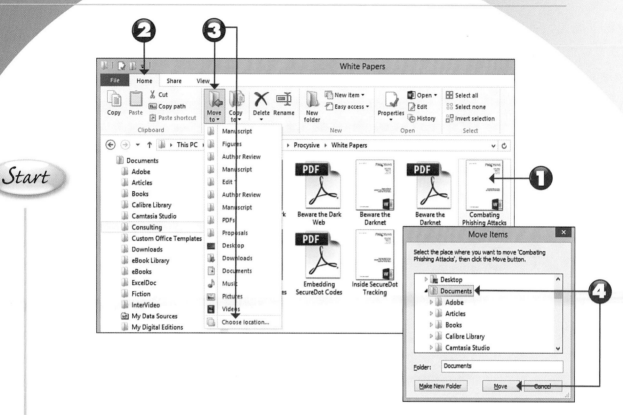

Start

① Click the item you want to move.

② Click the **Home** tab on the ribbon bar.

③ Click the **Move To** button and select one of the suggested locations, or click **Choose Location** to move the file another location.

④ When the Move Items dialog box appears, navigate to the new location for the item, and then click the **Move** button.

End

SEARCHING FOR A FILE

As organized as you might be, you might not always be able to find the specific files you want. Fortunately, Windows 8 offers an easy way to locate difficult-to-find files, via the new Instant Search function. Instant Search lets you find files by extension, filename, or keywords within the file.

Start

1. From within File Explorer, enter one or more keywords into the Search box and press **Enter.**

2. Windows now displays a list of files that match your search criteria. Double-click any item to open that file.

End

TIP

Search Index Instant Search indexes all the files stored on your hard disk (including email messages) by type, title, and contents. ■

DELETING A FILE OR FOLDER

Keeping too many files eats up too much hard disk space—which is a bad thing. Because you don't want to waste disk space, you should periodically delete those files (and folders) you no longer need. When you delete a file, you send it to the Windows Recycle Bin, which is kind of a trash can for deleted files.

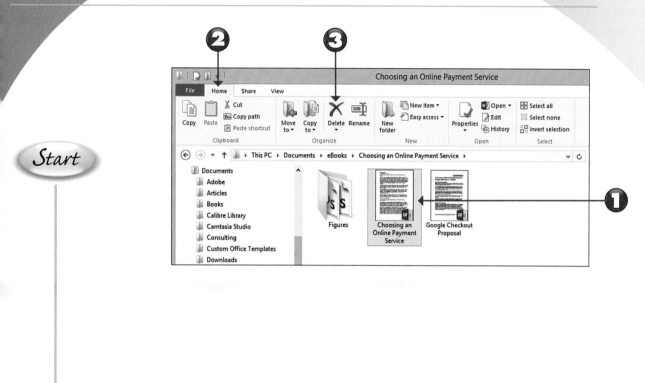

Start

1. Click the file you want to delete.

2. Click the **Home** tab on the ribbon bar.

3. Click the **Delete** button.

End

TIP

Other Ways to Delete You can also delete a file by dragging it from the folder window onto the Recycle Bin icon on the desktop or by highlighting it and pressing the **Delete** key on your computer keyboard. ■

RESTORING DELETED FILES

Have you ever accidentally deleted the wrong file? If so, you're in luck. Windows stores the files you delete in the Recycle Bin, which is actually a special folder on your hard disk. For a short period of time (in most instances, several days), you can "undelete" files from the Recycle Bin back to their original locations.

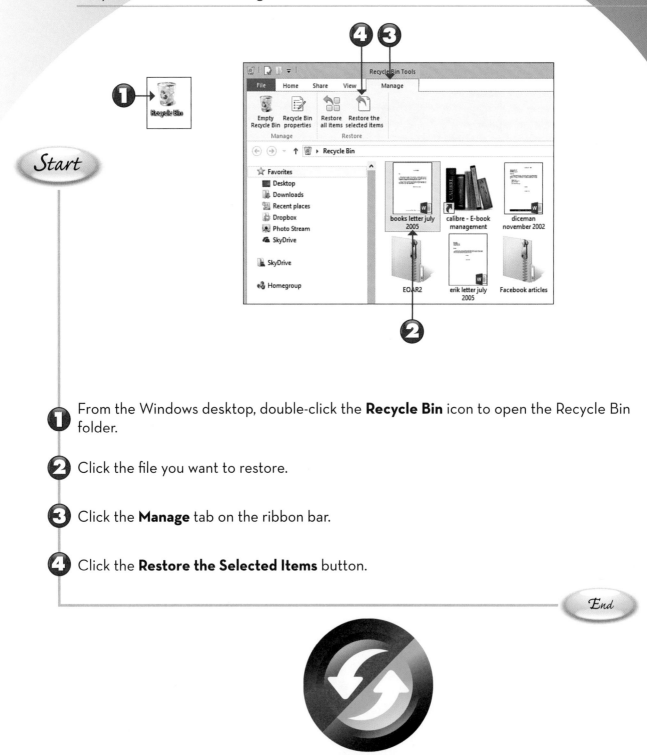

Start

1 From the Windows desktop, double-click the **Recycle Bin** icon to open the Recycle Bin folder.

2 Click the file you want to restore.

3 Click the **Manage** tab on the ribbon bar.

4 Click the **Restore the Selected Items** button.

End

EMPTYING THE RECYCLE BIN

By default, the deleted files in the Recycle Bin can occupy 4GB plus 5% of your hard disk space. When you've deleted enough files to exceed this limit, the oldest files in the Recycle Bin are automatically and permanently deleted from your hard disk. You can also manually empty the Recycle Bin and thus free up some hard disk space.

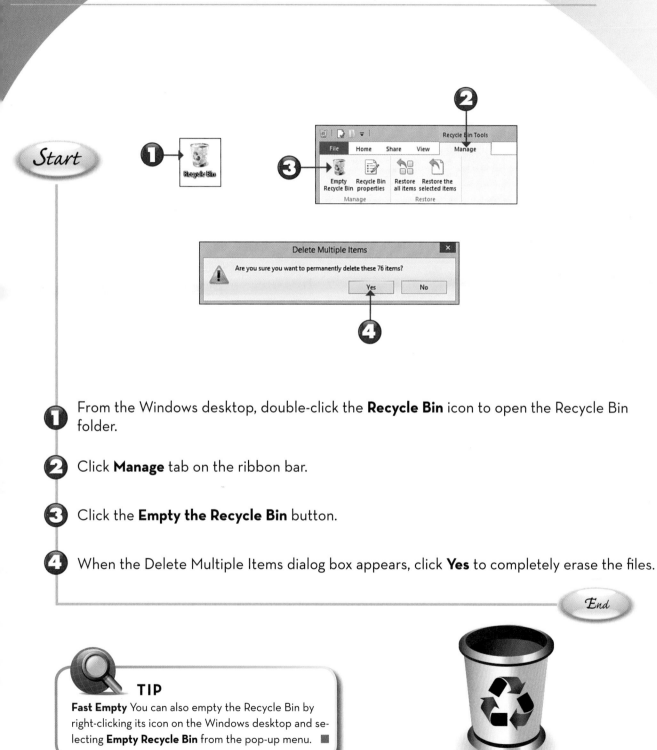

1 From the Windows desktop, double-click the **Recycle Bin** icon to open the Recycle Bin folder.

2 Click **Manage** tab on the ribbon bar.

3 Click the **Empty the Recycle Bin** button.

4 When the Delete Multiple Items dialog box appears, click **Yes** to completely erase the files.

TIP

Fast Empty You can also empty the Recycle Bin by right-clicking its icon on the Windows desktop and selecting **Empty Recycle Bin** from the pop-up menu. ▪

COMPRESSING A FILE

Really big files can be difficult to copy or share. Fortunately, Windows lets you create *compressed* folders, which take big files and compress them in size (called a "zipped" file). After the file has been transferred, you can then uncompress the file back to its original state.

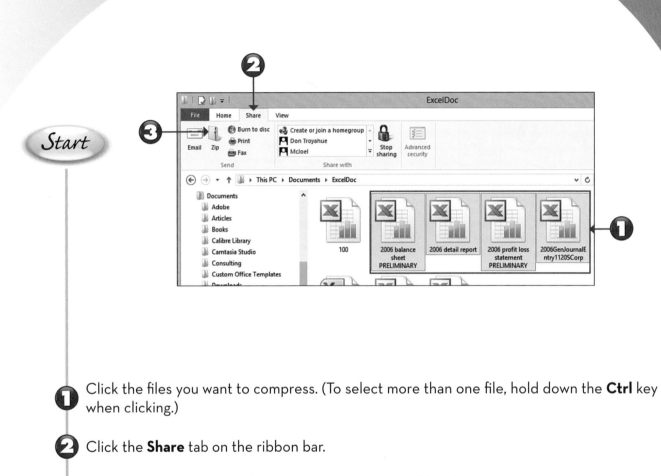

Start

1 Click the files you want to compress. (To select more than one file, hold down the **Ctrl** key when clicking.)

2 Click the **Share** tab on the ribbon bar.

3 Click the **Zip** button. Windows now creates a new folder that contains compressed versions of the files you selected.

End

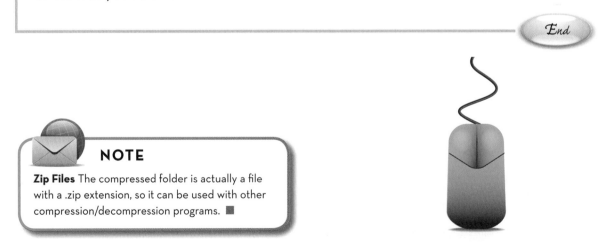

NOTE

Zip Files The compressed folder is actually a file with a .zip extension, so it can be used with other compression/decompression programs. ■

EXTRACTING FILES FROM A COMPRESSED FOLDER

The process of decompressing a file is actually an *extraction* process. That's because you extract the original files from the compressed folder to the desired location on your computer's hard drive.

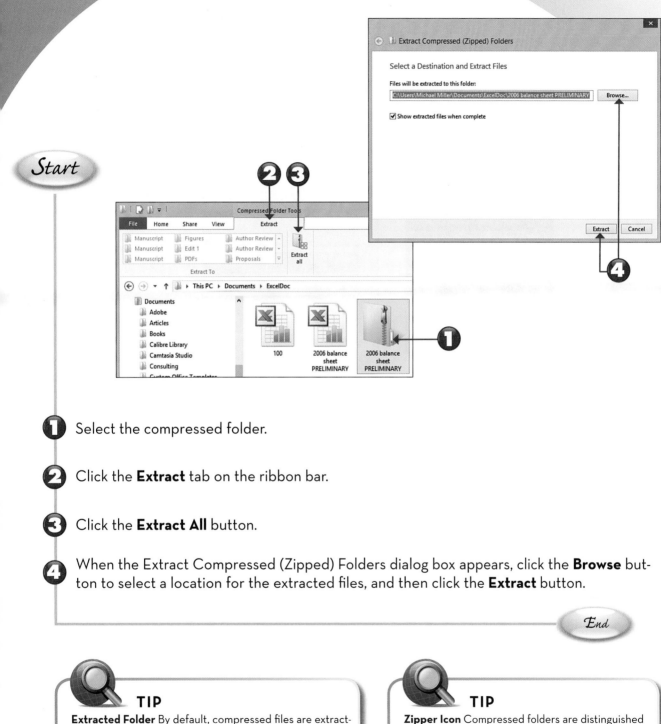

Start

End

1. Select the compressed folder.

2. Click the **Extract** tab on the ribbon bar.

3. Click the **Extract All** button.

4. When the Extract Compressed (Zipped) Folders dialog box appears, click the **Browse** button to select a location for the extracted files, and then click the **Extract** button.

WORKING WITH FILES ON SKYDRIVE

Microsoft offers online storage for all your documents and data via its SkyDrive service. When you store your files on SkyDrive, you can access them via any computer or mobile device connected to the Internet. You manage all your online files with the Windows SkyDrive app.

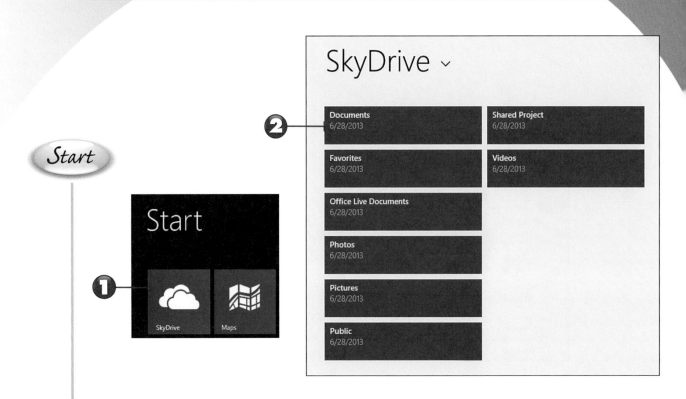

From the Windows Start screen, click or tap the **SkyDrive** tile to launch the SkyDrive app.

Your SkyDrive files are stored in folders—Documents, Favorites, Photos, and so forth. Click a folder to view its contents.

Continued

TIP

Local Files You can also use the SkyDrive app for basic management of local files. Click the **SkyDrive** down arrow and select **This PC** to access files stored on your computer's hard drive. ■

NOTE

Cloud Storage Online file storage, such as that offered by SkyDrive, Apple's iCloud, and Google Drive, is called *cloud storage*. The advantages of cloud storage is that files can be accessed from any computer (work, home, or other) at any location. You're not limited to using a given file on a single computer only. ■

SkyDrive ⌄ Documents

③→
| | A New Spreadsheet |
| | 10/30/2012   8.13 KB |

	Book1
	7/29/2013 10.9 KB
	Available offline

| | Book2 |
| | 1/24/2013   5.58 KB |

| | Document2 |
| | 10/30/2012   15.0 KB |

| | Document3 |
| | 10/30/2012   15.0 KB |

| | Presentation1 |
| | 1/24/2013   607 KB |

| 🗑 | 📋 | ✂ | ✏ | ☁ | 🗐 |
| Delete | Copy | Cut | Rename | Make offline | Open with |

④

③ Click a file to view it or, in the case of an Office document, open it in its host application.

④ To copy, cut, or rename a file, right-click the file to display the options bar, and then select the action you want to perform.

End

TIP
Download a File To download a file from SkyDrive to your local hard disk, right-click the file to display the options bar, and then click **Make Offline**. ■

NOTE
Storage Plans Microsoft gives you 7GB of storage in your free SkyDrive account, which is more than enough to store most users' documents, digital photos, and the like. If you need more storage, you can purchase an additional 20GB for $10/year. ■

USING THE INTERNET

It used to be that most people bought personal computers to do work—word processing, spreadsheets, databases, that sort of thing. But today, many people also buy PCs to access the Internet—to send and receive email, surf the Web, and chat with other users.

If you're using your notebook or tablet PC on the road, all you have to do is look for a public WiFi hotspot. Your notebook connects to the hotspot, which then connects you to the Internet, simple as pie.

Once you go online, you use the Internet Explorer (IE) *web browser* (included with Windows) to surf the World Wide Web. Information on the Web is presented in *web pages*, each of which contains text, graphics, and links to other web pages. A web page resides at a *website*, which is nothing more than a collection of web pages. The main page of a website is called the *home page*, which serves as an opening screen that provides a brief overview and a sort of menu of everything you can find at that site.

COMPARING THE MODERN AND DESKTOP VERSIONS OF IE

Internet Explorer
(Modern version)

Open tabs

Address box

Click to view Favorites

Internet Explorer
(desktop version)

Address box

Open tabs

Click to view
Favorites

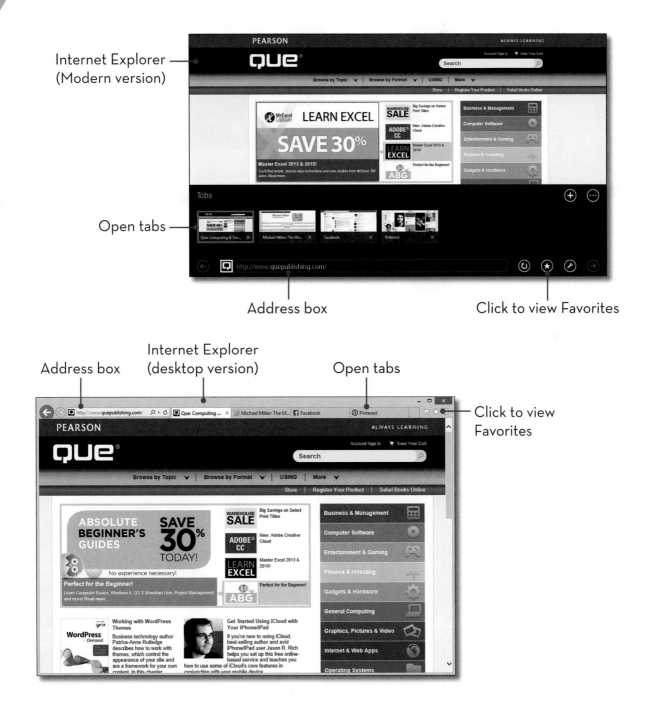

CONNECTING TO AN INTERNET WIFI HOTSPOT

If you have a notebook or tablet PC, you have the option to connect to the Internet when you're out and about. Many coffeehouses, libraries, hotels, and public spaces offer wireless WiFi Internet service, either free or for an hourly or daily fee.

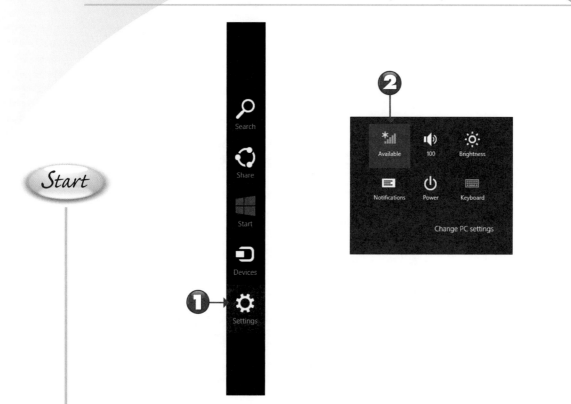

1 From the Start screen, display the charms bar, and then click or tap **Settings** to display the Settings panel.

2 Click or tap the **WiFi** icon. (If there are WiFi networks nearby, the icon should be labeled Available.)

Continued

NOTE

Wireless Hotspots A *hotspot* is a public place that offers wireless access to the Internet using WiFi technology. Some hotspots are free for all to access; others require some sort of payment. ■

NOTE

Finding the WiFi Signal When you're near a WiFi hotspot, your PC should automatically pick up the WiFi signal. Just make sure that your WiFi adapter is turned on (some notebooks have a switch for this, either on the front or on the side of the unit), and then follow these directions to find and connect to the nearest hotspot. ■

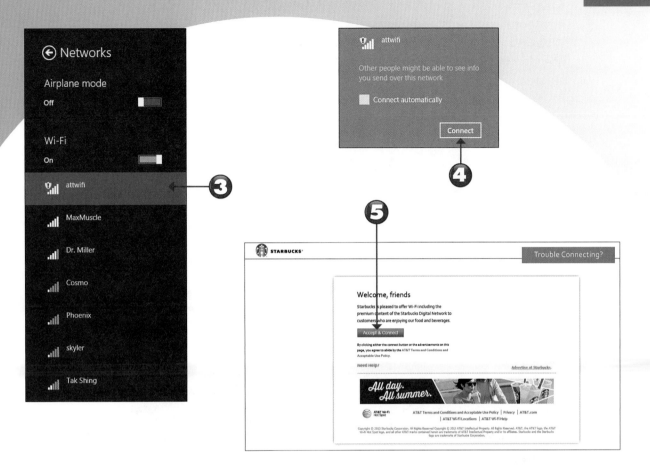

③ You now see a list of available wireless networks. Click or tap the network to which you want to connect.

④ This expands the panel. Click **Connect** to connect to the selected hotspot.

⑤ If the hotspot has free public access, you can now open IE (from the Start screen) and surf normally. If the hotspot requires a password, payment, or other logon procedure, Windows should open IE and display the hotspot's logon page. Enter the appropriate information to begin surfing.

End

TIP

Mobile Broadband If your notebook or tablet is configured to connect to your mobile phone carrier's data network, you'll see additional mobile broadband connection options within Windows. By default, Windows connects to available free or low-cost WiFi networks first. If no WiFi networks are available, it will connect to the data network you select. ■

TIP

Airplane Mode If you're using your notebook or tablet on an airplane, you can switch to Window's special Airplane mode so that you can use your computer while in the air. To switch into Airplane mode, go to the Start screen and display the charms bar, click **Settings**, and then click the **WiFi** icon. When the Networks pane appears, click "on" the **Airplane Mode** option. You can switch off Airplane mode when your plane lands. ■

USING INTERNET EXPLORER (MODERN VERSION)

Internet Explorer is a web browser that lets you quickly and easily browse the World Wide Web. Windows 8.1 includes two versions of IE: a Modern version optimized for full-screen use, and the traditional version found on the Windows desktop. We'll examine the Modern version first.

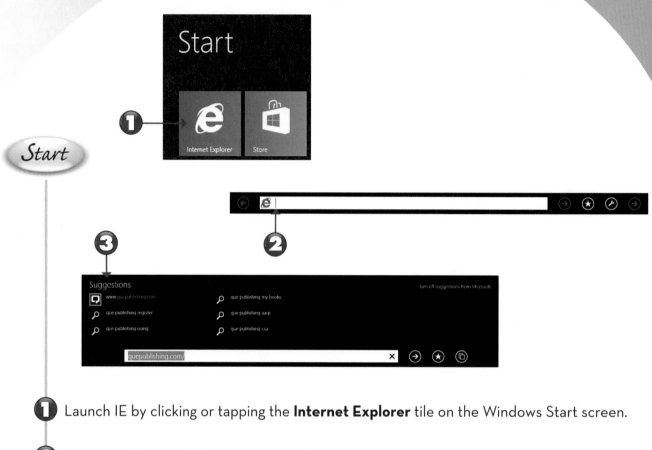

1 Launch IE by clicking or tapping the **Internet Explorer** tile on the Windows Start screen.

2 Enter a web page address into the Address box.

3 As you type, IE displays a list of suggested pages. Click one of these pages or finish entering the web page address and press **Enter**.

Continued

NOTE

Display the Address Bar Internet Explorer should launch with the Address bar displayed on the bottom of the screen. If you don't see the Address bar, right-click anywhere on the screen to display it. ■

TIP

New in Windows 8.1 Windows 8.1 includes Internet Explorer version 11, which is vastly improved over the previous version 10—especially in the Modern, full-screen version. New to the Modern version of IE11 are the capabilities to save Favorite sites and easily display different tabs. ■

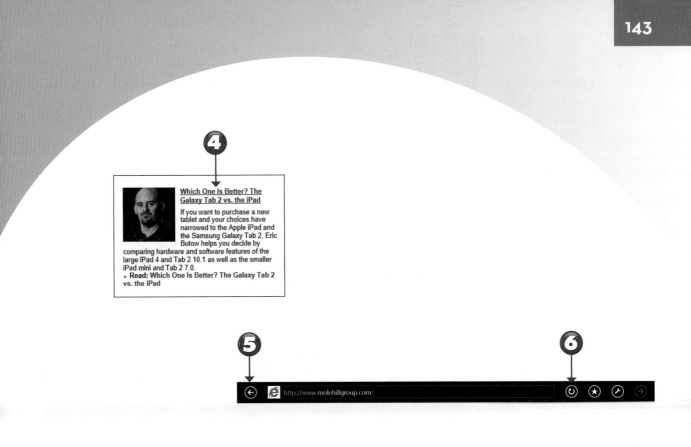

4 Pages on the web are linked via clickable *hyperlinks*. Click a link on a web page to display the linked-to page.

5 To return to the previous page, display the Address bar and click or tap the **Back** (left arrow) button.

6 To refresh or reload the current page, display the Address bar and click or tap the **Refresh** button.

End

TIP

InPrivate Browsing If you want to browse anonymously, without any traces of your history recorded, activate IE's InPrivate Browsing mode on a new tab. Display the Address bar and click the "three dot" (**...**) button, and then click **New InPrivate Tab** from the pop-up menu. ■

CAUTION

Default Browser If you change the default web browser on the desktop to something other than Internet Explorer, you will no longer be able to open the Modern version of Internet Explorer. To use the Modern, full-screen version of IE, Internet Explorer must be your default browser. ■

OPENING MULTIPLE PAGES IN TABS

If you're visiting more than one web page during a single session, you can display each page as a separate *tab* in the web browser. This use of tabs lets you keep multiple web pages open simultaneously—which is great when you want to reference different pages or want to run web-based applications in the background.

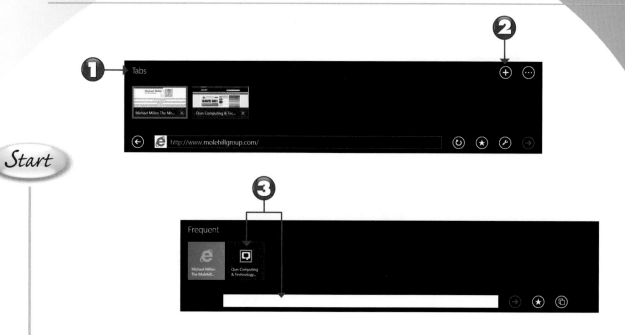

Start

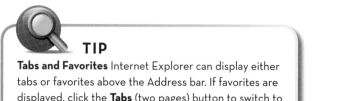

Right-click within the browser to display the Address bar at the bottom of the screen, then right-click again to display the row of tabs above the Address box.

Click or tap the New Tab (+) button to display the Frequent bar at the bottom of the screen.

Either click a tile on this screen or enter a new web page address in the Address box.

End

TIP

Tabs and Favorites Internet Explorer can display either tabs or favorites above the Address bar. If favorites are displayed, click the **Tabs** (two pages) button to switch to tabs view. If tabs are displayed, click the **Favorites** (star) button to switch to Favorites view. ■

SWITCHING BETWEEN TABS

Switching between open web pages is as easy as clicking different tabs. IE displays a small thumbnail of each open page/tab on the tab bar.

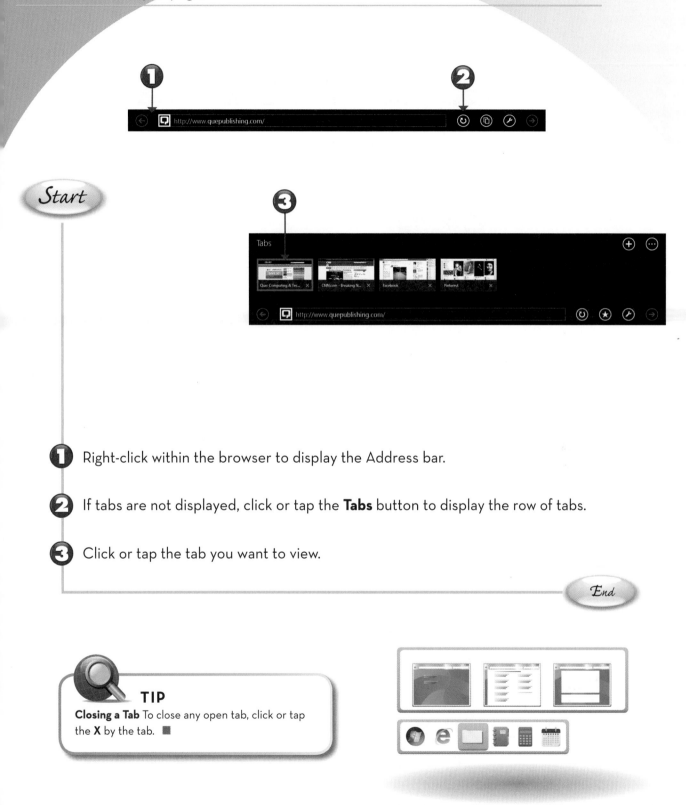

Start

1. Right-click within the browser to display the Address bar.

2. If tabs are not displayed, click or tap the **Tabs** button to display the row of tabs.

3. Click or tap the tab you want to view.

End

TIP

Closing a Tab To close any open tab, click or tap the **X** by the tab. ∎

SAVING FAVORITE PAGES

When you find a web page you like, you can save it in your Favorites list. Returning to a favorite page is as easy as clicking or tapping it in this list.

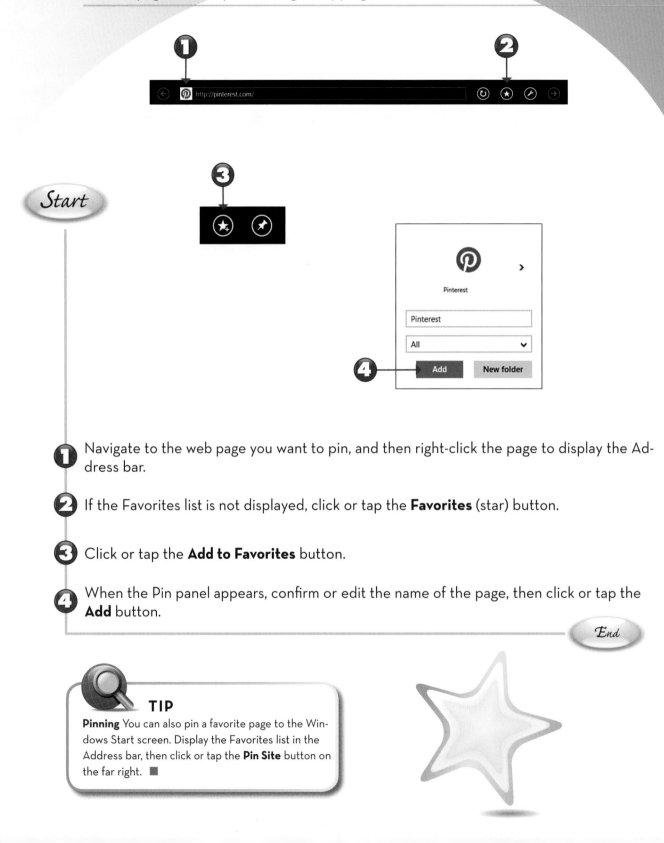

Navigate to the web page you want to pin, and then right-click the page to display the Address bar.

If the Favorites list is not displayed, click or tap the **Favorites** (star) button.

Click or tap the **Add to Favorites** button.

When the Pin panel appears, confirm or edit the name of the page, then click or tap the **Add** button.

TIP

Pinning You can also pin a favorite page to the Windows Start screen. Display the Favorites list in the Address bar, then click or tap the **Pin Site** button on the far right. ■

RETURNING TO A FAVORITE PAGE

To return to a page you've saved as a favorite, you can click or tap that page's tile in the Favorites list.

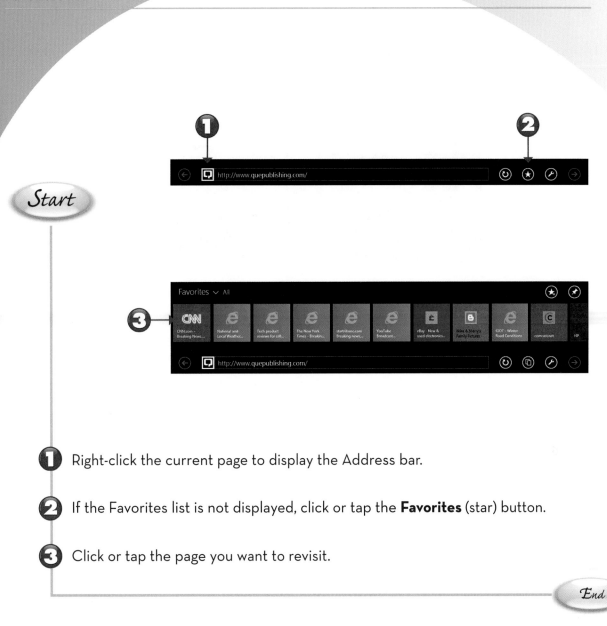

Start

1 Right-click the current page to display the Address bar.

2 If the Favorites list is not displayed, click or tap the **Favorites** (star) button.

3 Click or tap the page you want to revisit.

End

TIP

Favorites Folders You can organize favorite pages into folders in the Favorites list. To view favorites in a folder, click or tap the folder name. To return to the master Favorites list, click or tap **All** by the Favorites title. ■

USING INTERNET EXPLORER (DESKTOP VERSION)

The desktop version of Internet Explorer will be familiar to anyone who's used a previous version of Microsoft Windows. This web browser opens in its own window on the Windows desktop and features an Address bar and row of tabs that are always visible.

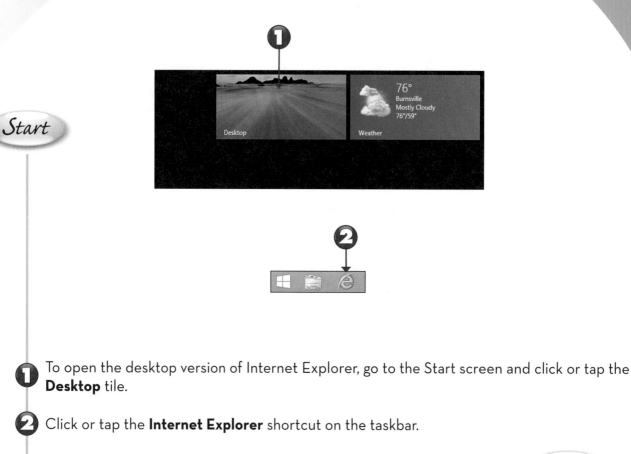

Start

To open the desktop version of Internet Explorer, go to the Start screen and click or tap the **Desktop** tile.

Click or tap the **Internet Explorer** shortcut on the taskbar.

Continued

TIP

Other Web Browsers Internet Explorer isn't the only web browser you can use. Other browsers you can install and use with the traditional Windows desktop include Google Chrome (www.google.com/chrome/), Mozilla Firefox (www.mozilla.org/firefox/), and Apple Safari (www.apple.com/safari/). ■

TIP

Home Page The desktop version of IE lets you set a *home page* that automatically opens whenever you launch the browser. To set the home page, navigate to that page, click the **Options** (gear) button, and select **Internet Options**. When the Internet Options dialog box opens, select the **General** tab, go to the Home Page section, and click the **Use Current** button. ■

To go to a specific web page, enter that page's page address into the Address box, and then press **Enter**.

To return to the previous web page, click or tap the **Back** (left arrow) button beside the Address box.

To reload or refresh the current page, click or tap the **Refresh** button.

Pages on the Web are linked via clickable *hyperlinks*. Click a link on a web page to display the linked-to page.

End

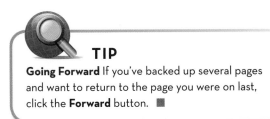

TIP

Going Forward If you've backed up several pages and want to return to the page you were on last, click the **Forward** button. ■

TIP

Revisit History To view a list of pages you've recently visited, click and hold the **Back** button. To view a list of even older pages, click and hold the **Back** button, and then click **History**. ■

OPENING MULTIPLE PAGES IN TABS

Just as the Modern version of Internet Explorer features tabbed browsing, so does the desktop version. You can display web pages as separate tabs in the browser, and thus easily switch between web pages—which is great when you want to reference different pages or want to run web-based applications in the background.

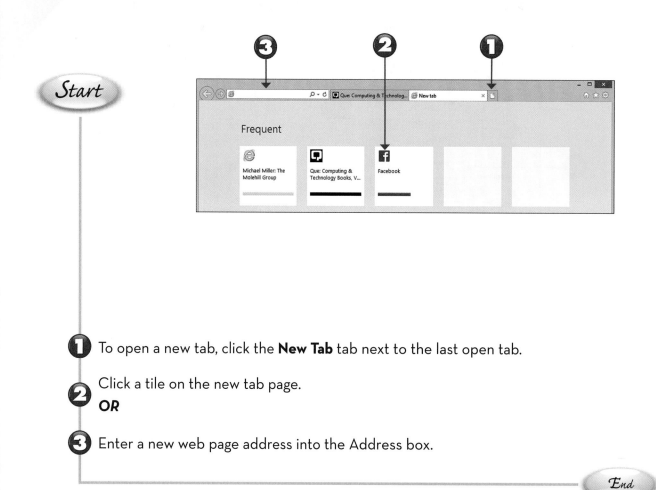

Start

1 To open a new tab, click the **New Tab** tab next to the last open tab.

2 Click a tile on the new tab page.
OR

3 Enter a new web page address into the Address box.

End

SWITCHING BETWEEN TABS

Switching between open web pages is as easy as clicking different tabs.

Start

Currently selected tab

1

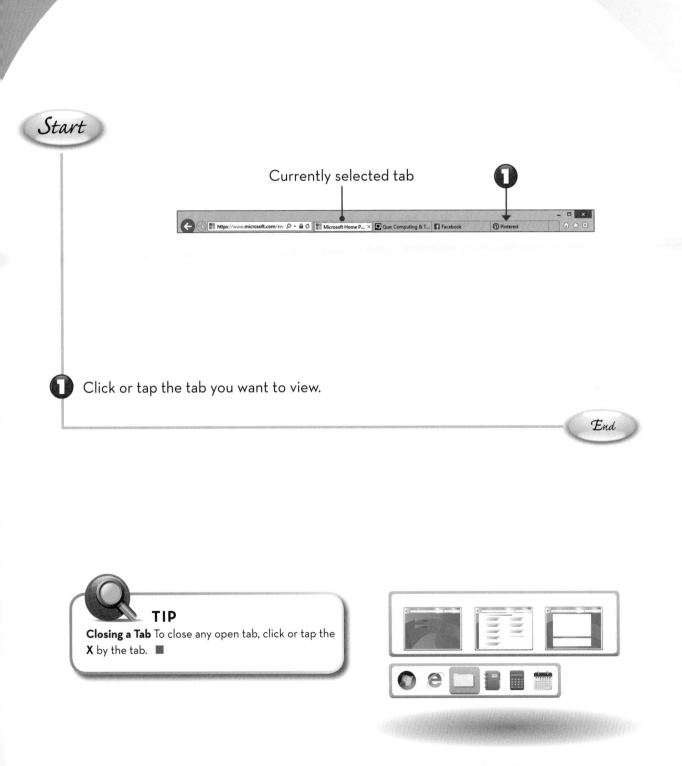

1 Click or tap the tab you want to view.

End

TIP

Closing a Tab To close any open tab, click or tap the **X** by the tab. ■

SAVING FAVORITE PAGES

The desktop version of IE also lets you save your favorite pages in the Favorites list.

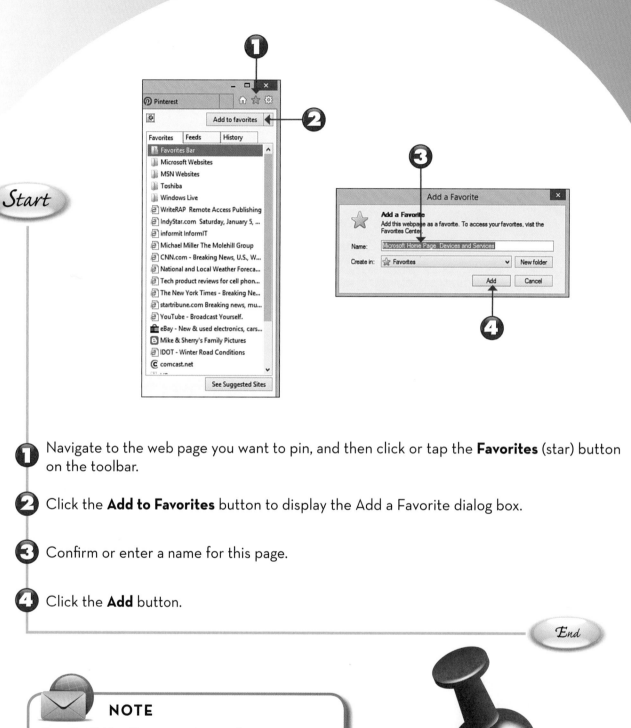

Start

Navigate to the web page you want to pin, and then click or tap the **Favorites** (star) button on the toolbar.

Click the **Add to Favorites** button to display the Add a Favorite dialog box.

Confirm or enter a name for this page.

Click the **Add** button.

End

NOTE

Favorites Folders You can organize your favorite pages into separate folders in the Favorites list. When the Add a Favorite dialog box appears, select a folder from the Create In list, or click the **New Folder** button to create a new folder. ■

RETURNING TO A FAVORITE PAGE

To return to a page you've saved as a favorite, open the Favorites list and make a selection.

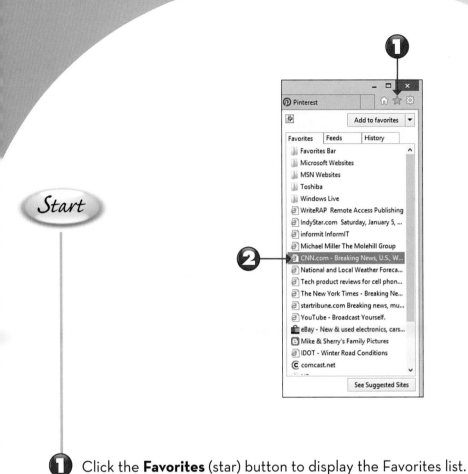

Start

1 Click the **Favorites** (star) button to display the Favorites list.

2 Click or tap the page you want to revisit.

End

TIP

Favorites Bar For even faster access to your favorite pages, display the Favorites bar at the top of the browser window, beneath the Address bar. Right-click any open area at the top of the browser, then select **Favorites Bar** from the pop-up menu. ■

SEARCHING THE WEB WITH GOOGLE

You can find just about anything you want online by using a web *search engine*. The most popular search engine today is Google (www.google.com), which indexes billions of individual web pages. Google is very easy to use and returns extremely accurate results.

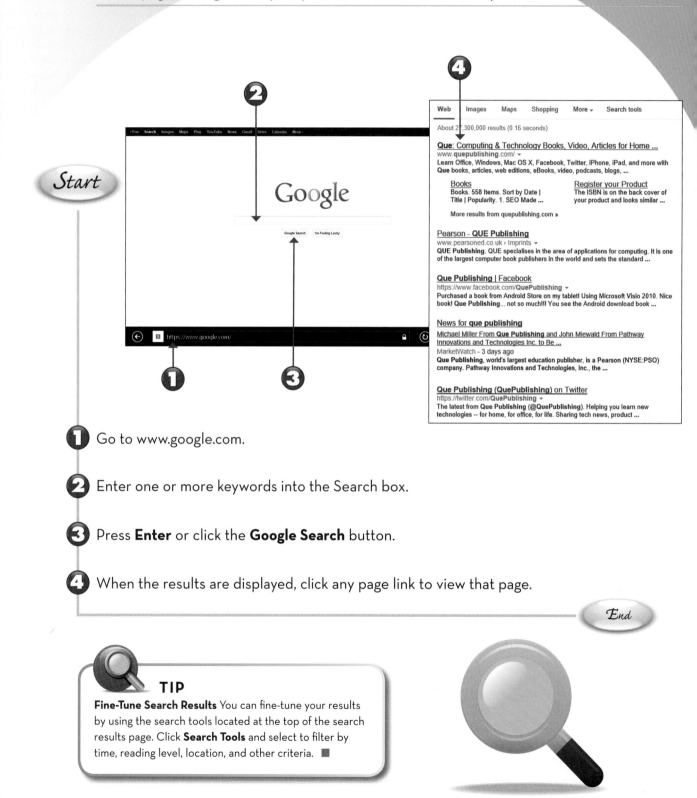

1. Go to www.google.com.

2. Enter one or more keywords into the Search box.

3. Press **Enter** or click the **Google Search** button.

4. When the results are displayed, click any page link to view that page.

TIP

Fine-Tune Search Results You can fine-tune your results by using the search tools located at the top of the search results page. Click **Search Tools** and select to filter by time, reading level, location, and other criteria. ■

SEARCHING THE WEB WITH BING

Google isn't the only search engine on the Web. Microsoft's Bing (www.bing.com) offers similar results, in a visual format that's particularly appealing in the full-screen version of Internet Explorer.

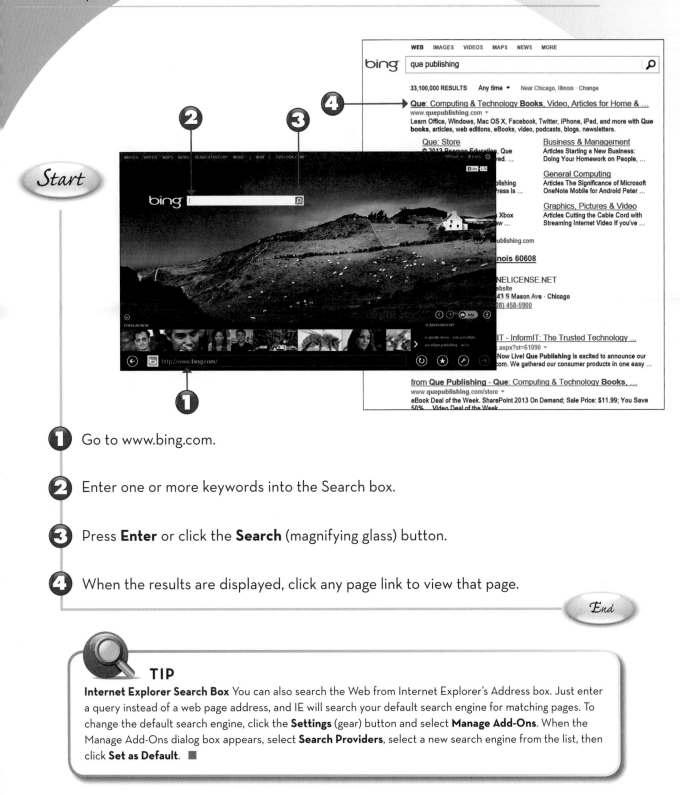

1 Go to www.bing.com.

2 Enter one or more keywords into the Search box.

3 Press **Enter** or click the **Search** (magnifying glass) button.

4 When the results are displayed, click any page link to view that page.

TIP

Internet Explorer Search Box You can also search the Web from Internet Explorer's Address box. Just enter a query instead of a web page address, and IE will search your default search engine for matching pages. To change the default search engine, click the **Settings** (gear) button and select **Manage Add-Ons**. When the Manage Add-Ons dialog box appears, select **Search Providers**, select a new search engine from the list, then click **Set as Default**. ◼

SMART SEARCHING FROM WINDOWS

Like previous versions, Windows 8.1 lets you search your computer for files and apps. New to Windows 8.1, however, is the capability to expand this internal search to the Web and use Bing to provide integrated web-based search results. This new global search is dubbed *Smart Search*, and it can make your searching more effective and efficient.

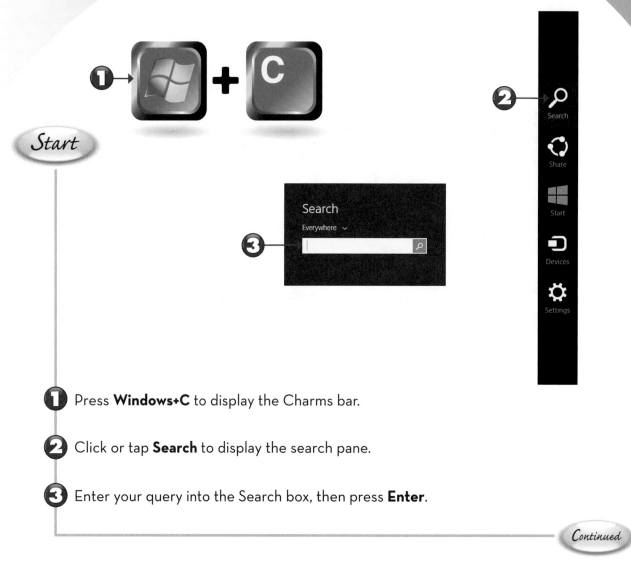

Start

1 Press **Windows+C** to display the Charms bar.

2 Click or tap **Search** to display the search pane.

3 Enter your query into the Search box, then press **Enter**.

Continued

TIP

New to Windows 8.1 The Smart Search feature, incorporating Bing web search results, is new to Windows 8.1. ■

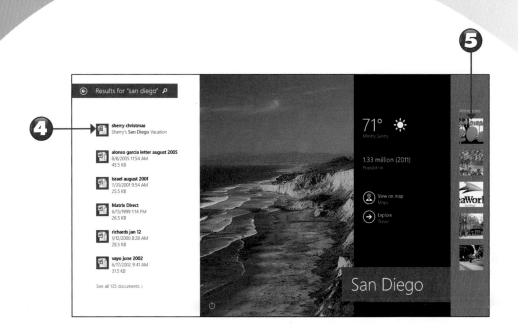

4 You now see a list of files and apps on your computer that match your query. Click or tap an item to open it.

5 Depending on your query, you might also see web results from Bing. Scroll to the right to see additional results, and then click an item to view that web page.

End

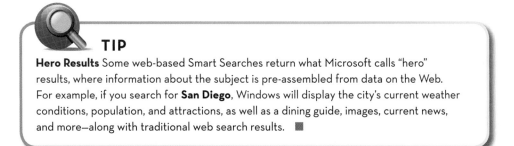

TIP

Hero Results Some web-based Smart Searches return what Microsoft calls "hero" results, where information about the subject is pre-assembled from data on the Web. For example, if you search for **San Diego**, Windows will display the city's current weather conditions, population, and attractions, as well as a dining guide, images, current news, and more—along with traditional web search results. ■

SHOPPING ONLINE

The Internet is a great place to buy things, from books to clothing to household items to cars. Online shopping is safe and convenient—all you need is your computer and a credit card.

 Start

1 Find an online store that sells the item you're shopping for.

2 Search or browse for the product you like.

Continued

 TIP

Traditional Retailers Online Most bricks-and-mortar retailers have equivalent online stores. For example, you can shop at Target online at www.target.com, or Macy's online at www.macys.com. Most catalog merchants also have their own websites where you can order online. ∎

 TIP

Online-Only Retailers Many big online-only retailers sell a variety of merchandise. The most popular of these include Amazon.com (www.amazon.com) and Overstock.com (www.overstock.com). ∎

3 Examine the product by viewing the photos and information on the product listing page.

4 Order the product by clicking a **Buy It Now** or **Add to Cart** button on the product listing page. This puts the item in your online shopping cart.

5 Check out by entering your shipping and payment (credit card) information.

End

TIP

In-Stock Items The better online retailers tell you either on the product description page or during the checkout process whether an item is in stock. Look for this information to help you decide how to group your items for shipment. ■

TIP

Shop Safely The safest way to shop online is to pay via credit card, as your credit card company offers various consumer protections. (Smaller merchants might accept credit cards via PayPal or a similar online payment service; this is also acceptable.) Also make sure that the retailer you buy from offers an acceptable returns policy, just in case. ■

Chapter 11

COMMUNICATING WITH EMAIL

An email message is like a regular letter, except that it's composed electronically and delivered almost immediately via the Internet. You can use email to send both text messages and computer files (such as digital photos) to pretty much anyone who's online.

You can use a dedicated email program, such as the Windows Mail app, to send and receive email from your personal computer. Or you can use a web mail service such as Gmail or Yahoo! Mail to manage all your email from any web browser on any computer. Either approach is good and lets you create, send, and read email messages from all your friends, family, and colleagues.

WINDOWS MAIL APP

Navigation
pane

Messages in
the Inbox

Current
message

Respond to
current
message

Delete current
message

Create new
message

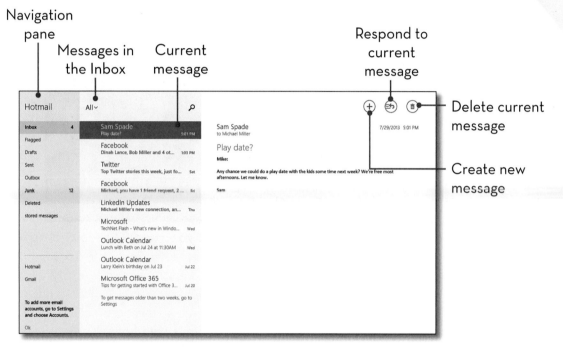

VIEWING YOUR INBOX AND READING MESSAGES

Windows 8.1 includes a built-in Mail app for sending and receiving email messages. By default, the Mail app manages email from the Outlook.com or Hotmail account linked to your Microsoft Account. This means you'll see Outlook and Hotmail messages in your Mail Inbox and be able to easily send emails from your Outlook or Hotmail account.

Start

1 From the Windows Start screen, click or tap the **Mail** tile.

Continued

TIP

Tile Info On the Start screen, the Mail app is a "live" tile; your most recent unread messages scroll across the face of the tile, and the number at the bottom left indicates how many unread messages you have. ■

NOTE

Read and Unread The headers for unread messages are displayed in bold. Messages you've read display normally. ■

Unread messages

2 When the Mail app launches, select **Inbox** from the navigation pane on the left.

3 This displays a list of all your incoming email messages. Tap a message to view it in the content pane on the right.

4 If the message has a file attached, click **Download** to download the file to your computer.

End

CAUTION

Attached Viruses Beware of receiving unexpected email messages with file attachments. Opening the attachment may infect your computer with a virus or spyware! You should *never* open email attachments that you weren't expecting—or from senders you don't know. ■

MOVING A MESSAGE TO ANOTHER FOLDER

New messages are stored in the Mail app's Inbox, which is actually a folder. Mail uses other folders, too; there are folders for Drafts, Sent Items, Outbox (messages waiting to be sent), Junk (spam), Deleted messages, and Stored messages. For better organization, you can easily move messages from one folder to another.

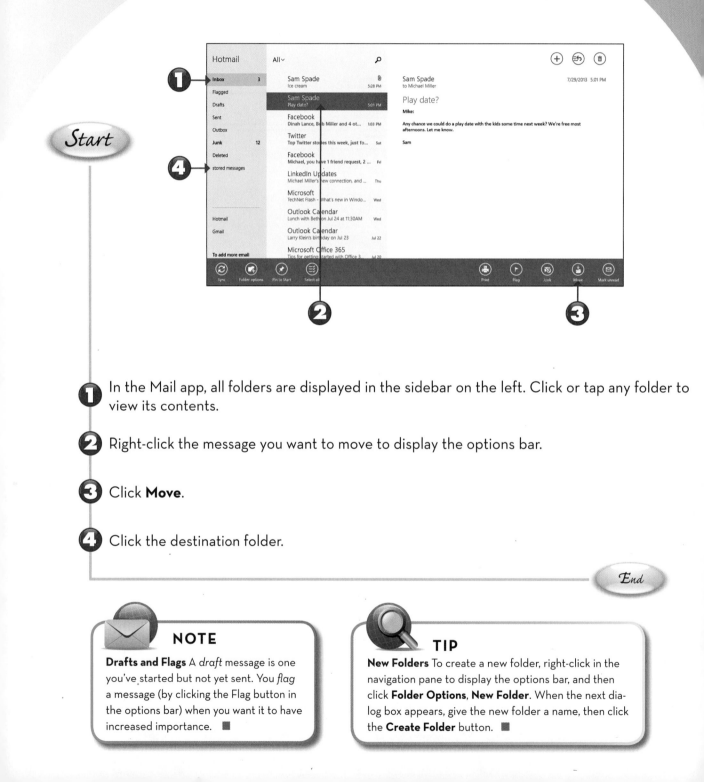

Start

1 In the Mail app, all folders are displayed in the sidebar on the left. Click or tap any folder to view its contents.

2 Right-click the message you want to move to display the options bar.

3 Click **Move**.

4 Click the destination folder.

End

NOTE

Drafts and Flags A *draft* message is one you've started but not yet sent. You *flag* a message (by clicking the Flag button in the options bar) when you want it to have increased importance. ■

TIP

New Folders To create a new folder, right-click in the navigation pane to display the options bar, and then click **Folder Options**, **New Folder**. When the next dialog box appears, give the new folder a name, then click the **Create Folder** button. ■

REPLYING TO AN EMAIL MESSAGE

Replying to an email message is as easy as clicking a button and typing your reply. The bottom of your reply "quotes" the text of the original message.

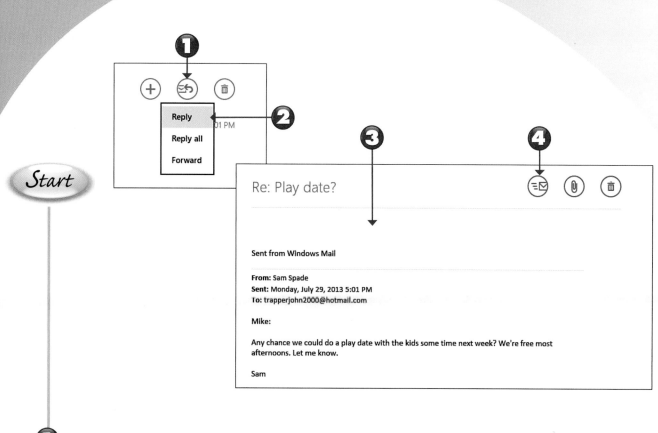

1. From an open message, click or tap the **Respond** button at the top of screen.

2. Select **Reply** from the pop-up menu to display the Reply screen.

3. Enter your reply at the top of the message; the bottom of the message "quotes" the original message.

4. Click or tap the **Send** button when you're ready to send the message.

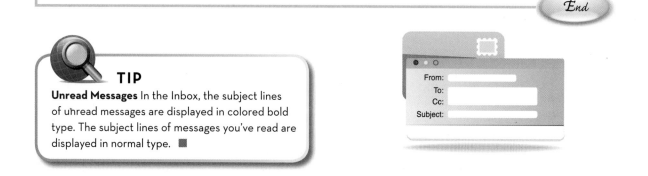

TIP

Unread Messages In the Inbox, the subject lines of unread messages are displayed in colored bold type. The subject lines of messages you've read are displayed in normal type. ■

COMPOSING A NEW EMAIL MESSAGE

Composing a new message is similar to replying to a message. The big difference is that you have to manually enter the recipient's email address.

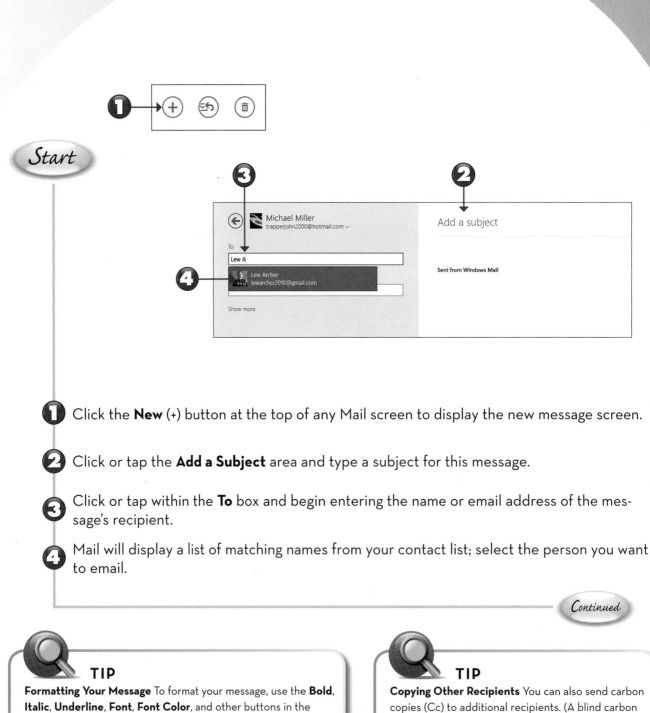

Start

1. Click the **New** (+) button at the top of any Mail screen to display the new message screen.

2. Click or tap the **Add a Subject** area and type a subject for this message.

3. Click or tap within the **To** box and begin entering the name or email address of the message's recipient.

4. Mail will display a list of matching names from your contact list; select the person you want to email.

Continued

TIP

Formatting Your Message To format your message, use the **Bold**, **Italic**, **Underline**, **Font**, **Font Color**, and other buttons in the options bar. You can even click the **Emoticons** button to insert smiley faces and other representations of facial expressions. ■

TIP

Copying Other Recipients You can also send carbon copies (Cc) to additional recipients. (A blind carbon copy, Bcc, is not visible to other recipients.) Just enter one or more email addresses into the CC box. ■

5 Click or tap within the main body of the message area and type your message.

6 To attach a file to this message, click the **Attachments** button.

7 When the Files screen appears, navigate to and select the file you want to attach, and then click the **Attach** button.

8 When you're ready to send the email, click the **Send** button at the top of the message.

End

TIP

Attaching Files One of the easiest ways to share a digital photo or other file with another user is via email, as an *attachment* to a standard email message. When the message is sent, the file travels along with it; when the message is received, the file is right there, waiting to be opened. ■

CAUTION

Large Files Be wary of sending extra-large files (2MB or more) over the Internet. They can take a long time to upload—and just as long for the recipient to download when received. ■

ADDING OTHER ACCOUNTS TO THE MAIL APP

By default, the Mail app sends and receives messages from the email account associated with your Microsoft account. You can, however, configure Mail to work with other email accounts, if you have them.

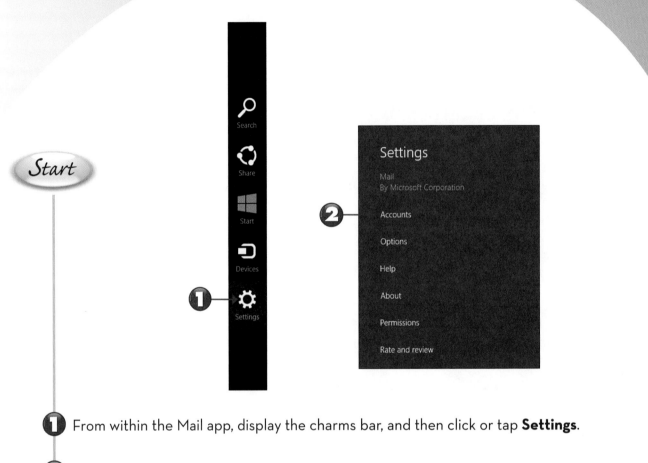

1 From within the Mail app, display the charms bar, and then click or tap **Settings**.

2 When the Settings pane appears, click or tap **Accounts**.

Continued

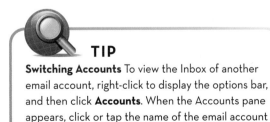

TIP
Switching Accounts To view the Inbox of another email account, right-click to display the options bar, and then click **Accounts**. When the Accounts pane appears, click or tap the name of the email account you want to view. ■

Accounts

⊕ Accounts ✉

Hotmail
trapperjohn2000@hotmail.com

Gmail
molehillgroup@gmail.com

3 → Add an account

⊕ Add an account ✉

Hotmail
Hotmail.com, Live.com, MSN

Outlook
Exchange, Office 365, Outlook.com

4 → Google
Connect

Other account
Connect

AOL
Connect

Yahoo!

Play date?

Add your Google account   g

Enter the information below to connect to your Google account.

Email address

5 →

Password

→

Connect   Cancel

6

3 When the Accounts pane appears, click or tap **Add an Account**.

4 When the next pane appears, click the type of account you want to add.

5 When the Add Your Account pane appears, enter your email address and password.

6 Click the **Connect** button when done.

End

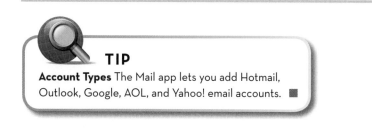

TIP
Account Types The Mail app lets you add Hotmail, Outlook, Google, AOL, and Yahoo! email accounts. ■

MANAGING YOUR CONTACTS FROM THE PEOPLE APP

The people you email regularly are known as *contacts*. When someone is in your contacts list, it's easy to send her an email; all you have to do is pick her name from the list instead of entering her email address manually. All your Windows contacts are managed from the People app; this app connects to the Microsoft account you used to create your Windows account, and so all the contacts from your main email account are automatically added.

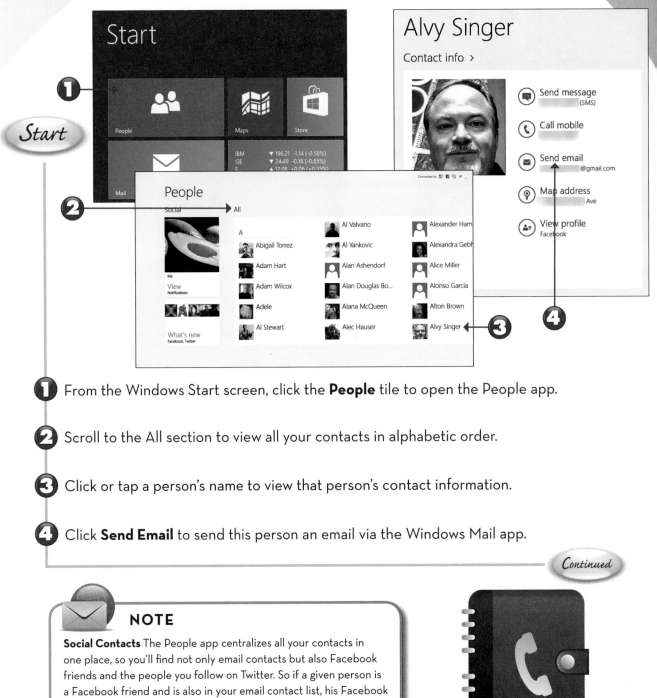

1 From the Windows Start screen, click the **People** tile to open the People app.

2 Scroll to the All section to view all your contacts in alphabetic order.

3 Click or tap a person's name to view that person's contact information.

4 Click **Send Email** to send this person an email via the Windows Mail app.

Continued

NOTE

Social Contacts The People app centralizes all your contacts in one place, so you'll find not only email contacts but also Facebook friends and the people you follow on Twitter. So if a given person is a Facebook friend and is also in your email contact list, his Facebook information and his email address appear in the People app. ■

5 **6**

+
New contact

8

New contact

Account
Hotmail ⌄

Email
Personal ⌄

Address
⊕ Address

Name
First name

⊕ Email

Other info
⊕ Other info

Last name

Phone
Mobile ⌄

Company

⊕ Phone

⊕ Name

5 To add a new contact, right-click anywhere on the screen to display the options bar.

6 Click New Contact to display the New Contact screen.

7 Enter this person's information into the appropriate boxes.

8 Click **Save This Contact** when done.

End

USING THE YAHOO! MAIL APP

Yahoo! Mail is one of the most popular free web mail services. Anyone can sign up for a free Yahoo! Mail account and then access email from any computer with an Internet connection, using any web browser—just go to mail.yahoo.com. Even better, you can use the full-screen Yahoo! Mail app to access your Yahoo! Mail account.

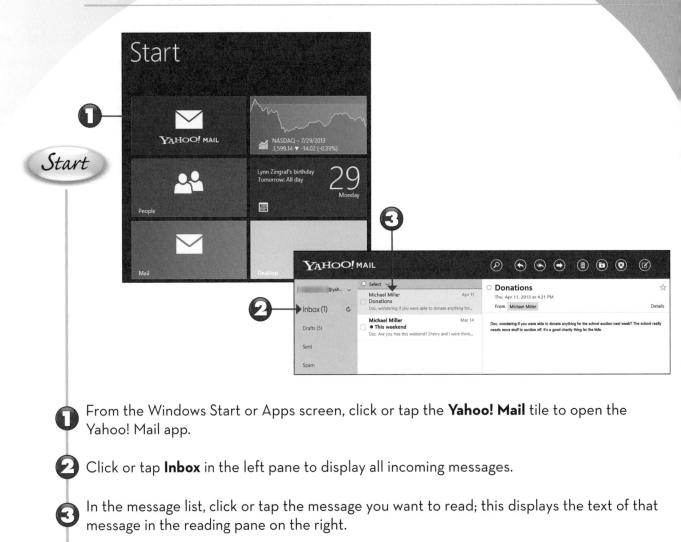

1 From the Windows Start or Apps screen, click or tap the **Yahoo! Mail** tile to open the Yahoo! Mail app.

2 Click or tap **Inbox** in the left pane to display all incoming messages.

3 In the message list, click or tap the message you want to read; this displays the text of that message in the reading pane on the right.

Continued

NOTE

Download the App To download and install the Yahoo! Mail app from the Windows Store, click the **Store** tile on the Start screen, and then search the Store for **yahoo mail**. The Yahoo! Mail app is free. ∎

NOTE

Other Web Mail Services Other popular web mail services include Microsoft's Outlook.com (www.outlook.com), AOL Mail (mail.aol.com), and Google's Gmail (mail.google.com). ∎

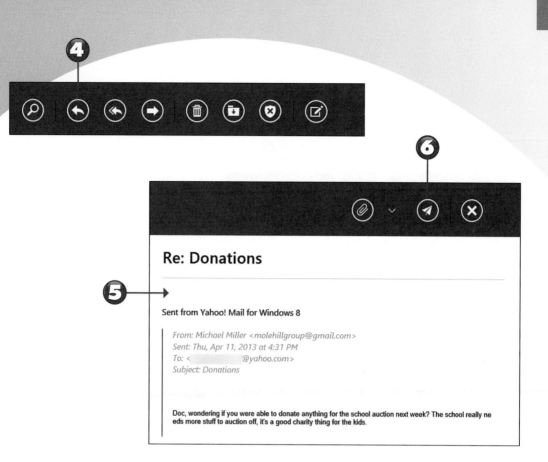

(4) To reply to an open message, click **Reply** to open the Reply screen.

(5) Enter your reply text in the message window, above the "quoted" original text.

(6) Click the **Send** button when you're finished and ready to send your message.

Continued

NOTE

POP Email Post Office Protocol (POP) email is available from most Internet service providers (ISPs). It requires the use of a dedicated email program and the configuration of that program with information about the ISP's incoming and outgoing email servers. ■

NOTE

POP Versus Web Mail POP email, like web mail, is typically free. However, you can only access POP email from the email program installed on a single computer; you can't send or receive email from other computers, as you can with web mail. ■

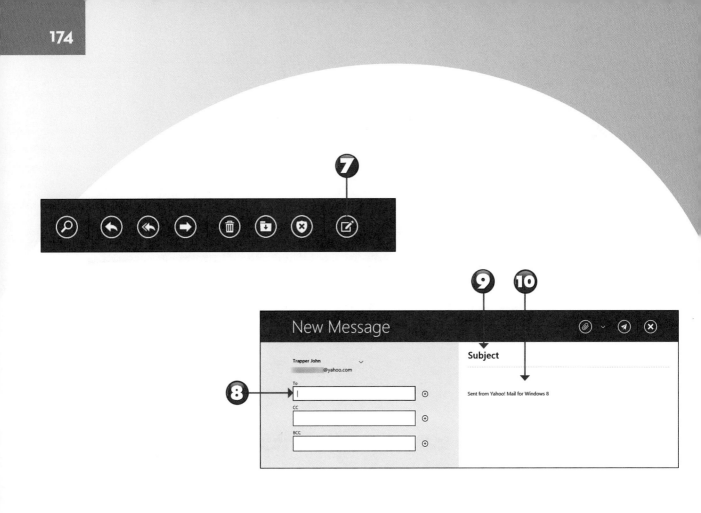

7 To send a new email message, return to the Inbox screen and click **Compose**.

8 Enter the email address of the recipient(s) in the **To** box.

9 Enter a subject in the **Subject** area.

10 Move your cursor to the main message area and type your message.

Continued

TIP

Send to Multiple Recipients You can enter multiple addresses in the To box as long as you separate the addresses with commas, like this: books@molehillgroup.com, gjetson@sprockets.com. ■

TIP

Cc and Bcc Yahoo! Mail also lets you send carbon copies (Cc) and blind carbon copies (Bcc) to additional recipients. Just enter those addresses into the CC and BCC boxes. ■

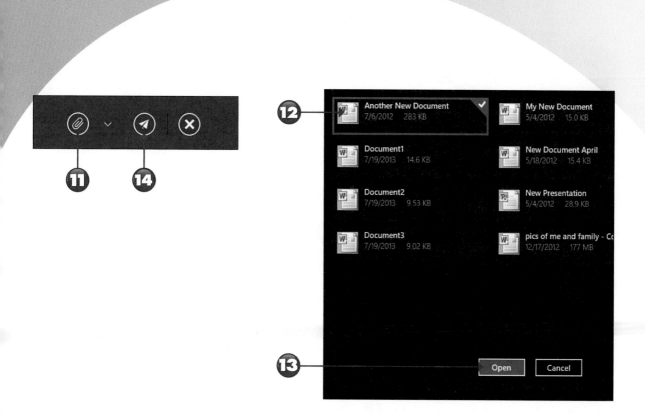

11 To attach a file to a message, click the **Attach** (paperclip) icon to launch the SkyDrive app.

12 Navigate to and select the file you want to attach.

13 Click the **Open** button to add the file to the in-progress message.

14 Click the **Send** button to send the message to the designated recipients.

End

SHARING WITH FACEBOOK AND OTHER SOCIAL NETWORKS

Social networking enables people to share experiences and opinions with each other via community-based websites. It's a great way to keep up-to-date on what your friends and family are doing.

In practice, a social network is just a large website that aims to create a community of users. Each user of the community posts his or her own personal profile on the site. You use the information in these profiles to connect with other people you know on the network or with those who share your interests.

The goal is to create a network of these online "friends," and then share your activities with them via a series of posts or status updates. All your online friends read your posts, as well as posts from other friends, in a continuously updated *News Feed*. The News Feed is the one place where you can read updates from all your online friends and family; it's where you find out what's really happening.

The biggest social network today is a site called Facebook; chances are all your friends are already using it. Other popular social networks include Pinterest and Twitter, both of which have their own unique characteristics.

COMPARING FACEBOOK, PINTEREST, AND TWITTER

Facebook

Pinterest

Twitter

FINDING FACEBOOK FRIENDS

Facebook (www.facebook.com) is the number-one social network today, with more than 1 billion active users worldwide. Once you've signed up, you can use Facebook to track down and keep in touch with all your friends and family—including old schoolmates and co-workers. You can then invite any of these people to be your Facebook friend; if they accept, they're added to your Facebook friends list.

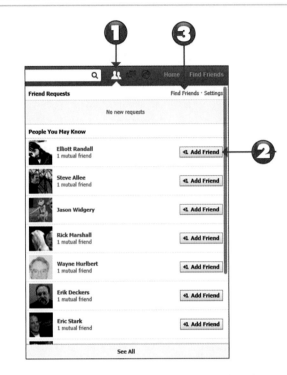

Start

1 Click the **Friends** button on the Facebook toolbar to display the drop-down menu, which lists any friend requests you've received and offers a number of friend suggestions from Facebook in the People You May Know section.

2 Click the **Add Friend** button next to a person's name to add that person to your friends list.

3 To search for more friends, click **Find Friends** at the top of the menu to display your Friends page.

Continued

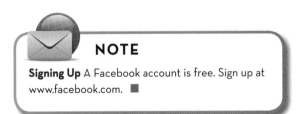

NOTE

Signing Up A Facebook account is free. Sign up at www.facebook.com. ■

NOTE

Suggested Friends Facebook automatically suggests friends based on your personal history (where you've lived, worked, or gone to school), people you might know (friends of people you're already friends with), and Facebook users who are in your email contacts lists. ■

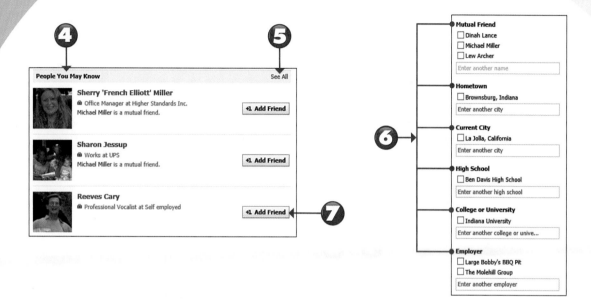

4 Scroll down the page to view other suggested friends from Facebook in the People You May Know section.

5 Click the **See All** link to view even more friend suggestions.

6 Filter the friend suggestions by making selections in the Mutual Friend, Hometown, Current City, High School, College or University, and Employer sections.

7 Click the **Add Friend** button for any person that you'd like to have on your friends list.

End

NOTE

Invitations Facebook doesn't automatically add a person to your friends list. Instead, that person receives an invitation to be your friend; she can accept or reject the invitation. ■

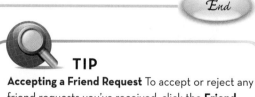

TIP

Accepting a Friend Request To accept or reject any friend requests you've received, click the **Friend Request** button on the Facebook toolbar. ■

READING THE NEWS FEED

Facebook's News Feed, found on your Facebook home page, is where you keep abreast of what all your friends are up to. When a person posts a status update to Facebook, it appears in your personal News Feed.

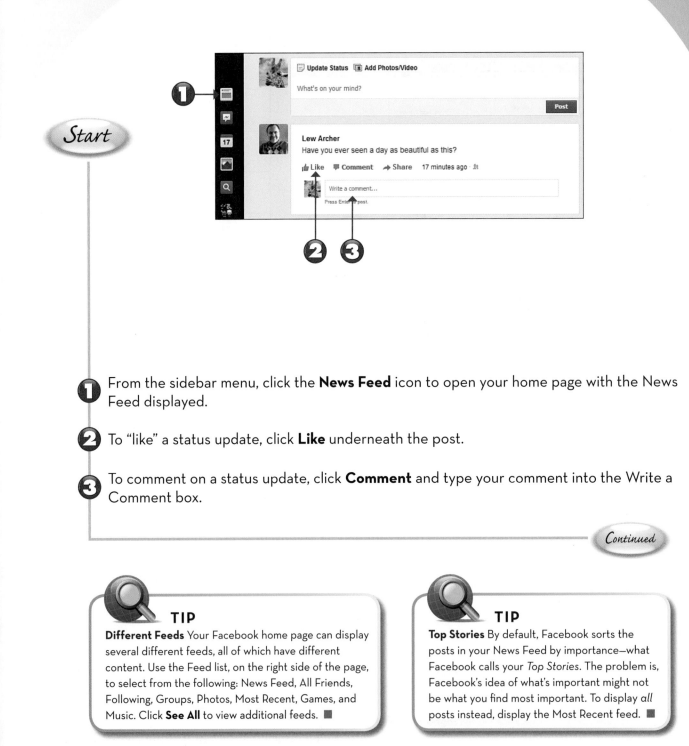

From the sidebar menu, click the **News Feed** icon to open your home page with the News Feed displayed.

To "like" a status update, click **Like** underneath the post.

To comment on a status update, click **Comment** and type your comment into the Write a Comment box.

Continued

TIP

Different Feeds Your Facebook home page can display several different feeds, all of which have different content. Use the Feed list, on the right side of the page, to select from the following: News Feed, All Friends, Following, Groups, Photos, Most Recent, Games, and Music. Click **See All** to view additional feeds. ■

TIP

Top Stories By default, Facebook sorts the posts in your News Feed by importance—what Facebook calls your *Top Stories*. The problem is, Facebook's idea of what's important might not be what you find most important. To display *all* posts instead, display the Most Recent feed. ■

4 If a status update includes a link to a web page, click that link to open that page.

5 If a status update includes one or more photos, click a photo to view it in its own *lightbox*—a special window displayed on top of the News Feed.

6 If a status update includes a video, click the **Play** arrow to play the video.

End

TIP

Sidebar Menu Use the sidebar menu on the left side of the home page to jump to different parts of the Facebook site. When you mouse over the menu, the sidebar expands, enabling you to see the names of each available item. ■

TIP

Share an Update If you'd like to share a friend's post with your own friends, click **Share** underneath the post to display the Share This Status dialog box. Click the **Share** button and select **On Your Own Timeline**, enter any comments you might have on this post into the Write Something box, and then click the **Share Status** button. ■

POSTING A STATUS UPDATE

The easiest way to let people know what's what is to post what Facebook calls a *status update*. Every status update you make is broadcast to everyone on your friends list, displayed in the News Feed on their home pages. A basic status update is text only, but you can also include photos, videos, and links to other web pages in your posts.

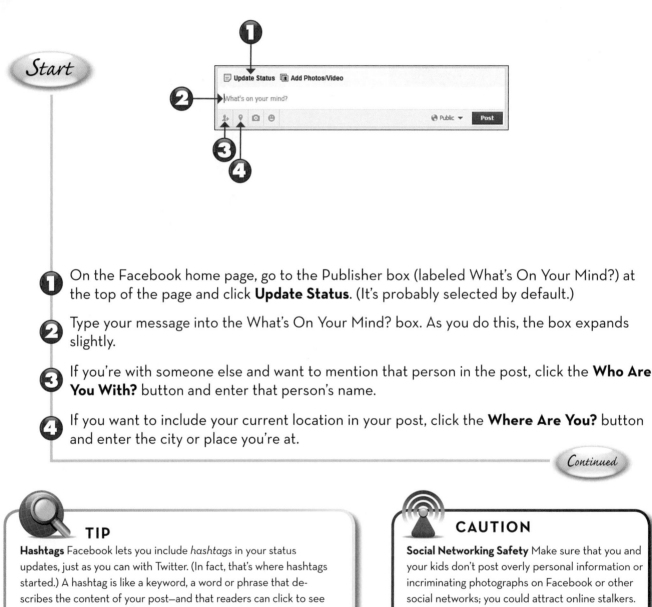

Start

1. On the Facebook home page, go to the Publisher box (labeled What's On Your Mind?) at the top of the page and click **Update Status**. (It's probably selected by default.)

2. Type your message into the What's On Your Mind? box. As you do this, the box expands slightly.

3. If you're with someone else and want to mention that person in the post, click the **Who Are You With?** button and enter that person's name.

4. If you want to include your current location in your post, click the **Where Are You?** button and enter the city or place you're at.

Continued

TIP

Hashtags Facebook lets you include *hashtags* in your status updates, just as you can with Twitter. (In fact, that's where hashtags started.) A hashtag is like a keyword, a word or phrase that describes the content of your post—and that readers can click to see similar posts with the same hashtag. A hashtag starts with the hash (#) character, followed by a single word that describes the content. Because hashtags cannot contain spaces, you must run multiple-word hashtags together into a single word, such as **#tennisgame**. ■

CAUTION

Social Networking Safety Make sure that you and your kids don't post overly personal information or incriminating photographs on Facebook or other social networks; you could attract online stalkers. Similarly, don't broadcast your every move on your profile page—and don't automatically accept friend requests from people you don't know. ■

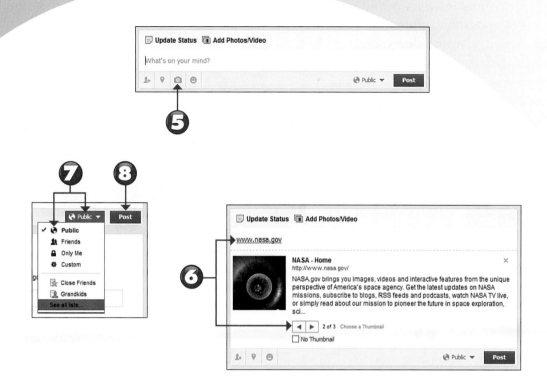

 5 To include a picture or video with your post, click the **Upload Photo** (camera) button, and then select the photos or video you want.

6 To include a link to another web page, simply enter that page's URL in your status update. Facebook should recognize the link and display a Link panel. Select a thumbnail image from the web page to accompany the link, or check the **No Thumbnail** box.

7 To determine who can read this post, click the **down arrow** next to the Public button and make a selection.

8 When you're ready to post your update, click the **Post** button.

End

TIP

Delete the URL If you don't want to display the web page's URL in the body of your status update, you can delete the address after the Link panel appears. The link and accompanying image still display under your status update even after you delete the web page URL from your text. ∎

TIP

Who Sees Your Posts? You can opt to make any post Public (anyone who's subscribed to your posts can read it), visible only to your Friends, visible only to yourself (Only Me), or Custom (you select individuals who can and can't view it). Alternatively, you can select which friends list can view the update. ∎

VIEWING A FRIEND'S TIMELINE

You can easily check up on what a friend is up to by visiting that person's Timeline page. A Timeline page is that friend's personal profile on Facebook; it contains all of that person's personal information, uploaded photos and videos, and a "timeline" of that person's posts and major life events.

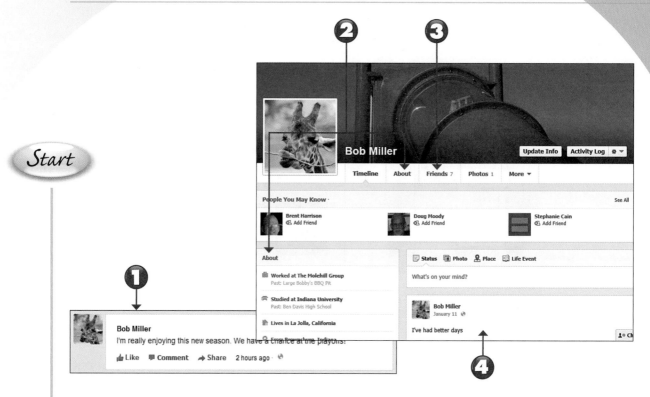

Start

1 Click a person's name anywhere on the Facebook site to display his or her profile or Timeline page.

2 View key personal information in the About box under the person's profile picture, or click About to view their full personal profile.

3 View a list of this person's friends by clicking Friends.

4 View a person's status updates in reverse chronological order (newest first) on the Timeline.

End

TIP

Read the Book Learn more about Facebook in my companion book, *Easy Facebook* (Que, 2012). ■

TIP

Posting on a Friend's Page You can post a message on your friend's profile page by entering your text into the Write Something box near the top of the Timeline. ■

PERSONALIZING YOUR TIMELINE PAGE

You can personalize your own profile page in a number of ways. You can change your profile and pictures, edit your personal information, and add and delete items to and from your Timeline.

Start

End

1 Click your name in the Facebook toolbar or your picture in the sidebar menu to display your Timeline page.

2 To change your profile picture, click the picture and select **Edit Profile Picture**.

3 To change your personal information, click the **Update Info** button.

4 To add a "life event" (something major in your life, such as getting a new job or getting married), go to the Publisher box, click **Life Event**, and then choose the kind of life event you're adding.

TIP

Cover Image To add a cover image (banner) to the top of your Timeline page, mouse over the image area and click the **Add a Cover** button. To change an existing cover image, click the **Change Cover** button. ■

TIP

Hide a Status Update If you've posted a status update that you'd rather not have, mouse over that update on the Timeline page and click the **Edit or Remove** button. Click **Hide from Timeline** to hide (but not delete) the status update. Click **Delete** to permanently remove the update from Facebook. ■

VIEWING A FRIEND'S PHOTOS

Facebook is a social network, and one of the ways we connect socially is through pictures. Facebook lets any user upload and store photos in virtual photo albums. It's easy, then, to view a friend's photos on the Facebook site.

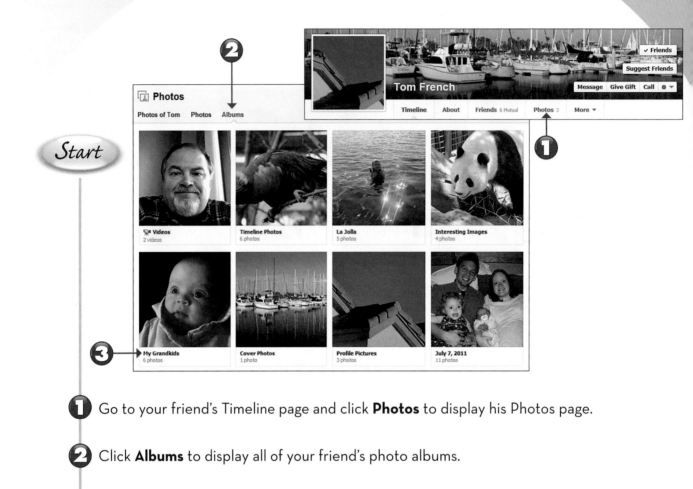

Start

1. Go to your friend's Timeline page and click **Photos** to display his Photos page.

2. Click **Albums** to display all of your friend's photo albums.

3. Click to open the desired photo album.

Continued

NOTE

Other Photos From the top of the Photos page, you can also select to view Photos of This Person (all photos in which this person appears) or This Person's Photos (all the photos this person has uploaded, not organized into albums). ∎

TIP

Photos Feed You can view the most recent photos uploaded by all your friends from the Photos Feed on your Facebook home page. Just click **Photos** in the Feed List. ∎

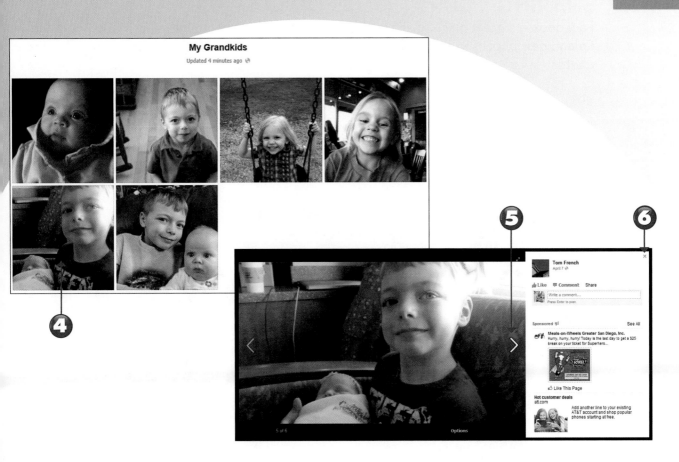

4 Click the thumbnail of the picture you want to view.

5 To go to the next picture, mouse over the current picture to display the navigational arrows, and then click the **right arrow**.

6 Click the **X** to close the photo viewer.

End

TIP

Commenting and Liking To comment on the current picture, enter your message into the comments box. To like a photo, click **Like**. ■

TIP

Downloading a Picture To download the current picture to your own computer, mouse over the photo, click **Options**, and then click **Download** from the pop-up menu. ■

SHARING YOUR PHOTOS ON FACEBOOK

Facebook is a great place to share your personal photos with family and friends. You can upload new photos to an existing photo album or create a new album for newly uploaded photos.

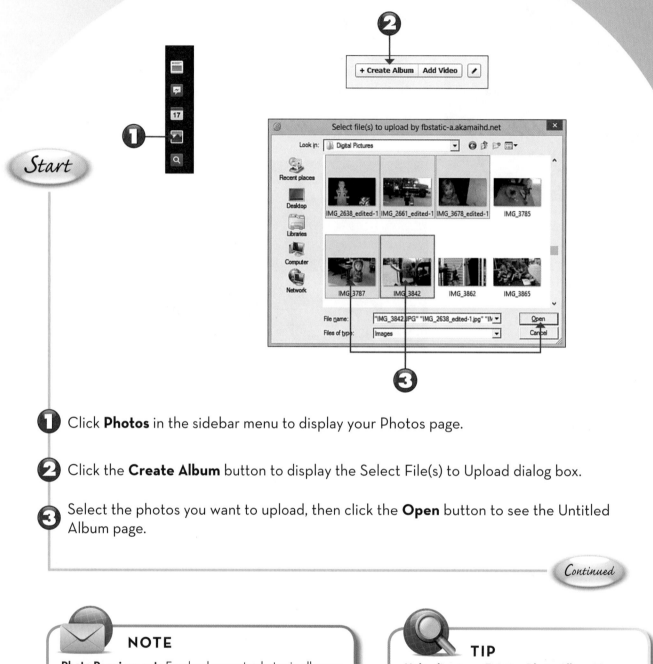

1. Click **Photos** in the sidebar menu to display your Photos page.

2. Click the **Create Album** button to display the Select File(s) to Upload dialog box.

3. Select the photos you want to upload, then click the **Open** button to see the Untitled Album page.

Continued

NOTE

Photo Requirements Facebook accepts photos in all popular file types, including JPG, PNG, GIF, TIFF, and BMP. Your picture files must be no larger than 15MB in size and can't contain any adult or offensive content. You're also limited to uploading your own photos—that is, you can't copy and then upload photos from another person's website. ■

TIP

Uploading to an Existing Photo Album You can also upload photos to an existing photo album. From your Photos page, click **Albums** to display your existing photo albums, then click to open the desired album. Click the **Add Photos** button to select new photos to upload to this album. ■

4 Enter information about this new album into the Untitled Album, Say Something About This Album, Where Were these Photos Taken, and other boxes.

5 Enter information about each new photo beneath each photo.

6 If there are people in the photo you've uploaded, Facebook displays the album page with boxes around the faces. To "tag" that person in Facebook, click a face and then enter that person's name.

7 Click the **Post Photos** button when ready.

End

TIP
High-Quality Photos To upload photos at their original resolution, check the **High Quality** option. This enables your friends to download your pictures at an acceptable resolution for printing. ■

TIP
Photo Privacy To determine who can view the photos in this album, click the **Privacy** button and make a selection—Public, Friends, Only Me, or Custom. ■

SHARING INTERESTING IMAGES WITH PINTEREST

Pinterest (www.pinterest.com) is a social network with particular appeal to women and people who like do-it-yourself projects. Unlike Facebook, which lets you post text-based status updates, Pinterest is all about images. The site consists of a collection of virtual online "pinboards" that people use to share pictures they find interesting. Users "pin" photos and other images to their personal message boards, and then share their pins with online friends.

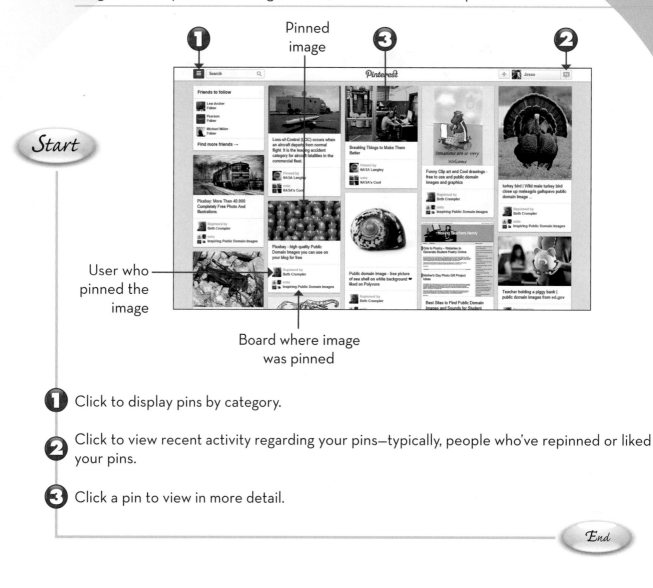

Pinned image

User who pinned the image

Board where image was pinned

Start

End

1 Click to display pins by category.

2 Click to view recent activity regarding your pins—typically, people who've repinned or liked your pins.

3 Click a pin to view in more detail.

NOTE

What's in a Name? Pinterest is all about pinning items of interest—hence the name, a combination of *pin* and *interest*. ■

NOTE

Pinterest Is Popular As of June, 2013, Pinterest had more than 70 million users. The average Pinterest user is a rural female, aged 30-49, with a college degree and household income in the $50,000 to $75,000 range. ■

FINDING PEOPLE TO FOLLOW ON PINTEREST

When you find someone who posts a lot of things you're interested in, you can follow that person on Pinterest. Following a person means that all that person's new pins will display on your Pinterest home page.

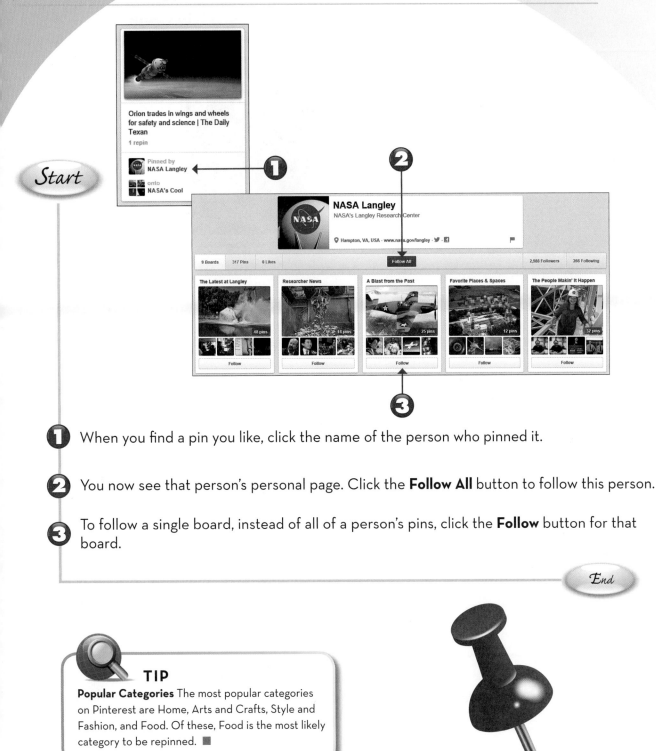

1 When you find a pin you like, click the name of the person who pinned it.

2 You now see that person's personal page. Click the **Follow All** button to follow this person.

3 To follow a single board, instead of all of a person's pins, click the **Follow** button for that board.

TIP

Popular Categories The most popular categories on Pinterest are Home, Arts and Crafts, Style and Fashion, and Food. Of these, Food is the most likely category to be repinned. ■

FINDING AND REPINNING INTERESTING PINS

Some people say that Pinterest is a little like a refrigerator covered with magnets holding up tons of photos and drawings. You can find lots of interesting items pinned from other users—and then "repin" them to your own personal pinboards.

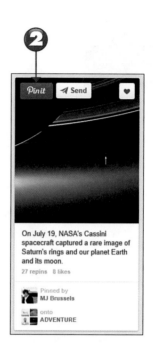

Start

1 Enter the name of something you're interested in into the Search box at the top of any Pinterest page, and then press **Enter**.

2 Pinterest now displays pins that match your query. Mouse over the item you want to repin and click the **Pin It** button.

Continued

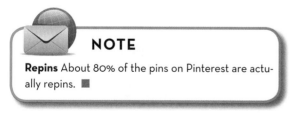

NOTE

Repins About 80% of the pins on Pinterest are actually repins. ■

TIP

Searching for Boards and People To search for boards instead of pins, click **Boards** at the top of the search results page. To display Pinterest users who match your query, click **Pinners**. ■

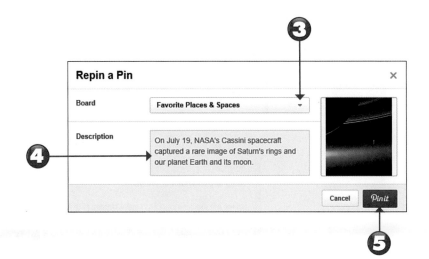

When the Repin a Pin panel appears, pull down the Board list and select which board you want to pin this item to.

Accept the previous user's description or add your own to the Description box.

Click the red **Pin It** button to repin the item.

End

TIP

Keep or Replace You can keep the original pinner's description or replace it with a new description of your own. If you want to truly personalize your pins, it's best to use your own descriptions, even when you repin. ■

PINNING FROM A WEB PAGE

You can also pin images you find on nearly any web page. It's as easy as copying and pasting the page's web address.

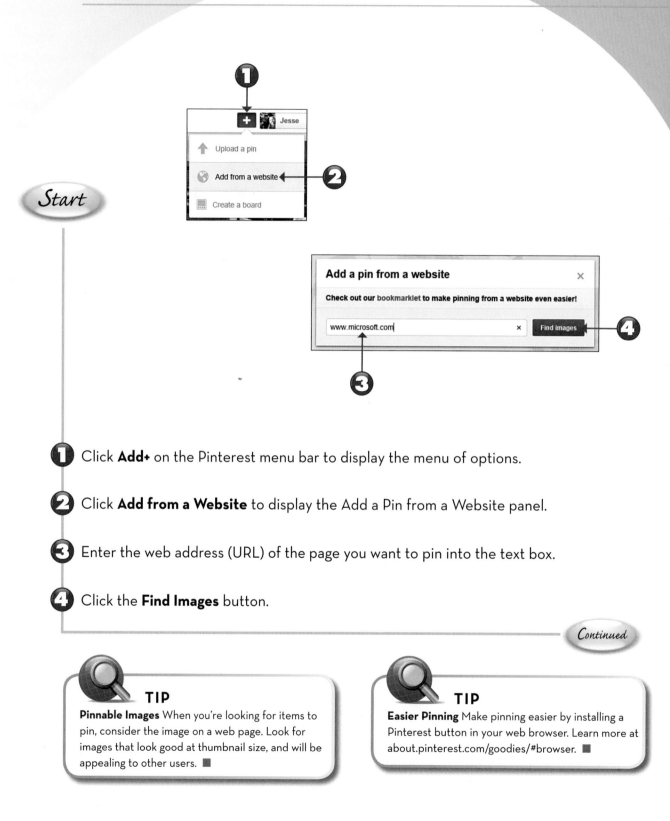

Start

1 Click **Add+** on the Pinterest menu bar to display the menu of options.

2 Click **Add from a Website** to display the Add a Pin from a Website panel.

3 Enter the web address (URL) of the page you want to pin into the text box.

4 Click the **Find Images** button.

Continued

TIP
Pinnable Images When you're looking for items to pin, consider the image on a web page. Look for images that look good at thumbnail size, and will be appealing to other users. ■

TIP
Easier Pinning Make pinning easier by installing a Pinterest button in your web browser. Learn more at about.pinterest.com/goodies/#browser. ■

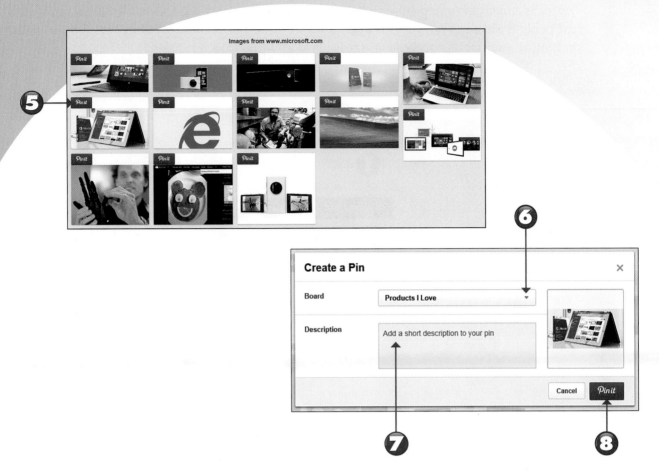

5 Pinterest now displays a page containing all the images found on the selected web page. Click the **Pin It** button for the image you want to pin.

6 When the Repin a Pin dialog box appears, pull down the Board list and select the board to which you want to pin this image.

7 Enter a short (500 characters or less) text description of or comment on this image into the Description box.

8 Click the red **Pin It** button when done.

End

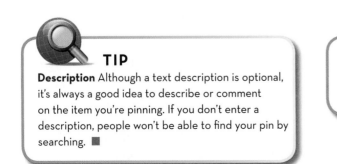

TIP

Description Although a text description is optional, it's always a good idea to describe or comment on the item you're pinning. If you don't enter a description, people won't be able to find your pin by searching. ∎

TIP

Read the Book Learn more about Pinterest in my companion book, *My Pinterest* (Que, 2012). ∎

TWEETING WITH TWITTER

Twitter is a *microblogging* service that lets you create short (up to 140 characters in length) text posts that keep your friends and family informed of your latest activities. Anyone subscribing to your posts receives updates via the Twitter site.

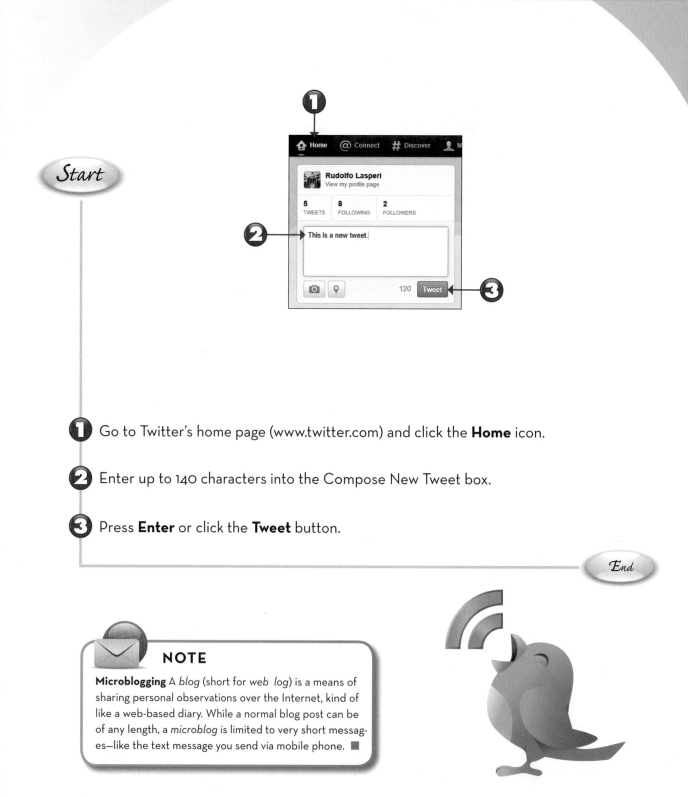

Start

End

1 Go to Twitter's home page (www.twitter.com) and click the **Home** icon.

2 Enter up to 140 characters into the Compose New Tweet box.

3 Press **Enter** or click the **Tweet** button.

NOTE

Microblogging A *blog* (short for *web log*) is a means of sharing personal observations over the Internet, kind of like a web-based diary. While a normal blog post can be of any length, a *microblog* is limited to very short messages—like the text message you send via mobile phone. ■

FOLLOWING OTHER TWITTER USERS

Twitter lets you "follow" what other users are doing on Twitter. Once you've registered and signed in, the Twitter home page displays *tweets* from users you've decided to follow.

Start

1 Go to the #Discover page on the Twitter site and click **Find Friends**.

2 Go to the Search Twitter for People section and enter a person's full name or Twitter username into the Search box.

3 Click the **Search Twitter** button to display a list of suggested friends.

4 Click the **Follow** button to follow a user.

End

NOTE

Other Ways to Search You can also search for Twitter users on other email networks (such as Gmail, Yahoo!, and Hotmail), invite nonusers to join Twitter, and view a list of suggested users you might want to follow. ■

VIEWING ALL YOUR SOCIAL ACTIVITY FROM THE WINDOWS PEOPLE APP

If you follow a lot of friends on multiple social networks, it can be quite time-consuming. Fortunately, the Windows People app consolidates messages from several major social networks and your email accounts. You can view the latest updates from your friends all in one place, as well as comment on and retweet those updates—without having to visit the social networking sites themselves.

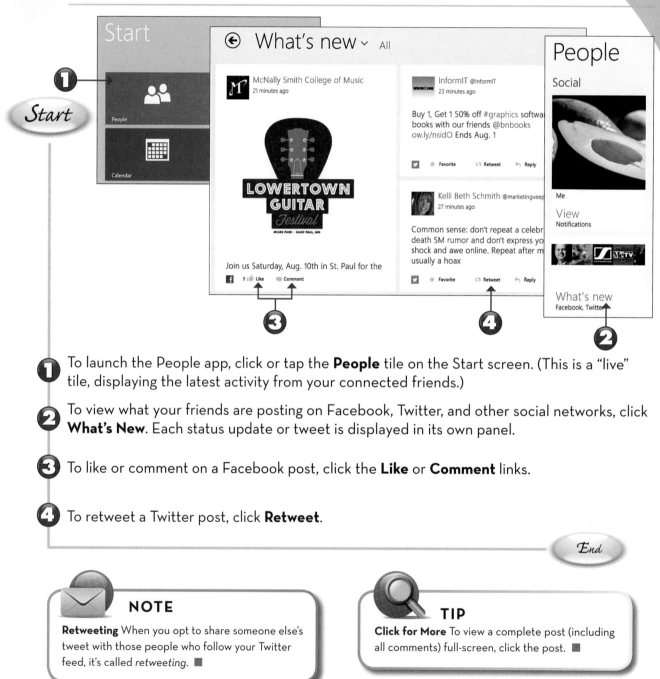

To launch the People app, click or tap the **People** tile on the Start screen. (This is a "live" tile, displaying the latest activity from your connected friends.)

To view what your friends are posting on Facebook, Twitter, and other social networks, click **What's New**. Each status update or tweet is displayed in its own panel.

To like or comment on a Facebook post, click the **Like** or **Comment** links.

To retweet a Twitter post, click **Retweet**.

NOTE

Retweeting When you opt to share someone else's tweet with those people who follow your Twitter feed, it's called *retweeting*. ■

TIP

Click for More To view a complete post (including all comments) full-screen, click the post. ■

POSTING NEW UPDATES FROM THE PEOPLE APP

In addition to displaying the most recent posts from your social networking friends, the People app also lets you post new status updates to your Facebook or Facebook account.

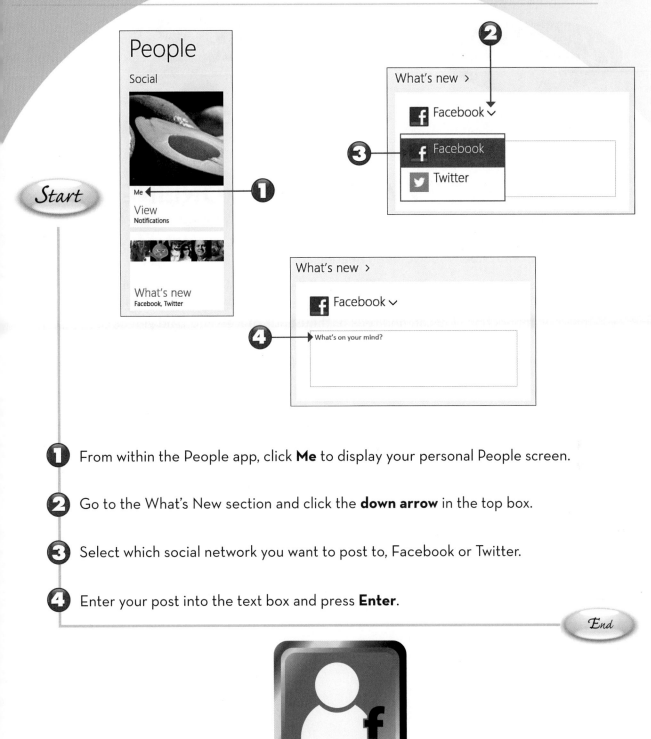

1 From within the People app, click **Me** to display your personal People screen.

2 Go to the What's New section and click the **down arrow** in the top box.

3 Select which social network you want to post to, Facebook or Twitter.

4 Enter your post into the text box and press **Enter**.

End

Chapter 13

WATCHING TV AND MOVIES ONLINE

Want to rewatch last night's episode of *The Voice*? Or the entire season of *Big Bang Theory*? How about a classic music video from your favorite band? Or that latest "viral video" you've been hearing about?

Here's the latest hot thing on the Web: watching your favorite television shows, movies, and videos online, via your web browser. If you have a fast enough Internet connection, you can find tens of thousands of free and paid videos to watch at dozens of different websites, including YouTube, Hulu, and Netflix. You can even use the Windows Xbox Video app to purchase and download videos to your PC—and watch them anytime, at your convenience.

PLAYING A VIDEO WITH THE XBOX VIDEO APP

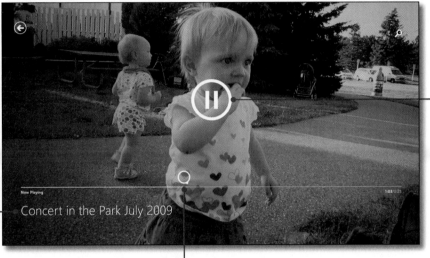

Pause control

Name of video — Concert in the Park July 2009

Scrub control

WATCHING MOVIES ON NETFLIX

Arguably the most popular site for streaming movies is Netflix (www.netflix.com), which offers a mix of both classic and newer movies, as well as classic television programming and some original programming. You can watch Netflix in your web browser or via the Netflix app for Windows.

Start

1 Click or tap the **Netflix** tile on the Start or Apps screen to launch the Netflix app.

2 By default, Netflix displays its Home screen, which is personalized based on your viewing habits. Click **Top 10 for You** to view your top 10 items.

3 Click **New Releases** to view the latest movies and shows on Netflix.

4 Click **Genres** to view a list of popular genres, then click a genre to view all films of that type.

Continued

NOTE

Netflix App Download the (free) Netflix app from the Windows Store. Once installed, you can create a new Netflix account or log in with an email address and password from an existing account. ■

TIP

Subscription Fees Netflix isn't free. You pay $7.99/month for unlimited streaming video online. ■

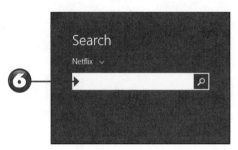

5 To search for a specific movie or show, click the **Search** (magnifying glass) icon to display the search pane.

6 Enter the name of the movie or show into the Search box, and then press **Enter**.

Continued

NOTE

Streaming Video Most movies and TV shows you watch online are not downloaded to your computer. Instead, they flow in real time from the host website to your PC, over the Internet, using a technology called *streaming video*. With streaming video, programs can start playing back almost immediately, with no time-consuming downloading necessary. ■

TIP

Recommendations Netflix analyzes your past viewing to suggest new movies you might like to watch. It also organizes programming by genre. ■

7 When you find a movie or show you want to watch, click it. The detail page for that movie or show displays.

8 Click the **Play** button on the image to watch the program.

Continued

TIP

TV Shows If you choose to watch a TV show, you can usually choose from different episodes in different seasons. Select a season to see all episodes from that season, and then click the episode you want to watch. ■

9 Netflix begins playing the movie or show you selected. Right-click anywhere on the screen to display the options bar.

10 Click the **Pause** button to pause playback; the Pause button changes to a Play button. Click the **Play** button to resume playback.

11 Click and drag the slider control to move directly to another part of the movie.

End

NOTE

DVD Rental Netflix also offers a separate DVD-by-mail rental service, with a separate subscription fee. ■

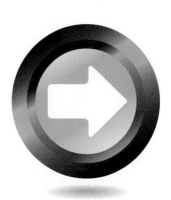

WATCHING TV SHOWS ON HULU PLUS

If Netflix is the best website for movies, Hulu is the best site for television programming. Hulu offers episodes from major-network TV shows, as well as new and classic feature films, for online viewing. The standard free membership offers access to a limited number of videos; upgrade to Hulu Plus ($7.99/month) for a larger selection of newer shows—and to use the Hulu Plus Windows app.

Start

① From the Windows Start screen, click or tap the **Hulu Plus** tile to open the Hulu Plus app.

② Hulu displays a series of featured programs on its main screen. Scroll right to view recommended programming by type.

③ From the list of programming categories, click **TV** to view available TV shows.

Continued

NOTE

Hulu Plus App Download the (free) Hulu Plus app from the Windows Store. To use this app, you must have a Hulu Plus membership. ■

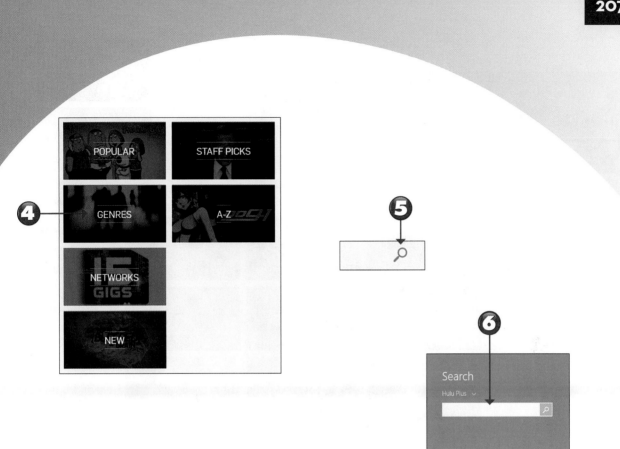

4 Scroll right to browse through TV programs by type or genre.

5 To search for specific shows, click the **Search** (magnifying glass) icon to display the search pane.

6 Enter the name of the program into the Search box and press **Enter**.

Continued

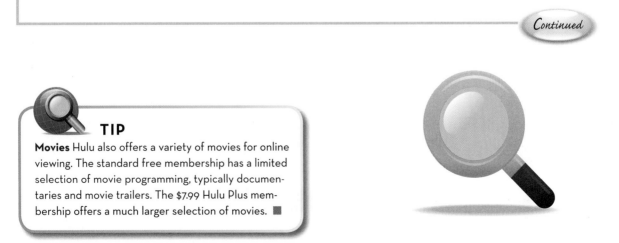

TIP

Movies Hulu also offers a variety of movies for online viewing. The standard free membership has a limited selection of movie programming, typically documentaries and movie trailers. The $7.99 Hulu Plus membership offers a much larger selection of movies. ■

POPULAR ▶

ALL SEASONS

SEASON 4

SEASON 3

SEASON 2

SEASON 1

EPISODES

Season 4, Episode 1
History 101

Season 4, Episode 5
Cooperative Escapism in Fa... (21 min)

Season 4, Episode 9
Intro to Felt Surrogacy

Season 4, Episode 2
Paranormal Parentage

Season 4, Episode 6
Advanced Documentary Film... (21 min)

Season 4, Episode 10
Intro to Knots

Season 4, Episode 3
Conventions of Space and Ti... (21 min)

Season 4, Episode 7
Economics of Marine Biology

Season 4, Episode 11
Basic Human Anatomy

Season 4, Episode 4
Alternative History of the Ge... (21 min)

Season 4, Episode 8
Herstory of Dance

Season 4, Episode 12
Heroic Origins

7 Select the show you want to watch.

8 When the detailed program page appears, scroll right to view episodes by season.

9 Click the episode you want to watch.

Continued

10 Hulu begins playing the program you selected. Move your mouse over the screen to display the playback controls.

11 Click the **Pause** button to pause playback; the Pause button changes to a Play button. Click the **Play** button to resume playback.

12 Click and drag the scrub control (slider) to move directly to another part of the program.

End

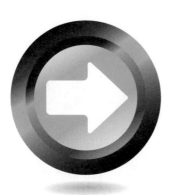

WATCHING VIDEOS ON YOUTUBE

The most popular video site on the Web is YouTube. This site is a video-sharing community; users can upload their own videos and watch videos uploaded by other members. (YouTube also offers a number of commercial movies, TV shows, and music videos.)

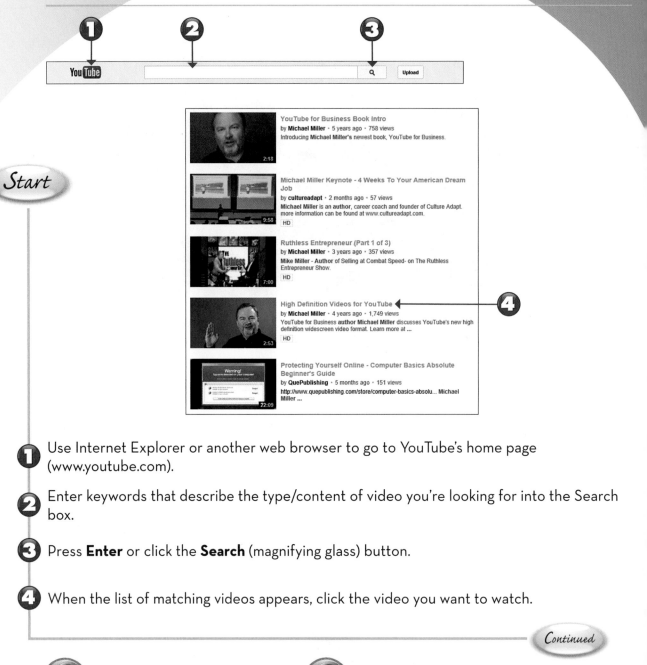

Start

1 Use Internet Explorer or another web browser to go to YouTube's home page (www.youtube.com).

2 Enter keywords that describe the type/content of video you're looking for into the Search box.

3 Press **Enter** or click the **Search** (magnifying glass) button.

4 When the list of matching videos appears, click the video you want to watch.

Continued

TIP

Movies To view commercial movies on YouTube, click **Movies** at the top of any page. Some movies are free; others can be rented on a 48-hour pass for as low as $1.99. ■

TIP

Playlists To add a video to a playlist, click the **Add To** button under the video player, and then click a playlist. You can view your playlists favorites by clicking the **down arrow** next to your name (at the top of the page); click a playlist to begin playback. ■

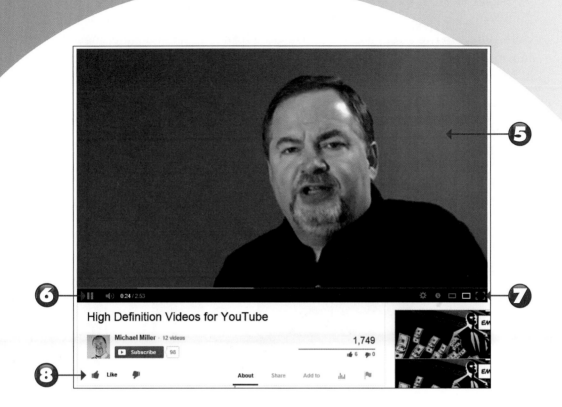

5 When the video page appears, the video begins playing automatically.

6 Click the **Pause** button to pause playback; click the button again to resume playback.

7 Click the **full-screen** button to view the video on your entire computer screen.

8 Click the **thumbs-up** button to "like" the video.

End

TIP

Sharing Videos Find a video you think a friend would like? Click the **Share** button under the video player. You can then opt to email a link to the video, like the video on Facebook, or tweet a link to the video on Twitter. ◼

TIP

Uploading Your Own Videos To upload your own home movies to YouTube, click **Upload** at the top of any page. On the next screen, click **Select Files from Your Computer**, and then navigate to and select the video you want to upload. After the video is uploaded, you can add a title and description and choose a thumbnail image for the video. ◼

PURCHASING AND DOWNLOADING MOVIES WITH THE XBOX VIDEO APP

The Windows Xbox Video app lets you download movies and TV shows to your PC. This is different from the streaming video available from Netflix and Hulu; these are usually newer movies than you find on those other services, and you can watch these downloaded videos at your convenience.

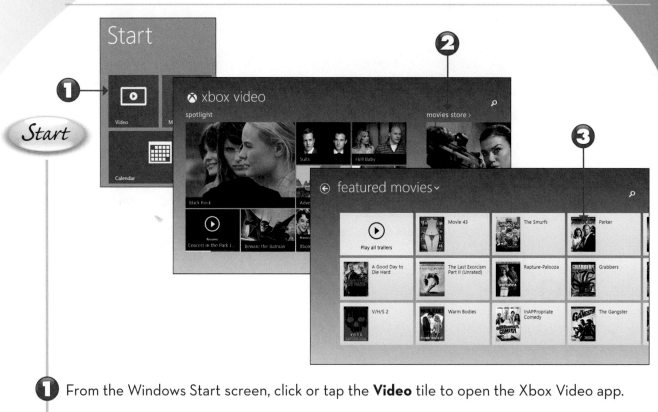

① From the Windows Start screen, click or tap the **Video** tile to open the Xbox Video app.

② The main screen displays Spotlight videos; scroll right to purchase movies (click **New Movies** or **Featured Movies**) and TV shows (click **New TV Shows** or **Featured TV Shows**).

③ When you find an item you want to purchase, click or tap the tile for that item.

Continued

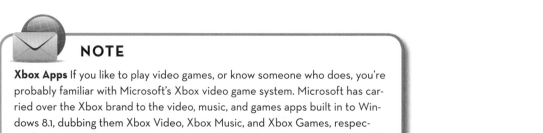

NOTE

Xbox Apps If you like to play video games, or know someone who does, you're probably familiar with Microsoft's Xbox video game system. Microsoft has carried over the Xbox brand to the video, music, and games apps built in to Windows 8.1, dubbing them Xbox Video, Xbox Music, and Xbox Games, respectively. Versions of these apps are also available on the Xbox game console. ∎

4 Click or tap the **Buy** button to purchase and download the selected item.

5 Click or tap the **Rent** button to rent the item for a specific number of days.

End

NOTE

Renting Movies Many movies can be rented for a limited time (14 days), in addition to being available for permanent purchase.

VIEWING VIDEOS WITH THE XBOX VIDEO APP

All the items you've purchased or rented are displayed within the Xbox Video app and can be viewed within the app.

Start

From the Xbox Video app, scroll to the *left* and click **My Videos** to view all the videos in your collection—including your own home videos and those you've downloaded from the Xbox Video store.

Click or tap the video you want to view.

Continued

TIP

Other Online Video Stores You can purchase movies and TV shows from several other sites online. These include Amazon Instant Video (www.amazon.com), Apple's iTunes Store (www.apple.com/itunes/), CinemaNow (www.cinemanow.com), and Vudu (www.vudu.com). ∎

3 When the video begins to play, move your mouse to display program information and play-back controls.

4 Click the **Pause** control to pause playback; click the **Play** control to resume playback.

5 Click and drag the slider bar to move to any specific part of the program.

End

TIP

Jumping Tap or click the **left** or **right arrows** to jump back 15 seconds or forward 30 seconds in the video. This is great for skipping recorded commercials. ■

Chapter 14

PLAYING DIGITAL MUSIC

Your personal computer can do more than just compute. It can also serve as a fully functional music player!

That's right, you can use your PC to listen to your favorite music, either on CD or downloaded from the Internet. Windows 8.1 includes the full-featured Xbox Music app for downloading, streaming, and playing back all your favorite music. You can also use Apple's iTunes software to purchase and play the music you love.

EXPLORING THE XBOX MUSIC APP

Collection

Radio

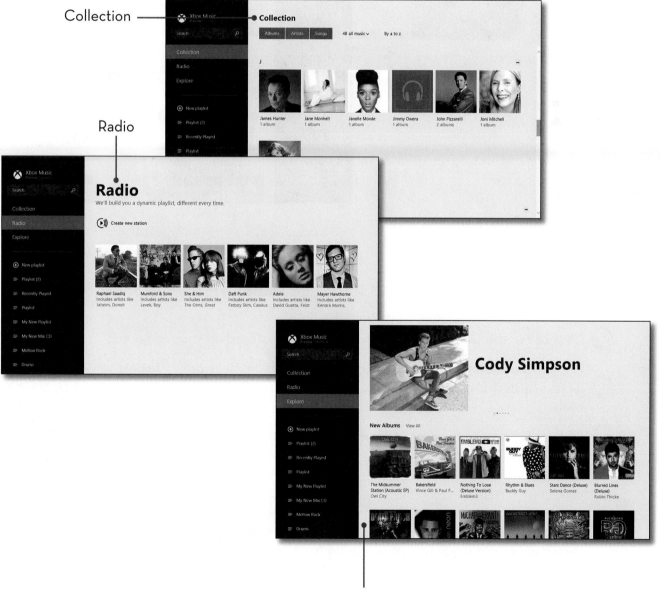

Explore

PLAYING YOUR OWN MUSIC IN WINDOWS

The Xbox Music app lets you play any songs you've downloaded from the Internet or ripped from your own CDs. Your music is available from the Collection page of the app.

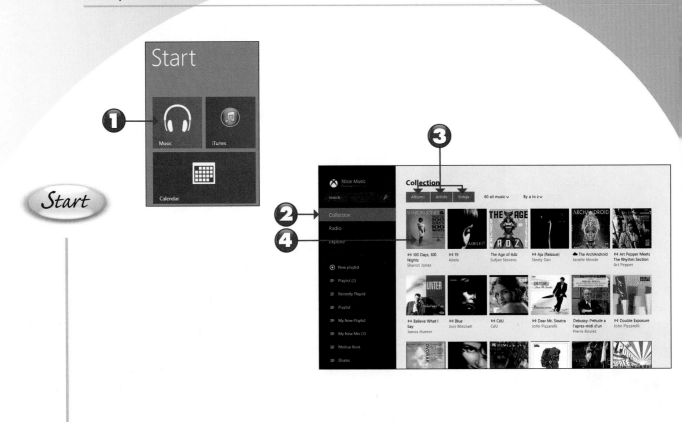

Start

1 From the Start or Apps screen, click or tap the **Music** tile to launch the Xbox Music app.

2 Click or tap the **Collection** tab to view the tracks stored on your computer.

3 Click or tap **Albums** to view your collection by album. Click or tap **Artists** to view your collection by performing artist. Click or tap **Songs** to view your collection on a track by track basis.

4 Click or tap an album cover to view all the tracks in that album.

Continued

 TIP

Windows Media Player If you need more fully featured music playback and management, check out the Windows Media Player app that runs on the traditional Windows desktop. To launch this app, go to the Apps screen, and then scroll to and click the **Windows Media Player** icon. ∎

 **TIP**

Playlists To add a track to an existing playlist, click or tap the + button, and then click the playlist name. To create a new playlist, click or tap **New Playlist** in the navigation pane on the left side of the app window. To play a playlist, click or tap the list name in the navigation pane. ∎

5

100 Days, 100 Nights
Sharon Jones, 2007, R&B / Soul

(•) 1	100 Days, 100 Nights	3:45	Sharon Jones
(•) 2	Nobody's Baby	2:27	Sharon Jones
(•) 3	Tell Me	2:46	Sharon Jones
(•) 4	Be Easy	3:03	Sharon Jones
(•) 5	When The Other Foot Drops, Uncle	3:15	Sharon Jones
(•) 6	Let Them Knock	4:29	Sharon Jones

6

8

7

5 Click or tap the **Play** button to play all the tracks in this album.

6 Click or tap any individual track to play that song.

7 Right-click the screen to display the Options bar and playback controls.

8 Click the **Pause** button to pause playback. Click the **Play** button to resume playback.

End

TIP
Artist Info To display more information about the current artist, click the **Info** button (next to the + button) on the album page. ■

TIP
Next and Previous Tracks To play the next track in an album or playlist, click the **Next** button in the options bar. To play the previous track, click the **Previous** button. ■

PURCHASING AND DOWNLOADING NEW MUSIC

Want to listen to some new music? If so, pull out your credit card, fire up the Xbox Music App, and get ready to go shopping!

1 From the Xbox Music App, click the **Explore** tab to display the Xbox Music Store.

2 You now see a selection of new albums for purchase. Scroll to the Top Albums section and click **View All**.

3 By default, Xbox Music displays albums for purchase. Click the **down arrow** next to Albums to view artists or individual songs instead.

4 Click a genre to view all music in that genre.

Continued

Big Bad Voodoo Daddy

Big Bad Voodoo Daddy, 1993, Jazz, Coolsville

1	The Boogie Bumper Big Bad Voodoo Daddy	3:41
2	Mr. Pinstripe Suit Big Bad Voodoo Daddy	3:37
3	King Of Swing Big Bad Voodoo Daddy	4:58
4	Minnie The Moocher Big Bad Voodoo Daddy	4:42
5	You & Me & The Bottle Makes 3 Toni...	3:33

(▶) Play album

(+) Add to

5 → (🛒) Buy album

(☰) Explore artist

6

Explore artist Buy song

Tatatango
Minor Swing Quinte...
0:05 / 3:25

Verify your Microsoft account info

Music needs to confirm your identity.

Michael Miller
trapperjohn2000@hotmail.com

7 → Password

Can't access your account?

OK   Cancel

5 To purchase an entire album, click the album to display the purchase pane, then click **Buy Album**.

6 To purchase an individual song, right-click the track to display the options bar, then click **Buy Song**.

7 When prompted, sign in to your Microsoft account and confirm your purchase via credit card.

End

STREAMING MUSIC ONLINE

There's an entire world of music out there on the Internet that you don't have to purchase and download. Microsoft offers millions of tracks through its Xbox Music Pass streaming music service. You can listen to individual tracks on demand or create your own personalized online radio stations.

1 From the Xbox Music Store, navigate to and click a track you want to play.

2 Click the **Play** button to begin streaming this track in real time.

Continued

NOTE

Free and Premium Microsoft offers both a free and premium version of the Xbox Music Pass service. The free version makes you listen to occasional ads and limits you to just 10 hours of music a month. Xbox Music Pass Premium costs $9.99/month but gets rid of the ads and gives you unlimited music streaming. A yearly subscription and 30-day free trial are also available. ■

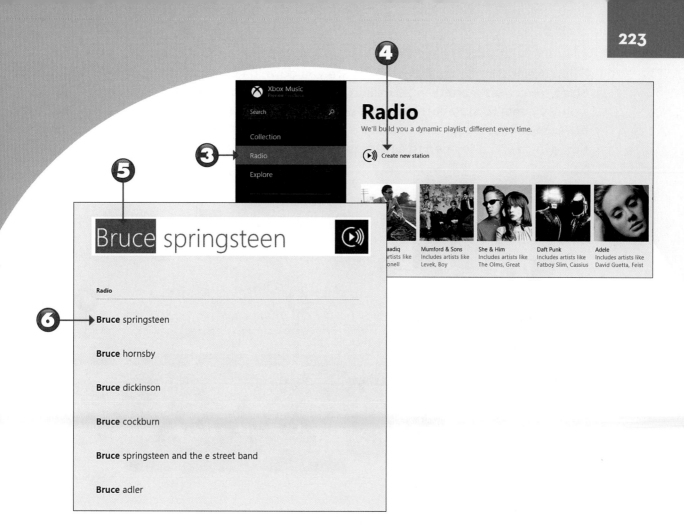

3 To create a new online radio station, go to the main screen of the Xbox Music app and click **Radio**.

4 Click **Create New Station**.

5 Enter the name of an artist. As you type, Xbox Music lists matching artists.

6 Click the name of the artist you want. Xbox Music creates a radio station based on this artist and begins playback.

End

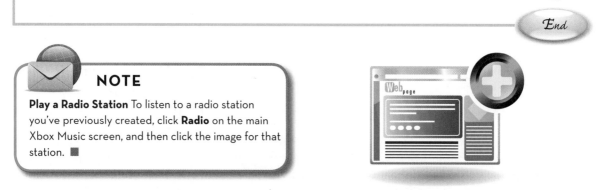

NOTE

Play a Radio Station To listen to a radio station you've previously created, click **Radio** on the main Xbox Music screen, and then click the image for that station. ■

DOWNLOADING MUSIC FROM THE ITUNES STORE

If you use an iPhone or iPad, chances are you download your music from Apple's iTunes Store, which has more than 20 million tracks available for downloading at prices ranging from 69 cents to $1.29 each. You can play music purchased at the iTunes Store in the Windows Xbox Music app, on your iPod or iPhone, or with Apple's iTunes music player application—which you also need to access the iTunes Store.

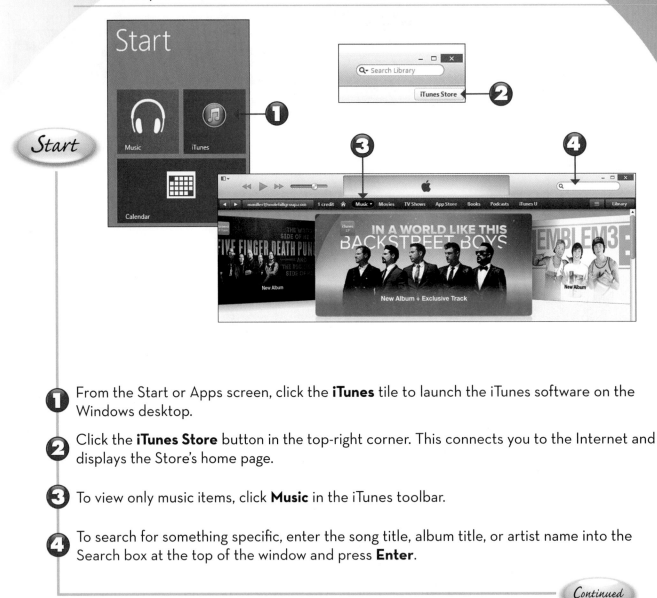

① From the Start or Apps screen, click the **iTunes** tile to launch the iTunes software on the Windows desktop.

② Click the **iTunes Store** button in the top-right corner. This connects you to the Internet and displays the Store's home page.

③ To view only music items, click **Music** in the iTunes toolbar.

④ To search for something specific, enter the song title, album title, or artist name into the Search box at the top of the window and press **Enter**.

Continued

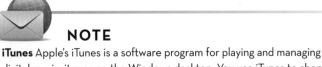

NOTE

iTunes Apple's iTunes is a software program for playing and managing digital music; it runs on the Windows desktop. You use iTunes to shop the iTunes Store, as well as to manage the content of your iPhone, iPad, or iPod. You can download the iTunes app for free at www.apple.com/itunes/. ■

TIP

More in the Store The iTunes Store offers more than just music for download. iTunes also sells movies, TV shows, music videos, podcasts, audiobooks, and eBooks (in the ePub format). ■

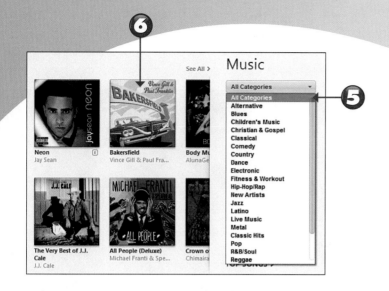

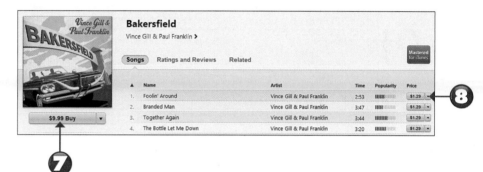

5 To browse music by category, click the **All Categories** list and select a category.

6 To view all the tracks in an album, click the album cover.

7 To purchase an individual track, click the **Buy** (price) button for that track.

8 To purchase an entire album, click the **Buy** button for that album.

End

TIP

Apple Account Before you can purchase items from the iTunes Store, you must create an Apple account and enter your credit card information. You might be prompted to do this the first time you click to purchase, or you can create your account manually, at any time, by clicking the **Sign In** button at the top right of the iTunes window and, when prompted, clicking the **Create New Account** button. ■

PLAYING A CD WITH ITUNES

You can also use the iTunes program to play audio CDs—if your computer has a CD drive, that is.

Start

① Insert a CD into your PC's CD drive and launch the iTunes software.

② The CD automatically appears in the iTunes window. Click the **Play** button to begin playback; the button now changes to a Pause button. Click the **Pause** button to pause playback.

③ Click the right arrow button to skip to the next track. Click the **back arrow** button to skip to the previous track.

④ Double-click a specific track to jump to that track.

End

RIPPING A CD TO YOUR HARD DISK WITH ITUNES

You can use iTunes to copy songs from any CD to your PC's hard drive; this is called *ripping* the CD. Ripping a CD lets you take all your music with you, on your computer, without having to carry dozens (or hundreds) of CDs along for the ride. In addition, when you rip a CD to your PC using iTunes, you can then transfer it to your iPhone or iPod for listening on the go.

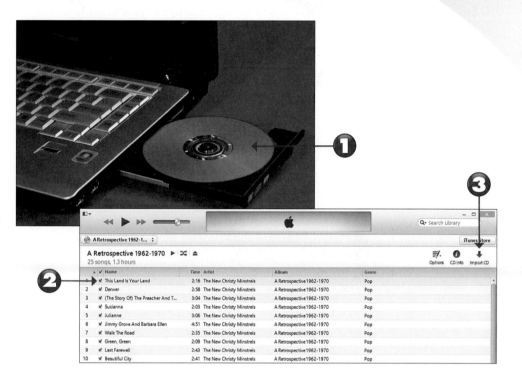

Start

1 Launch the iTunes software and insert the original music CD into your computer's CD/DVD drive.

2 The CD should automatically appear in the iTunes window, with all the tracks listed. Leave checked those tracks that you want to copy to your computer, and uncheck those that you don't want to copy.

3 Click the **Import CD** button. The selected tracks are now copied to your PC's hard disk and automatically added to the iTunes library.

End

TIP

Ripping and Burning The process of copying music from a CD to a computer's hard drive, in digital format, is called *ripping*. The reverse process, copying music from your PC to a blank CD, is called *burning*. ■

TIP

Connect Before You Rip Make sure you're connected to the Internet before you start ripping so that iTunes can download album and track details. If you don't connect, you won't encode track names or CD cover art—and will have to do so manually, later. ■

PLAYING DIGITAL MUSIC WITH ITUNES

You can use the iTunes software to play any digital music you've downloaded from the iTunes Store or ripped from CDs.

1 Launch the iTunes software and make sure **Music** is selected in the top-left corner.

2 To view all the tracks in your library, click **Songs**. To view your music organized by original album, click **Albums**. To view your music organized by artist, click **Artists**. To view your music organized by genre, click **Genres**.

3 Navigate to the track, album, artist, or genre you want to play, and then double-click that item.

4 Click the **Pause** button to pause playback; click the **Play** button to resume playback.

TIP

Playlists You can put multiple songs together into a single *playlist* for future playback. To view and play back your playlists, click the **Playlists** button at the top of the iTunes window. To create a new playlist, click the + button at the bottom of the playlists pane, and then click **New Playlist**. To add songs to a playlist, drag individual tracks from the content pane into the playlists pane. ■

TIP

Shuffle and Repeat To play an album or playlist in a random order, click the **Shuffle** icon in the mini-player at the top of the iTunes window. Click the **Repeat** icon in the mini-player to repeat the selected songs over and over. ■

CONNECTING AN IPOD TO YOUR PC

To manage the music stored on your iPod or iPhone, you have to connect your device to your computer. The actual music management is done with Apple's iTunes software. This is called *synchronizing* or *syncing* tracks from your computer to your portable device.

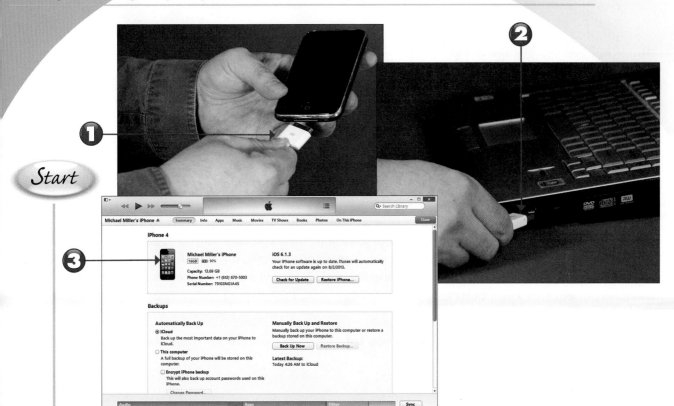

 Start

1. Connect one end of the USB cable to your iPod.

2. Connect the other end of the USB cable to a USB port on your PC.

3. The iTunes software now launches on your PC and displays the screen for your device. iTunes automatically syncs all selected tracks and playlists to your portable device.

End

TIP

Manually Syncing You can also manually select which tunes are copied to your iPod or iPhone. Just access the **Music** tab on the connection screen and opt to sync only selected tracks and playlists—those items checked in your iTunes library. ■

TIP

Autofill and the iPod Shuffle If you have an iPod shuffle, iTunes offers an Autofill option. This lets the software automatically choose songs to sync to your iPod—which is useful if you have more songs on your hard disk than you have storage capacity on your shuffle. ■

VIEWING DIGITAL PHOTOS

The traditional film camera is a thing of the past. These days, everybody uses a digital camera or cell phone camera—which you can easily connect to your PC. Once connected, you can transfer all the photos you take to your computer's hard disk, view them on your computer monitor, share them with friends and family via Facebook and social media, and even edit your pictures to make them look even better.

The Windows full-screen Photos app helps you find and view all the photos stored on your PC. It even lets you touch up your photos with easy-to-use editing functions.

NAVIGATING THE PHOTOS APP

Click to return to
main Pictures folder

Name of current
folder

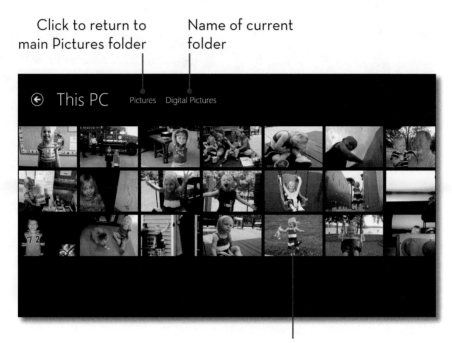

Click to view picture
full-screen

TRANSFERRING PICTURES FROM A MEMORY CARD

If your PC includes a memory card reader, it may be easier to copy your digital photos via your camera's memory card. When you insert a memory card, your PC recognizes the card as if it were another disk on your system. You can then copy files from the memory card to your computer's hard disk.

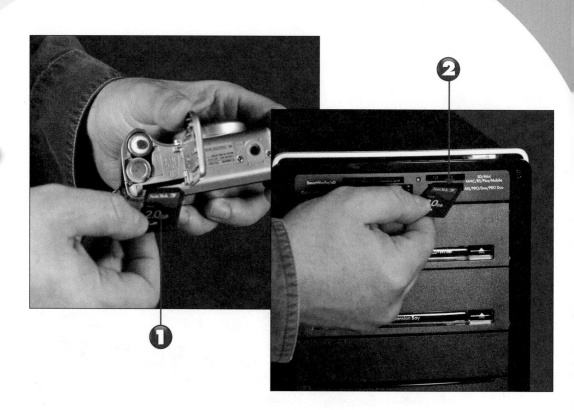

1. Turn off your digital camera and remove the flash memory card.

2. Insert the memory card from your digital camera into the memory card slot on your PC.

Continued

TIP

Connecting via USB You can also transfer photos by connecting your digital camera to your computer via USB. Windows should recognize when your camera is connected and automatically download the pictures in your camera, while displaying a dialog box that notifies you of what it's doing. ■

NOTE

Copying Automatically Windows might recognize that your memory card contains digital photos and start to download those photos automatically—no manual interaction necessary. ■

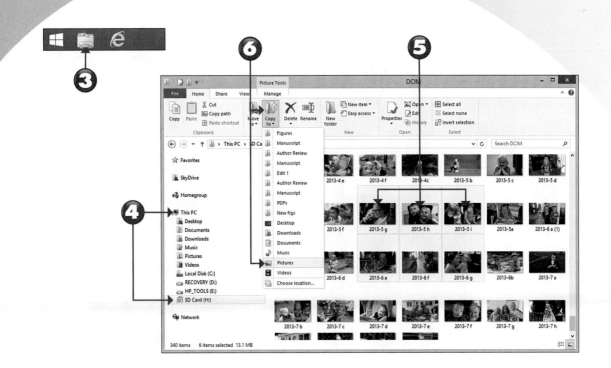

3 Open the Windows desktop and click **File Explorer** on the taskbar.

4 When File Explorer opens, click **This PC** in the navigation pane, click the drive for your memory card reader drive, and then navigate to and open the folder where the photos reside—usually labeled DCIM.

5 Hold down the **Ctrl** key and click each photo you want to transfer.

6 Select the **Home** ribbon and click **Copy To**, and then select **Pictures**.

End

CAUTION

Other Opening Apps Depending on what apps you have installed on your system, you may get multiple prompts to download photos when you connect your camera. If this happens, pick the program you prefer to work with and close the other dialog boxes. ■

TIP

Different Folder Names Some cameras might use a name other than DCIM for the main folder. ■

VIEWING YOUR PHOTOS IN WINDOWS

To view your photos, you can use the Windows Photos app.

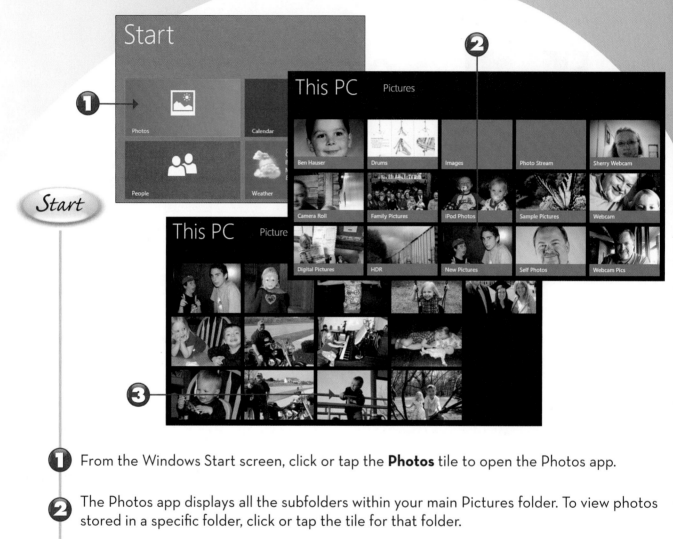

From the Windows Start screen, click or tap the **Photos** tile to open the Photos app.

The Photos app displays all the subfolders within your main Pictures folder. To view photos stored in a specific folder, click or tap the tile for that folder.

Click through the folders and subfolders until you find a photo you want to view, and then click that photo to view it full-screen.

Continued

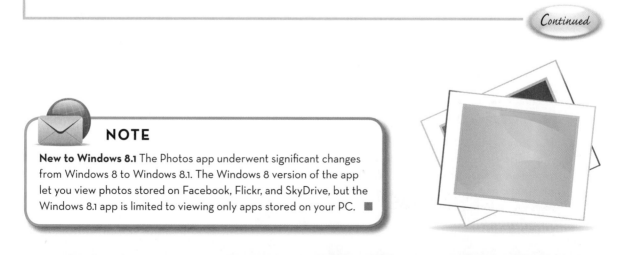

NOTE

New to Windows 8.1 The Photos app underwent significant changes from Windows 8 to Windows 8.1. The Windows 8 version of the app let you view photos stored on Facebook, Flickr, and SkyDrive, but the Windows 8.1 app is limited to viewing only apps stored on your PC. ■

Delete	Open with	Set as	Slide show

④ To enlarge the picture, click the **+** button at the lower-right corner of the screen. To make a picture smaller, click the **–** button.

⑤ To move to the next picture in the folder, click the **right arrow** on screen or press the **right arrow** key on your keyboard. To return to the previous picture, click the **left arrow** on screen or press the **left arrow** key on your keyboard.

⑥ To view a slide show of the pictures in this folder, starting with the current picture, right-click the open photo to display the options bar, and then click or tap **Slide Show.**

⑦ To delete the current picture, right-click the screen to display the options bar, and then click or tap **Delete.**

End

TIP

Lock Screen Picture To use the current picture as the image on the Windows lock screen, display the photo full-screen, and then right-click the screen to display the options bar and click or tap **Set As** and then select **Lock Screen**. ■

EDITING YOUR PHOTOS IN WINDOWS

Not all your pictures turn out perfect. Maybe you need to crop a picture to highlight the important area. Maybe you need to brighten a dark picture, or darken a bright one. Or maybe you need to adjust the tint or color saturation. Fortunately, you're in luck—you can do all these basic touchups within the Windows Photos app.

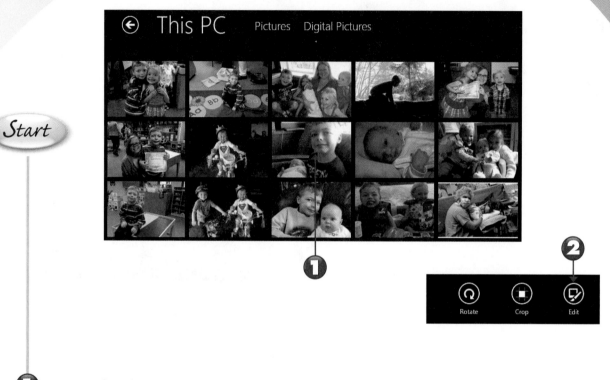

Start

1 From within the Photos app, navigate to and click the photo you want to edit.

2 Right-click the photo to display the options bar, then click **Edit** to display the editing screen.

Continued

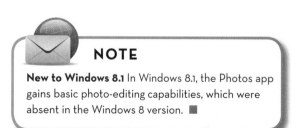

NOTE

New to Windows 8.1 In Windows 8.1, the Photos app gains basic photo-editing capabilities, which were absent in the Windows 8 version. ■

3 Click the **Auto Fix** button to let the Photos app try to automatically touch up your picture.

4 Click the best suggested result on the right side of the screen.

Continued

5 Click **Basic Fixes** to access four basic fixes.

6 Click **Rotate** to rotate the picture 90 degrees clockwise. Continue clicking to further rotate the picture.

7 Click **Crop** to crop the edges of the picture.

8 When the crop screen appears, use your mouse to drag the corners of the white border until the picture appears as you like, and then click **Apply**.

Continued

TIP

Aspect Ratio By default, Windows maintains the original aspect ratio when you crop a photo. To crop to a different aspect ratio, click the **Aspect Ratio** button and make a new selection. ■

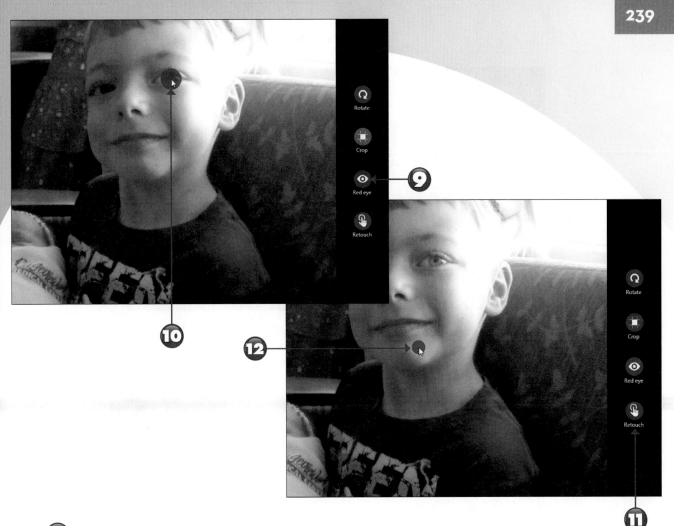

9 Click **Red Eye** to remove the red eye effect from the picture.

10 The cursor changes to a blue circle. Move the circle to the eye(s) you want to fix, and then click the mouse button to remove red eye.

11 Click **Retouch** to smooth out or remove blemishes from the photo.

12 The cursor changes to a blue circle. Move the circle to the area you want to repair, and then click the mouse button to do so.

Continued

NOTE

Red Eye Red eye is caused when a camera's flash causes the subject's eyes to appear a devilish red. Removing the red eye effect involves changing the red color to black in the edited photo. ■

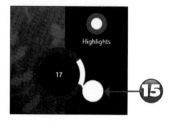

13 Click **Light** to edit the brightness and contrast of the photo.

14 Click the control you want to adjust—**Brightness**, **Contrast**, **Highlights**, or **Shadows**.

15 The selected control changes to a circular control. Click/tap and drag the control clockwise to increase the effect, or counterclockwise to decrease the effect.

Continued

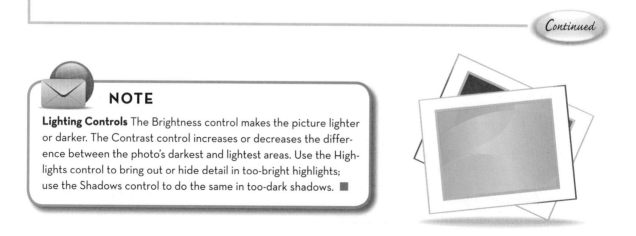

NOTE

Lighting Controls The Brightness control makes the picture lighter or darker. The Contrast control increases or decreases the difference between the photo's darkest and lightest areas. Use the Highlights control to bring out or hide detail in too-bright highlights; use the Shadows control to do the same in too-dark shadows. ■

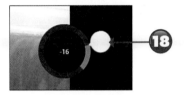

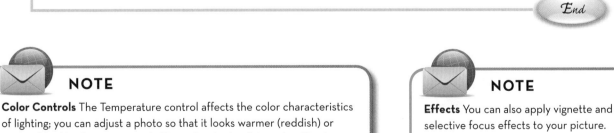

16 Click **Color** to edit the tint and saturation of the photo.

17 Click the control you want to adjust—**Temperature**, **Tint**, **Saturation**, or **Color Enhance**.

18 The selected control changes to a circular control. Click/tap and drag the control clockwise to increase the effect, or counterclockwise to decrease the effect.

End

NOTE

Color Controls The Temperature control affects the color characteristics of lighting; you can adjust a photo so that it looks warmer (reddish) or cooler (bluish). The Tint control affects the shade of the color. The Saturation control affects the amount of color in the photo; completely desaturating a photo makes it black and white. And the Color Enhance control lets you click an area of the photo to increase or decrease color saturation. ■

NOTE

Effects You can also apply vignette and selective focus effects to your picture. Click **Effects** in the left sidebar, and then click the effect you want to apply. ■

Chapter 16

PROTECTING YOUR COMPUTER

"An ounce of prevention is worth a pound of cure" is a bit of a cliché, but it's also true—especially when it comes to your computer system. Spending a few minutes a week on preventive maintenance can save you from costly computer problems in the future.

To ease the task of protecting and maintaining your system, Windows 8.1 includes several utilities to help you keep your computer running smoothly—and recover your data in case of some sort of malfunction.

PC SETTINGS

Configure the Windows Lock and Start screens and connected devices

Manage SkyDrive cloud storage

Manage privacy settings

Add and edit user accounts

Configure search and application settings

Control Ease of Access functions

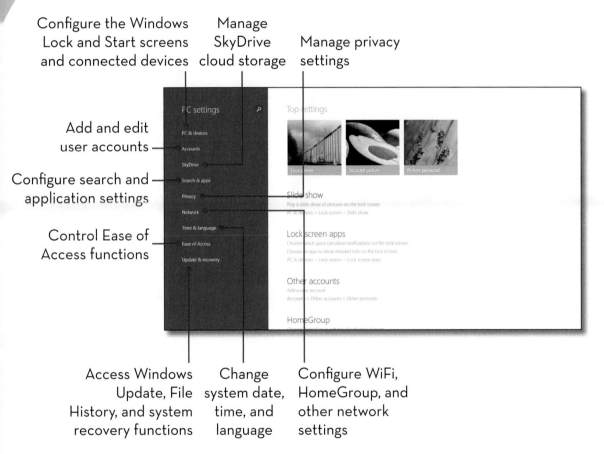

Access Windows Update, File History, and system recovery functions

Change system date, time, and language

Configure WiFi, HomeGroup, and other network settings

USING THE WINDOWS ACTION CENTER

In Windows 8.1, the best way to manage your PC's maintenance and security is via the Action Center. This built-in utility centralizes many maintenance operations, error reporting, and troubleshooting operations and will alert you to any action you need to take to protect and maintain your system.

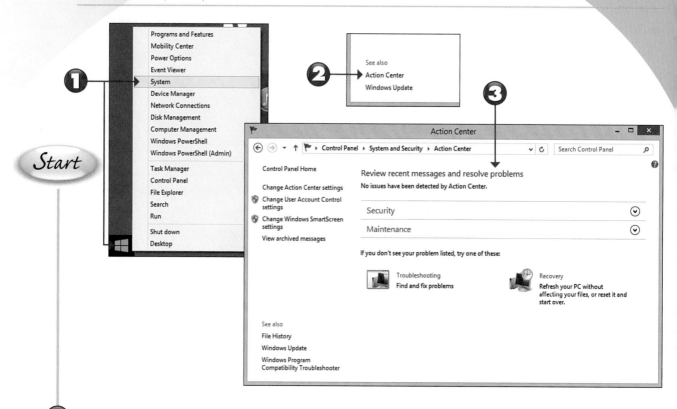

Start

1 Right-click the Start button and select **System** to display the System window.

2 Go to the See Also section in the left sidebar and click **Action Center** to open the Windows Action Center.

3 The main Action Center screen notifies you of actions you need to take or problems you need to resolve.

End

NOTE

Control Panel Another useful utility is the Windows Control Panel, which runs on the desktop and offers control of many system settings. To open the Control Panel, right-click the **Start** button and click **Control Panel**. ■

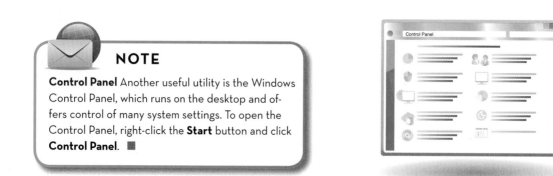

DEFENDING AGAINST MALWARE WITH WINDOWS DEFENDER

Computer viruses and spyware (collectively known as malicious software, or *malware*) install themselves on your computer, typically without your knowledge, and then either damage critical system files or surreptitiously send personal information to some devious third party. You can protect your system from viruses and spyware by using an antimalware program, such as Windows Defender, which is built in to Windows 8.1.

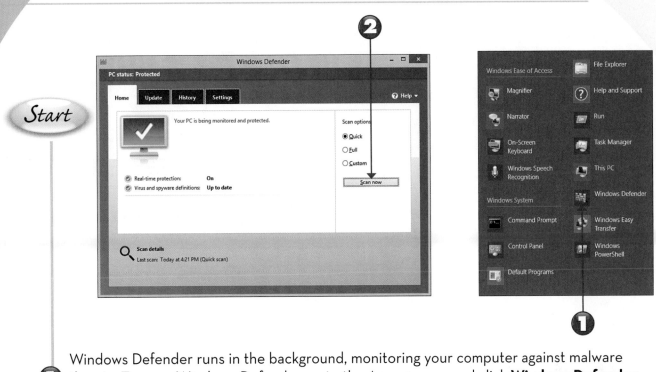

1 Windows Defender runs in the background, monitoring your computer against malware threats. To open Windows Defender, go to the Apps screen and click **Windows Defender** (in the Windows System section).

2 Defender automatically scans your system on its own schedule, but you can perform a manual scan at any time by clicking the **Scan Now** button.

End

TIP

Other Antimalware Utilities Your computer manufacturer may substitute or supplement Windows Defender with other antivirus utilities, such as AVG Anti-Virus (www.avg.com), Kaspersky Anti-Virus (www.kaspersky.com), McAfee VirusScan AntiVirus Plus (www.mcafee.com), and Norton AntiVirus (www.symantec.com). Other antispyware utilities include Ad-Aware (www.lavasoftusa.com) and Spybot Search & Destroy (www.safer-networking.org). ∎

CAUTION

How to Catch a Virus Computer viruses and spyware are most commonly transmitted via infected computer files. You can receive virus-infected files via email or instant messaging, by downloading files from unsecure websites, or by clicking links in Facebook or Twitter that link to malware-infested sites. ∎

DELETING UNNECESSARY FILES

Even with today's humongous hard disks, you can still end up with too many useless files taking up too much hard disk space. Fortunately, Windows includes a utility that identifies and deletes unused files. The Disk Cleanup tool is what you should use when you need to free up extra hard disk space for more frequently used files.

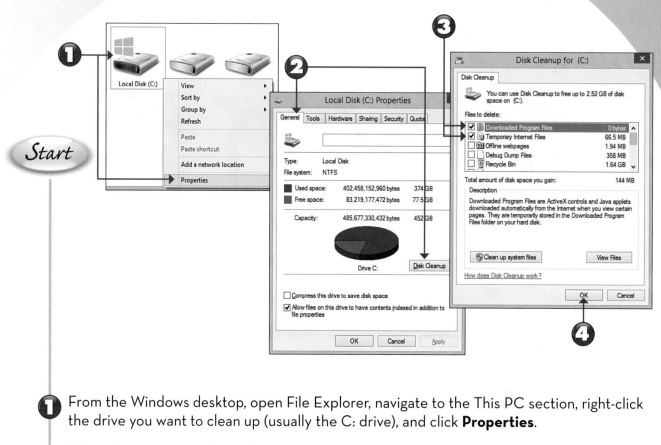

From the Windows desktop, open File Explorer, navigate to the This PC section, right-click the drive you want to clean up (usually the C: drive), and click **Properties**.

When the Properties dialog box opens, select the **General** tab (displayed by default), and click the **Disk Cleanup** button.

Disk Cleanup automatically analyzes the contents of your hard disk drive. When it's finished analyzing, it presents its results in the Disk Cleanup dialog box. Select which types of files you want to delete.

Click **OK** to begin deleting.

TIP

Which Files to Delete? You can safely choose to delete all these files *except* the setup log files and hibernation files, which are needed by the Windows operating system. ■

DELETING UNUSED PROGRAMS

Another way to free up valuable hard disk space is to delete those programs you never use.
This is accomplished using the Uninstall or Change a Program utility.

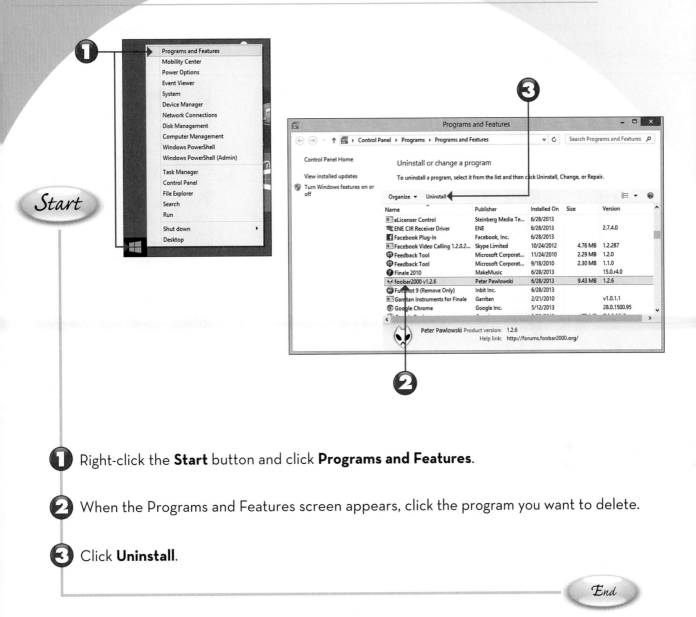

Right-click the **Start** button and click **Programs and Features**.

When the Programs and Features screen appears, click the program you want to delete.

Click **Uninstall**.

TIP

New PC Bloatware Most brand-new PCs come with
unwanted programs and trial versions installed at the
factory. Many users choose to delete these "bloatware" programs when they first run their PCs. ■

BACKING UP YOUR FILES WITH FILE HISTORY

The data stored on your computer's hard disk is valuable, and perhaps irreplaceable. That's why you want to keep a backup copy of all these valuable files, preferably on an external hard disk or another computer on your network. You can do this with the Windows File History feature, which lets you keep copies of all the different versions of your files and then restore them in case they get lost or destroyed.

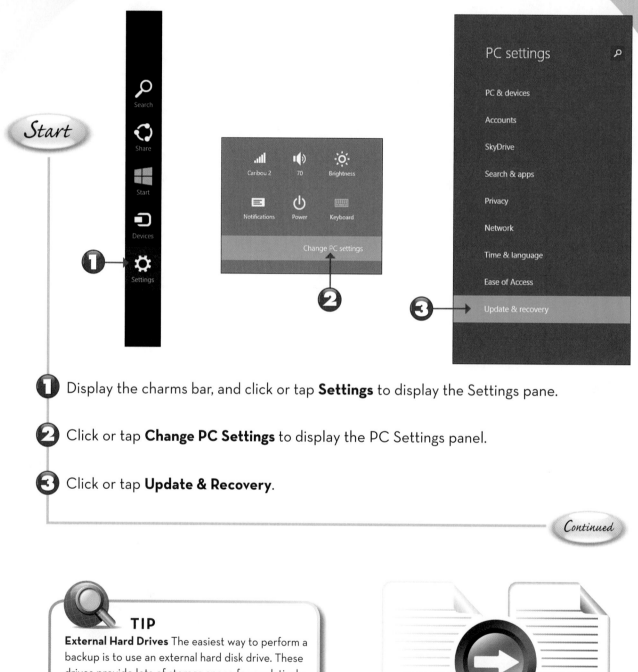

1 Display the charms bar, and click or tap **Settings** to display the Settings pane.

2 Click or tap **Change PC Settings** to display the PC Settings panel.

3 Click or tap **Update & Recovery**.

Continued

TIP

External Hard Drives The easiest way to perform a backup is to use an external hard disk drive. These drives provide lots of storage space for a relatively low cost, and they connect to your PC via USB. There's no excuse not to do it! ■

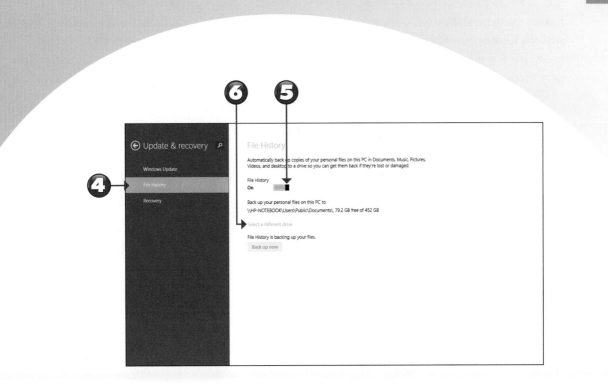

4 Click or tap **File History** to display the File History screen.

5 Click "on" the **File History** control.

6 File History automatically uses the first external drive on your system for its backup. If you want to use a different backup drive, click **Select a Different Drive** and, when the drive pane appears, select a different drive or network location.

End

TIP

Restoring Files To restore any lost or changed files you've previously backed up, go to the File History screen and click **Restore Personal Files**. Navigate to and select those files that you want to restore, and then click the **Restore** button to copy these files to their original locations. ■

RESTORING YOUR COMPUTER AFTER A CRASH

If your computer system ever crashes or freezes, your best course of action is to run the System Restore utility. This utility can automatically restore your system to the state it was in before the crash occurred—and save you the trouble of reinstalling any damaged software programs. It's a great safety net for when things go wrong!

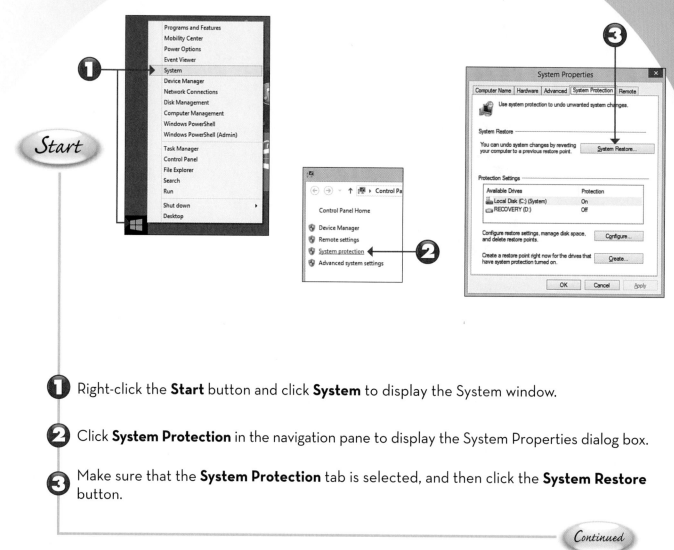

1 Right-click the **Start** button and click **System** to display the System window.

2 Click **System Protection** in the navigation pane to display the System Properties dialog box.

3 Make sure that the **System Protection** tab is selected, and then click the **System Restore** button.

Continued

TIP
Restoring Your System Be sure to close all programs before you use System Restore because Windows will need to be restarted when it's done. The full process might take half an hour or more. ■

CAUTION
System Files Only—No Documents System Restore will help you recover any damaged programs and system files, but it won't help you recover any documents or data files. This is why you need to use the File History utility to back up all your data on a regular basis—and restore that backed-up data in the case of an emergency. ■

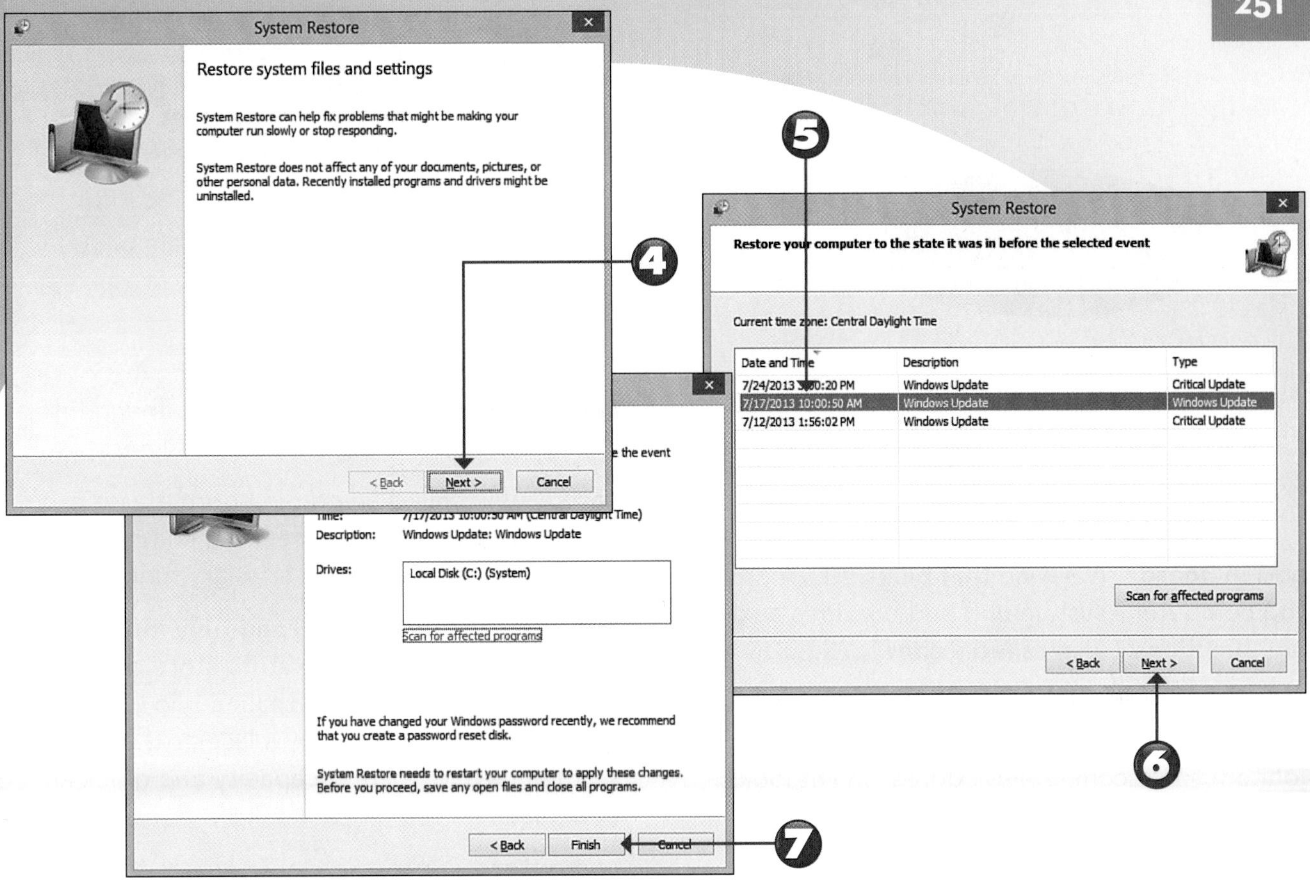

System Restore

Restore system files and settings

System Restore can help fix problems that might be making your computer run slowly or stop responding.

System Restore does not affect any of your documents, pictures, or other personal data. Recently installed programs and drivers might be uninstalled.

< Back   Next >   Cancel

System Restore

Restore your computer to the state it was in before the selected event

Current time zone: Central Daylight Time

Date and Time	Description	Type
7/24/2013 3:00:20 PM	Windows Update	Critical Update
7/17/2013 10:00:50 AM	Windows Update	Windows Update
7/12/2013 1:56:02 PM	Windows Update	Critical Update

Scan for affected programs

< Back   Next >   Cancel

the event

Time: 7/17/2013 10:00:50 AM (Central Daylight Time)
Description: Windows Update: Windows Update

Drives: Local Disk (C:) (System)

Scan for affected programs

If you have changed your Windows password recently, we recommend that you create a password reset disk.

System Restore needs to restart your computer to apply these changes. Before you proceed, save any open files and close all programs.

< Back   Finish   Cancel

④ When the System Restore window appears, click the **Next** button.

⑤ Click the restore point you want to return to.

⑥ Click the **Next** button to display the Confirm Your Restore Point screen.

⑦ Click the **Finish** button to begin the restore process.

End

TIP

Refreshing System Files Windows 8.1 lets you "refresh" your system with the current versions of important system files, in case those files become damaged or deleted. To use the Refresh utility, go to the PC Settings page and click **Update & Recovery**. On the next screen, click **Recovery**, go to the Refresh Your PC Without Affecting Your Files section, and click **Get Started**. ■

TIP

Resetting Your System In the event of a catastrophic system problem, you can reset your system to its factory-fresh condition by wiping clean the hard disk and reinstalling Windows from scratch. To reinstall Windows in this fashion, go to the PC Settings page and click **Update & Recovery**. On the next screen, click **Recovery**, go to the Remove Everything and Reinstall Windows section, and click **Get Started**. Note, however, that this option will delete all the programs and files on your computer. ■

Glossary

A

add-in board   A device that plugs in to a desktop computer's system unit and provides auxiliary functions. (Also called a *card*.)

address   The location of an Internet host. An email address might take the form johndoe@xyz.com; a web address might look like www.xyztech.com. See also *URL*.

all-in-one computer   A desktop computer where the system unit, monitor, and speakers are housed in a single unit. Often the monitor of such a system has s touchscreen display.

app   See *application*.

application   A computer program designed for a specific task or use, such as word processing, accounting, or missile guidance.

attachment   A file, such as a Word document or graphics image, attached to an email message.

B

backup   A copy of important data files.

boot   The process of turning on your computer system.

broadband   A high-speed Internet connection; it's faster than the older dial-up connection.

browser   A program, such as Internet Explorer, that translates the Hypertext Markup Language (HTML) of the Web into viewable web pages.

bug   An error in a software program or the hardware.

C

cable modem   A high-speed broadband Internet connection via digital cable TV lines.

card   Also called an *add-in board*, this is a device that plugs in to a desktop computer's system unit and provides auxiliary functions.

CD-ROM (compact disc read-only memory)   A CD that can be used to store computer data. A CD-ROM, similar to an audio CD, stores data in a form readable by a laser, resulting in a storage device of great capacity and quick accessibility.

computer   A programmable device that can store, retrieve, and process data.

CPU (central processing unit)   The group of circuits that direct the entire computer system by (1) interpreting and executing program instruction and (2) coordinating the interaction of input, output, and storage devices.

cursor   The highlighted area or pointer that tracks with the movement of your mouse or arrow keys onscreen.

D

data   Information—on a computer, in digital format.

database   A program for arranging facts in the computer and retrieving them—the computer equivalent of a filing system.

desktop   The graphical user interface within Windows that runs older non-Metro apps.

desktop computer   A personal computer designed for use on a typical office desktop. A traditional desktop computer system consists of a system unit, monitor, keyboard, mouse, and speakers.

device   A computer file that represents some object—physical or nonphysical—installed on your system.

disk   A device that stores data in magnetic or optical format.

disk drive   A mechanism for retrieving information stored on a magnetic disk. The drive rotates the disk at high speed and reads the data with a magnetic head similar to those used in tape recorders.

domain   The identifying portion of an Internet address. In email addresses, the domain name follows the @ sign; in website addresses, the domain name follows the www.

download   A way to transfer files, graphics, or other information from the Internet to your computer.

driver   A support file that tells a program how to interact with a specific hardware device, such as a hard disk controller or video display card.

DSL (digital subscriber line)   A high-speed Internet connection that uses the ultra-high frequency portion of ordinary telephone lines, allowing users to send and receive voice and data on the same line at the same time.

DVD   An optical disc, similar to a CD, that can hold a minimum of 4.7GB, enough for a full-length movie.

E

email   Electronic mail; a means of corresponding with other computer users over the Internet through digital messages.

encryption   A method of encoding files so only the recipient can read the information.

Ethernet   A popular computer networking technology; Ethernet is used to network, or hook together, computers so that they can share information.

executable file   A program you run on your computer system.

F

favorite   A bookmarked site in Internet Explorer.

file   Any group of data treated as a single entity by the computer, such as a word processor document, a program, or a database.

File Explorer   The utility used to navigate and display files and folders on your computer system. Previously known as Windows Explorer.

FiOS   A type of broadband Internet service delivered over fiber-optic cable.

firewall   Computer hardware or software with special security features to safeguard a computer connected to a network or to the Internet.

FireWire   A high-speed bus used to connect digital devices, such as digital cameras and video cameras, to a computer system. Also known as *i.LINK* and *IEEE-1394*.

folder   A way to group files on a disk; each folder can contain multiple files or other folders (called *subfolders*). Folders are sometimes called *directories*.

freeware   Free software available over the Internet. This is in contrast with *shareware*, which is available freely but usually asks the user to send payment for using the software.

G

gigabyte (GB)   One billion bytes.

graphics   Pictures, photographs, and clip art.

H

hard disk   A sealed cartridge containing a magnetic storage disk(s) designed for long-term mass storage of computer data.

hardware   The physical equipment, as opposed to the programs and procedures, used in computing.

home page   The first or main page of a website.

HomeGroup   A small network of computers all running Windows.

hover   See *mouse over.*

hybrid computer   A portable computer that combines the functionality of a touchscreen tablet and traditional notebook PC.

hyperlink   A connection between two tagged elements in a web page, or separate sites, that makes it possible to click from one to the other.

I–J

icon   A graphic symbol on the display screen that represents a file, peripheral, or some other object or function.

instant messaging   Text-based, real-time, one-on-one communication over the Internet.

Internet   The global network of networks that connects millions of computers and other devices around the world.

Internet service provider (ISP)   A company that provides end-user access to the Internet via its central computers and local access lines.

K–L

keyboard   The typewriter-like device used to type instructions to a personal computer.

kilobyte (KB)   A unit of measure for data storage or transmission equivalent to 1024 bytes; often rounded to 1000.

LAN (local-area network)   A system that enables users to connect PCs to one another or to minicomputers or mainframes.

laptop   A portable computer small enough to operate on one's lap. Also known as a *notebook* computer.

LCD (liquid crystal display)   A flat-screen display where images are created by light transmitted through a layer of liquid crystals.

M–N

megabyte (MB)   One million bytes.

megahertz (MHz)   A measure of microprocessing speed; 1MHz equals one million electrical cycles per second.

memory   Temporary electronic storage for data and instructions, via electronic impulses on a chip.

microprocessor   A complete central processing unit assembled on a single silicon chip.

modem (modulator demodulator)   A device capable of converting a digital signal into an analog signal, which can be transmitted via a telephone line, reconverted, and then "read" by another computer.

Modern   The flat, tiled graphical user interface used in Windows 8 and 8.1. Previously known as the Metro interface.

monitor   The display device on a computer, similar to a television screen.

motherboard   Typically the largest printed circuit board in a computer, housing the CPU chip and controlling circuitry.

mouse   A small handheld input device connected to a computer and featuring one or more button-style switches. When moved around on a flat surface, the mouse causes a symbol on the computer screen to make corresponding movements.

mouse over   The act of selecting an item by placing your cursor over an icon without clicking. Also known as *hovering*.

network   An interconnected group of computers.

notebook computer   A portable computer with all components (including keyboard, screen, and touchpad) contained in a single unit. Notebook PCs can typically be operated via either battery or wall power.

O-P

operating system   A sequence of programming codes that instructs a computer about its various parts and peripherals and how to operate them. Operating systems, such as Windows, deal only with the workings of the hardware and are separate from software programs.

parallel   A type of external port used to connect printers and other similar devices; typically not found on newer PCs.

path   The collection of folders and subfolders (listed in order of hierarchy) that hold a particular file.

peripheral   A device connected to the computer that provides communication or auxiliary functions.

phishing   The act of trying to "fish" for personal information via means of a deliberately deceptive email or website.

pixel   The individual picture elements that combine to create a video image.

Plug and Play (PnP)   Hardware that includes its manufacturer and model information in its ROM, enabling Windows to recognize it immediately upon startup and install the necessary drivers if not already set up.

port   An interface on a computer to which you can connect a device, either internally or externally.

printer   The piece of computer hardware that creates hard copy printouts of documents.

Q-R

RAM (random-access memory)   A temporary storage space in which data can be held on a chip rather than being stored on disk or tape. The contents of RAM can be accessed or altered at any time during a session but will be lost when the computer is turned off.

resolution   The degree of clarity an image displays, typically expressed by the number of horizontal and vertical pixels or the number of dots per inch (dpi).

ribbon   A toolbar-like collection of action buttons, used in many newer Windows programs.

ROM (read-only memory)   A type of chip memory, the contents of which have been permanently recorded in a computer by the manufacturer and cannot be altered by the user.

root   The main directory or folder on a disk.

router   A piece of hardware or software that handles the connection between your home network and the Internet.

S

scanner   A device that converts paper documents or photos into a format that can be viewed on a computer and manipulated by the user.

screensaver   A display of moving designs on your computer screen when you haven't typed or moved the mouse for a while.

serial   A type of external port used to connect communication devices; typically not found on newer PCs.

server   The central computer in a network, providing a service or data access to client computers on the network.

shareware   A software program distributed on the honor system; providers make their programs freely accessible over the Internet, with the understanding that those who use them will send payment to the provider after using them. See also *freeware*.

snaps   The actions that enable you to maximize and "snap" windows to either side of the screen.

software   The programs and procedures, as opposed to the physical equipment, used in computing.

spam   Junk email. As a verb, it means to send thousands of copies of a junk email message.

spreadsheet   A program that performs mathematical operations on numbers arranged in large arrays; used mainly for accounting and other record keeping.

spyware   Software used to surreptitiously monitor computer use (that is, spy on other users).

system unit   The part of a desktop computer system that looks like a big beige or black box. The system unit typically contains the microprocessor, system memory, hard disk drive, floppy disk drives, and various cards.

T-U-V

tablet computer   A small, handheld computer with no keyboard or mouse, operated solely via its touchscreen display.

terabyte (TB)   One trillion bytes.

touchscreen display   A computer display that is touch sensitive and can be operated with a touch of the finger.

trackpad   The pointing device used on most notebook PCs, in lieu of an external mouse.

ultrabook   A type of small and thin notebook computer with no built-in CD/DVD drive and a smaller display.

upgrade   To add a new or improved peripheral or part to your system hardware. Also to install a newer version of an existing piece of software.

upload   The act of copying a file from a personal computer to a website or Internet server. The opposite of *download*.

URL (uniform resource locator)   The address that identifies a web page to a browser. Also known as a *web address*.

USB (universal serial bus)   An external bus standard that supports data transfer rates of up to 4.8Gbps; an individual computer can connect up to 127 peripheral devices via USB.

virus   A computer program segment or string of code that can attach itself to another program or file, reproduce itself, and spread from one computer to another. Viruses can destroy or change data and in other ways sabotage computer systems.

W-X-Y-Z

web page   An HTML file, containing text, graphics, and/or mini-applications, viewed with a web browser.

website   An organized, linked collection of web pages stored on an Internet server and read using a web browser. The opening page of a site is called a *home page*.

WiFi   The radio frequency (RF)-based technology used for home and small business wireless networks and for most public wireless Internet connections. It operates at 11Mbps (802.11b), 54Mbps (802.11g), or 600Mbps (802.11n). Short for wireless fidelity.

window   A portion of the screen display used to view simultaneously a different part of the file in use or a part of a different file than the one in use.

Windows   The generic name for all versions of Microsoft's graphical operating system.

Windows Explorer   See *File Explorer*.

Windows Store   Microsoft's online store that offers Windows 8/8.1-specific apps for sale and download.

World Wide Web (WWW)   A vast network of information, particularly business, commercial, and government resources, that uses a hypertext system for quickly transmitting graphics, sound, and video over the Internet.

Zip file   A file that has been compressed for easier transmission.

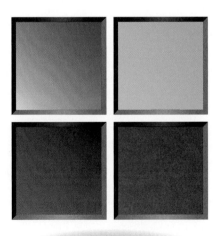

Index

Symbols

\# (hash) character, 182

A

accepting Facebook friend requests, 179

accessing
    HomeGroup computers, 38
    wireless network computers, 39

accounts
    adding to Mail app, 168-169
    Apple accounts, creating, 225
    user accounts
        configuring, 74-76
        logging out, 77
        switching between, 77

Action Center, 244

Ad-Aware, 245

adapters, wireless, 30-32

additional PCs, connecting to home networks, 32-34

Airplane mode, 141

alarms, adding to Lock Screen, 59

Alarms app, 91

all-in-one PCs, 5, 22-23

Amazon.com, 158

anti-malware software, 245

AOL Mail, 172

Apple accounts, creating, 225

Apple Safari, 148

applications. *See* apps

apps, 78
    adding to Lock Screen, 58-59
    Alarms, 91
    Apps screen, 83

Bing Food & Drink, 93
Bing Health & Fitness, 93
Calculator, 91
Calendar, 91
closing, 81
Finance, 92
finding in Windows Store, 94-95
Hulu Plus, 206-209
launching, 80
Mail. *See* Mail app
Maps, 90
Netflix, 202-205
News, 92
People, 170-171
    posting updates from, 199
    viewing social activity from, 198
Photos
    editing photos, 236-241
    navigating, 231
    transferring photos from memory cards, 232-233
    transferring photos with USB connections, 232
    viewing photos, 234-235
pinning to taskbar, 100
pricing, 95
searching for, 84
SkyDrive. *See* SkyDrive
snapping two apps side by side, 88-89
Sports, 92
on Start screen, 79, 85
switching between, 86-87
Travel, 93
trial versions, 95
unused programs, deleting, 247
updating, 94
Video, 201
viewing all, 82
Weather, 90
Word. *See* Word (Microsoft)

Xbox Music
    downloading music, 220-221
    navigating, 217
    playing music, 218-219
    streaming music, 222-223
Xbox Video
    downloading movies, 212-213
    watching movies, 214-215
Yahoo! Mail, 172-175

Apps button, 47

Apps screen, 83

arrow keys, 47

attachments (email), 167

audio systems, connecting, 19

Auto Fix option (Photos app), 237

Autofill option (iTunes), 229

AVG Anti-Virus, 245

B

backgrounds
    changing, 101
    displaying on Start screen, 68-69

backing up files, 248-249

Bcc (blind carbon copies), 166, 174

Bing, 155

Bing Food & Drink app, 93

Bing Health & Fitness app, 93

Bing Maps, 90

black-and-white printers, 15

blind carbon copies (Bcc), 166, 174

bloatware, 247

blogs, 196

Blu-ray drives, 13

booting computers, 24-25

Brightness control (Photos app), 240

broadband routers, 30

Browse button, 55

browsers
    Apple Safari, 148
    Google Chrome, 148
    Internet Explorer. See Internet Explorer
    Mozilla Firefox, 148

browsing
    help topics, 51
    web, 142, 148-149
        Bing searches, 155
        Google searches, 154
        opening multiple pages, 144, 150
        private browsing, 143
        returning to favorite pages, 147, 153
        saving favorite pages, 146, 152
        shopping online, 158-159
        Smart Searches, 156-157
        switching between tabs, 145, 151

burning CDs, 227

buttons
    Apps, 47
    Browse, 55
    Choose Picture, 55
    Maximize, 104
    Minimize, 104
    Restore Down, 104
    Start, 46, 99
    Zoom (-), 62

buying. See purchasing

C

cables (power), connecting, 18

Calculator app, 91

Calendar app, 91

carbon copies (Cc), 166, 174

cards (video), 14

cathode ray tube (CRT) monitors, 14

Cc (carbon copies), 166, 174

CD drives, 13

CDs
    burning, 227
    playing, 226
    ripping, 227

changing. See personalization

charms, 48

charms bar, 48-49

Choose Picture button, 55

Chrome, 148

clicking mouse, 42-43

closing
  apps, 81
  tabs, 145, 151
  windows, 104
cloud storage, 136. *See also* SkyDrive
Color Enhance control (Photos app), 241
color printers, 15
color schemes, changing, 66-67, 102
commenting on Facebook photos, 187
composing email
  in Windows Mail app, 166-167
  in Yahoo! Mail app, 174
compressed folders, extracting files from, 135
compressing files, 134
computer system setup, 16
  all-in-one PCs, 5, 22-23
  audio systems, 19
  CD and DVD drives, 13
  connectors, 8
  desktop PCs, 4, 18-20
  hard disk drives, 9
  hybrid PCs, 7
  keyboards, 10, 18
  logging on to Windows, 25
  memory card readers, 12
  monitors, 14, 18
  mouse, 11, 18
  notebook PCs, 3, 6, 21
  powering on, 24-25
  printers, 15
  restoring after crashes, 250
  solid-state storage, 9
  system power cables, 18
  tablet PCs, 7
  touchpad, 11
  USB, 27
  video cards, 14
  Windows 8 Lock Screen, 17
configuring
  user accounts, 74-76
  Windows 8 settings, 72-73
connecting, 16
  additional PCs to home networks, 32-34
  all-in-one PCs, 22-23
  audio systems, 19
  desktop PCs, 18-20
  to Internet
    with mobile broadband, 141
    with WiFi hotspots, 140-141
  iPods to PCs, 229
  logging on to Windows, 25
  monitors, 18
  mouse and keyboard, 18
  new devices to computer systems, 27
  notebook PCs, 21
  powering on, 24-25
  system power cables, 18
  Windows 8 Lock Screen, 17
connectors, 4, 8
contacts, managing from People app, 170-171
Control Panel, 73, 244
convertible PCs, 7
Copy command (Word Edit menu), 115
Copy Items dialog box, 128
copying
  files/folders, 128, 137
  text, 115
cost of apps, 95
crashes, restoring computers after, 250-251
creating
  Apple accounts, 225
  folders, 126
cropping photos, 238
CRT (cathode ray tube) monitors, 14
cursor, 11
customization. *See* personalization
Cut command (Word Edit menu), 115
cutting
  SkyDrive files, 137
  text, 115

D

Delete Multiple Items dialog box, 133
deleted files, restoring, 132
deleting
  files, 131
  folders, 131
  Start screen tiles, 64
  unnecessary files, 246
  unused programs, 247
desktop. *See also* Start screen
  background
    changing, 101
    displaying on Start screen, 68-69

color schemes, 102
  overview, 97
  themes, 102
  traditional desktop, displaying, 98
desktop app (Word), launching, 112
desktop PCs, 4, 18-20
desktop replacement notebooks, 6
devices, adding to computer systems, 27
dialog boxes
  Copy Items, 128
  Delete Multiple Items, 133
  Extract Compressed (Zipped) Folders, 135
  Move Items, 129
digital music. *See* music
digital photos. *See* photos
Digital Video Interface (DVI), 18
disabling
  live tiles (Start screen), 61
  slide shows, 57
displaying. *See also* viewing
  apps, 82
  charms bar, 48-49
  files, 124
displays. *See* monitors
documents (Word)
  creating, 114
  definition of, 114
  keyboard shortcuts, 115
  naming, 118
  paragraph formatting, 117
  printing, 119
  saving, 118
  text editing, 115
  text entry, 114
  text formatting, 116
double-clicking mouse, 42
downloading
  iTunes, 224
  music
    from iTunes Store, 224-225
    with Xbox Music app, 220-221
  photos from Facebook, 187
  SkyDrive files, 137
  video, 212-213
  Yahoo! Mail app, 172
draft messages, 164
dragging and dropping, 43

drives
  CD and DVD drives, 13
  hard disk drives, 9
DVD drives, 13
DVI (Digital Video Interface), 18

E

Edit menu commands (Word)
  Copy, 115
  Cut, 115
  Paste, 115
editing
  photos, 236-241
  Word documents, 115
Effects (Photos app), 241
email, 160
  Post Office Protocol (POP) email, 173
  Windows Mail app
    adding accounts, 161, 168-169
    composing messages, 166-167, 174
    draft messages, 164
    email attachments, 167
    flagging messages, 164
    formatting messages, 166
    moving messages, 164
    reading messages, 162-163, 172
    replying to messages, 165, 173
    viewing Inbox, 162-163, 172
  Yahoo! Mail app, 172-175
emptying Recycle Bin, 133
extensions, 127
external mouse, 11
external peripherals, 6, 21
external speakers, 23
Extract Compressed (Zipped) Folders dialog box, 135
extracting files from compressed folders, 135

F

Facebook
  commenting on photos, 187
  compared to Pinterest and Twitter, 177
  finding friends on, 178-179
  hiding status updates, 185
  liking photos, 187
  personalizing your Timelines, 185
  posting status updates, 182-183
  reading News Feed, 180-181

sharing status updates, 181

uploading photos, 188-189

viewing friends' photos, 186-187

viewing friends' Timelines, 184

favorite web pages

returning to, 147, 153

saving, 146, 152

Favorites folder, 123

File Explorer, 121

file extensions, 127

File History, 248-249

files, 120

backing up, 248-249

compressing, 134

copying, 128

deleting, 131

displaying, 124

extensions, 127

extracting from compressed folders, 135

File Explorer, 121

files, 134

moving, 129

renaming, 127

restoring deleted files, 132

searching for, 130

SkyDrive files, 136-137

sorting, 125

unnecessary files, deleting, 246

Finance app, 92

finding

apps

in Windows Store, 94-95

on your computer, 84

Facebook friends, 178-179

files, 130

pins on Pinterest, 192-193

WiFi signals, 140

Firefox, 148

flagging email messages, 164

flash memory cards, transferring pictures from, 232-233

folders, 120

compressed folders, extracting files from, 135

copying, 128

creating, 126

deleting, 131

displaying files, 124

File Explorer, 121

moving, 129

navigating, 122-123

Public, 39

Recycle Bin

emptying, 133

restoring files from, 132

renaming, 127

sorting, 125

This PC, 123

following

Pinterest boards, 191

Twitter users, 197

Food & Drink app, 93

formats (memory card), 12

formatting

email in Mail app, 166

hard disk drives, 9

Word documents

paragraph formatting, 117

text formatting, 116

friends (Facebook), finding, 178-179

G

Gmail, 172

Google, 154

Google Chrome, 148

Google Gmail, 172

grouping tiles on Start screen, 62

H

hard disk drives, 9

hardware

adding to computer systems, 27

all-in-one PCs, 5

CD and DVD drives, 13

connectors, 8

desktop PCs, 4

hard disk drives, 9

hybrid PCs, 7

keyboards, 10

memory card readers, 12

monitors, 14

mouse, 11

notebook PCs, 3, 6

printers, 15

solid-state storage, 9

tablet PCs, 7

touchpad, 11

video cards, 14

hashtags, 182

HDMI connections, 8, 18

Health & Fitness app, 93

help
    ToolTips, 42
    Windows 8 help, 50-51

Help and Support window, 51

hiding Facebook status updates, 185

Highlights control (Photos app), 240

home networks (wireless), 28
    accessing computers in, 39
    additional PCs, connecting, 32-34
    broadband routers, 30
    HomeGroups
        accessing computers in, 38
        adding computers to, 35-37
    how they work, 29
    main PC, setting up, 30-31
    security, 31, 34
    wireless adapters, 30-32
    wireless routers, 30

home pages, 138, 148

HomeGroups
    accessing computers in, 38
    adding computers to, 35-37

hotspots (WiFi)
    connecting to, 140-141
    definition of, 140

hovering, 42

Hulu Plus, 206-209

hybrid PCs, 7

hyperlinks, 149

I

icons, 107

IE. See Internet Explorer

illegal characters, 126

images
    icons, 107
    photos. See photos
    sharing with Pinterest, 190
        finding and repinning interesting pins, 192-193
        finding people to follow, 191
        pinning from web pages, 194-195

Inbox, viewing
    in Windows Mail app, 162-163
    in Yahoo! Mail app, 172

inkjet printers, 15

InPrivate browsing, 143

insertion points (Word), 114

Instant Search, 130

Internet connections
    with mobile broadband, 141
    with WiFi hotspots, 140-141

Internet Explorer
    Bing searches, 155
    Google searches, 154
    InPrivate browsing, 143
    opening multiple pages, 144, 150
    returning to favorite pages, 147, 153
    saving favorite pages, 146, 152
    shopping online, 158-159
    Smart Searches, 156-157
    switching between tabs, 145, 151
    web browsing with, 142, 148-149

Internet WiFi hotspots
    connecting to, 140-141
    definition of, 140

iPods, connecting to PCs, 229

iTunes
    CDs
        playing, 226
        ripping, 227
    downloading, 224
    music
        downloading, 224-225
        playing, 228

K

Kaspersky Anti-Virus, 245

keyboards, 10
    connecting, 18
    keyboard shortcuts
        renaming files, 127
        Word, 115
    scrolling with, 47

L

laptops. *See* notebook PCs

laser printers, 15

launching
    apps, 80
    Word desktop app, 112
    Word Web App, 110-111

LCD monitors, 14

left arrow key, 47

lighting controls (Photos app), 240

liking Facebook photos, 187

live information on Lock Screen, 59

live tiles (Start screen), 61

local accounts, 74-76

Lock Screen, 17, 25, 53
    alarms, displaying, 59
    apps, adding, 58-59
    picture
        changing, 54-55
        setting, 235
    slide show, displaying, 56-57

logging into accounts, 75

logging out of user accounts, 77

M

Mail app, 161
    adding accounts, 168-169
    composing messages, 166-167, 174
    draft messages, 164
    email attachments, 167
    flagging messages, 164
    formatting messages, 166
    moving messages, 164
    reading messages
        in Windows Mail app, 162-163
        in Yahoo! Mail app, 172
    replying to messages, 165, 173
    viewing Inbox, 162-163, 172

maintenance
    computer systems, restoring after crashes, 250
    deleting unnecessary files, 246
    deleting unused programs, 247

malware, preventing with Windows Defender, 245

managing contacts, 170-171

Maps app, 90

Maximize button, 104

maximizing windows, 104

McAfee VirusScan AntiVirus Plus, 245

memory cards
    memory card readers, 12
    transferring pictures from, 232-233

menu bars, 106

menus, 106
    Quick Access menu, 100

messages (email)
    composing
        in Windows Mail app, 166-167
        in Yahoo! Mail app, 174
    drafts, 164
    email attachments, 167
    flagging, 164
    formatting, 166
    moving, 164
    reading
        in Windows Mail app, 162-163
        in Yahoo! Mail app, 172
    replying to
        in Windows Mail app, 165
        in Yahoo! Mail app, 173

Metro interface, 40

microblogging, 196

Microsoft Accounts, 74-75

Microsoft Office Suite editions, 112

Microsoft Support website, 51

Microsoft website, 50

Microsoft Word, 108
    desktop app, launching, 112
    documents
        creating, 114
        naming, 118
        printing, 119
        saving, 118
    keyboard shortcuts, 115
    paragraph formatting, 117
    text editing, 115
    text entry, 114
    text formatting, 116
    versions of, 109
    Word Web App
        launching, 110-111
        navigating, 113

Minimize button, 104

minimizing windows, 104

mobile broadband, 141

monitors, 14
  connecting, 18
  notebook PCs, 6
  touchscreen monitors, 5, 14

mouse, 11
  clicking, 42-43
  connecting, 18
  dragging and dropping, 43
  mouse over, 42
  pointing and clicking, 42

mouse over, 42

Move Items dialog box, 129

movies
  downloading with Xbox Video app, 212-213
  watching
    on Hulu Plus, 206-209
    on Netflix, 202-205
    with Video app, 201
    with Xbox Video app, 214-215

moving
  email messages, 164
  files, 129
  folders, 129
  insertion point, 114

Mozilla Firefox, 148

multifunction printers, 15

multiple web pages, opening, 144, 150

music, 216
  CDs
    burning, 227
    playing, 226
    ripping, 227
  downloading
    from iTunes Store, 224-225
    with Xbox Music app, 220-221
  iPods, connecting to PCs, 229
  playing
    with iTunes, 228
    with radio stations, 223
    with Windows Media Player, 218
    with Xbox Music app, 218-219
  purchasing
    from iTunes Store, 224-225
    with Xbox Music app, 220-221
  streaming, 222-223
  Xbox Music app
    downloading music, 220-221
    navigating, 217

    playing music, 218-219
    streaming music, 222-223

My Computer folder. See File Explorer

My Documents folder. See File Explorer

N

naming
  files, 127
  folders, 127
  groups of tiles, 63
  illegal characters, 126
  Word documents, 118

navigating
  folders, 122-123
  Photos app, 231
  Start screen, 46-47
  Word Web App, 113
  Xbox Music app, 217

Navigation pane, 123

netbooks, 6

Netflix, 202-205

networks (wireless home networks), 28
  accessing computers in, 39
  additional PCs, connecting, 32-34
  broadband routers, 30
  HomeGroups
    accessing computers in, 38
    adding computers to, 35-37
  how they work, 29
  main PC, setting up, 30-31
  security, 31, 34
  wireless adapters, 30-32
  wireless routers, 30

News app, 92

News Feed (Facebook), reading, 180-181

Norton AntiVirus, 245

notebook mouse, 11

notebook PCs, 3, 6, 21

notification panel, 49

O

Office Web Apps, 110

one-button wireless setup, 34

online accounts, 74

online shopping, 158-159

opening multiple web pages, 144, 150

operating systems, 40

organizing
    Start screen tiles, 62
    windows, 105

Outlook.com, 172

Overstock.com, 158

P

PageDown key, 47

PageUp key, 47

Paragraph dialog box (Word), 117

paragraph formatting in Word documents, 117

Paste command (Word Edit menu), 115

PDF viewers, 119

People app, 170-171
    posting updates from, 199
    viewing social activity from, 198

peripherals, 4-6, 21

personalization
    desktop
        background, 101
        color schemes, 102
        themes, 102
    Facebook Timeline, 185
    Lock Screen, 53
        adding apps, 58-59
        changing picture, 54-55
        displaying alarms, 59
        displaying slide show, 56-57
    profile pictures, 70-71
    Start screen
        adding tiles, 65
        changing color schemes, 66-67
        deleting tiles, 64
        displaying desktop background, 68-69
        naming groups of tiles, 63
        organizing into groups, 62
        rearranging tiles, 60
        resizing tiles, 61
    user accounts
        configuring, 74-76
        logging out, 77
        switching between, 77
    Windows 8 settings, 72-73

photos, 230
    editing in Windows, 236-241
    Facebook photos
        commenting on, 187
        liking, 187
        uploading, 188-189
        viewing friends' photos, 186-187
    on Lock Screen
        changing, 54-55
        slide shows, 56-57
    navigating, 231
    setting for Lock screen, 235
    sharing with Pinterest, 190
        finding and repinning interesting pins, 192-193
        finding people to follow, 191
        pinning from web pages, 194-195
    transferring
        from memory cards, 232-233
        with USB connections, 232
    viewing in Windows, 234-235

Photos app
    editing photos, 236-241
    navigating, 231
    transferring photos
        from memory cards, 232-233
        with USB connections, 232
    viewing photos, 234-235

pictures. See photos

pinning apps
    to Start screen, 65, 85
    to taskbar, 100

pins (Pinterest)
    finding and repinning, 192-193
    pinning from web pages, 194-195

Pinterest, 190
    compared to Facebook and Twitter, 177
    finding and repinning interesting pins, 192-193
    finding people to follow, 191
    pinning from web pages, 194-195

playing
    music
        CDs, 226-227
        with iTunes, 228
        radio stations, 223
        with Windows Media Player, 218
        with Xbox Music app, 218-219

video
on Hulu Plus, 206-209
on Netflix, 202-205
on YouTube, 210-211
with Video app, 201
with Xbox Video app, 214-215
playlists, 210, 228
pointing and clicking mouse, 42
POP (Post Office Protocol) email, 173
pop-up menus, 43
ports, 4, 8
Post Office Protocol (POP) email, 173
posting Facebook updates, 182-183, 199
power cables, connecting, 18
power surges, 20
powering on, 24-25
preventive maintenance
computer systems, restoring after crashes, 250
deleting unnecessary files, 246
deleting unused programs, 247
pricing for apps, 95
printers, 15
printing Word documents, 119
private web browsing, 143
profile pictures, changing, 70-71
protecting computers
Action Center, 244
backups, 248-249
Control Panel, 244
PC settings, 243
preventive maintenance
deleting unnecessary files, 246
deleting unused programs, 247
System Restore, 250-251
Windows Defender, 245
Public folder, 39
purchasing
music
from iTunes Store, 224-225
with Xbox Music app, 220-221
video, 212-213

Q-R

Quick Access menu, 100

radio stations, listening to, 223
reading
email messages
in Windows Mail app, 162-163
in Yahoo! Mail app, 172
Facebook News Feed, 180-181
rearranging Start screen tiles, 60
rebooting, 24
Recycle Bin
emptying, 133
restoring files from, 132
red eye, removing, 239
rejecting Facebook friend requests, 179
removing. *See also* deleting
apps from Start screen, 85
red eye, 239
renaming
files, 127
folders, 127
SkyDrive files, 137
repeating music in iTunes, 228
repinning pins on Pinterest, 192-193
replying to email
in Windows Mail app, 165
in Yahoo! Mail app, 173
resetting system, 251
resizing Start screen tiles, 61
responding to email
in Windows Mail app, 165
in Yahoo! Mail app, 173
Restore Down button, 104
restoring
computers after crashes, 250
files, 132
system, 250-251
windows, 104
retouching photos, 239
returning
to favorite web pages, 147, 153
to Start screen, 99

retweeting, 198

ribbons, 107, 113

right arrow key, 47

right-clicking mouse, 43

ripping CDs, 227

rotating photos, 238

routers, 30

S

Safari, 148

Saturation control (Photos app), 241

saving
  favorite web pages, 146, 152
  Word documents, 118

screens. See monitors

scrolling
  Start screen, 47
  windows, 103

scrollwheels, 11

searching
  for apps
    in Windows Store, 94-95
    on your computer, 84
  for Facebook friends, 178-179
  for files, 130
  web
    Bing searches, 155
    Google searches, 154
    Smart Searches, 156-157

security
  Action Center, 244
  backups, 248-249
  Control Panel, 244
  online shopping, 159
  PC settings, 243
  preventive maintenance
    deleting unnecessary files, 246
    deleting unused programs, 247
  System Restore, 250-251
  Windows Defender, 245
  wireless home networks, 31, 34

setting up computer systems, 16
  all-in-one PCs, 5, 22-23
  audio systems, 19
  CD and DVD drives, 13
  connectors, 8
  desktop PCs, 4, 18-20

hard disk drives, 9

hybrid PCs, 7

keyboards, 10, 18

logging on to Windows, 25

memory card readers, 12

monitors, 14, 18

mouse, 11, 18

notebook PCs, 3, 6, 21

powering on, 24-25

system power cables, 18

printers, 15

restoring after crashes, 250

solid-state storage, 9

tablet PCs, 7

touchpad, 11

USB, 27

video cards, 14

Windows 8 Lock Screen, 17

Shadows control (Photos app), 240

sharing
  Facebook status updates, 181
  photos on Facebook, 188-189
  YouTube videos, 211

shopping online, 158-159

shuffling music in iTunes, 228

shutting down, 26

SkyDrive
  browsing photos on, 71
  files
    copying, 137
    cutting, 137
    downloading, 137
    renaming, 137
    viewing, 136-137
  storage space, 137

SkyDrive app, 110

Sleep mode, 26

slide shows
  displaying on Lock Screen, 56-57
  turning off, 57

Smart Searches, 156-157

snapping
  apps side by side, 88-89
  windows, 105

social media
  comparison of, 177
  Facebook
    commenting on photos, 187
    finding friends on, 178-179

hiding status updates, 185
liking photos, 187
personalizing your Timelines, 185
posting status updates, 182-183
reading News Feed, 180-181
sharing status updates, 181
uploading photos, 188-189
viewing friends' photos, 186-187
viewing friends' Timelines, 184
People app
posting updates from, 199
viewing social activity from, 198
Pinterest, 190
finding and repinning interesting pins, 192-193
finding people to follow, 191
pinning from web pages, 194-195
safety issues, 182
Twitter, 196-197
solid-state storage, 9
sorting files/folders, 125
sound systems, connecting, 19
speakers
connecting, 19
external speakers, 23
special characters in filenames, 126
spell checking in Microsoft Word, 117
Sports app, 92
Spybot Search & Destroy, 245
Start button, 46, 99
Start screen, 41
apps on, 79
color schemes, 66-67
desktop background, 68-69
navigating, 46-47
pinning apps to, 85
removing apps from, 85
returning to, 99
scrolling, 47
tiles
adding, 65
deleting, 64
naming groups of tiles, 63
organizing into groups, 62
rearranging, 60
resizing, 61
starting. See launching

status updates (Facebook)
hiding, 185
posting, 182-183
sharing, 181
storage, solid-state, 9
streaming music, 222-223
surfing the web. See web surfing
surge suppressors, 20
swiping touchscreen, 45
switching
between apps, 86-87
between browsers tabs, 145, 151
between user accounts, 77
to local accounts, 76
syncing iPods, 229
system power cables, connecting, 18
System Restore, 250-251
system unit, 4

T

tablet PCs, 7
tapping touchscreen, 44
Target, 158
taskbar, pinning apps to, 100
Temperature control (Photos app), 241
text in Word documents
editing, 115
entering, 114
formatting, 116
themes, 102
This PC folder, 123
tiles (Start screen)
adding, 65
deleting, 64
naming groups of, 63
organizing into groups, 62
rearranging, 60
resizing, 61
Timeline (Facebook)
personalizing, 185
viewing, 184
toolbars, 107
ToolTips, 42
Top Stories (Facebook), 180
touchpad, 11

touchscreen displays, 5, 14, 45
  scrolling, 45
  scrolling with, 47
  swiping, 45
  switching between apps, 87
  tapping, 44
  zooming in, 45
  zooming out, 45
traditional desktop, displaying, 98
transferring photos
  from memory cards, 232-233
  with USB connections, 232
Travel app, 93
trial versions of apps, 95
turning off
  live tiles, 61
  slide shows, 57
turning on computer systems, 24-25
TV shows, watching on Hulu Plus, 206-209
tweeting, 196-197
Twitter, 196
  compared to Facebook and Pinterest, 177
  following users, 197

U

ultrabooks, 6
unnecessary files, deleting, 246
unused programs, deleting, 247
updating apps, 94
uploading
  photos to Facebook, 188-189
  video to YouTube, 211
USB connections, 8, 27
  transferring pictures with, 232
user accounts
  configuring, 74-76
  logging out, 77
  profile pictures, 70-71
  switching between, 77
user interfaces, 40

V

video
  downloading with Xbox Video app, 212-213
  uploading to YouTube, 211

watching
  on Hulu Plus, 206-209
  on Netflix, 202-205
  on YouTube, 210-211
  with Video app, 201
  with Xbox Video app, 214-215
Video app, 201
video cards, 14
viewing. *See also* displaying
  Facebook Timelines, 184
  friends' Facebook photos, 186-187
  Inbox
    in Windows Mail app, 162-163
    in Yahoo! Mail app, 172
  photos, 234-235
  SkyDrive files, 136-137
  social activity from People app, 198
viruses, preventing with Windows Defender, 245

W

watching video
  on Hulu Plus, 206-209
  on Netflix, 202-205
  on YouTube, 210-211
  with Video app, 201
  with Xbox Video app, 214-215
Weather app, 90
web blogs, 196
web browsers
  Apple Safari, 148
  Google Chrome, 148
  Internet Explorer. *See* Internet Explorer
  Mozilla Firefox, 148
web surfing, 142, 148-149
  Bing searches, 155
  Google searches, 154
  opening multiple pages, 144, 150
  pinning web content to Pinterest, 194-195
  private browsing, 143
  returning to favorite pages, 147, 153
  saving favorite pages, 146, 152
  shopping online, 158-159
  Smart Searches, 156-157
  switching between tabs, 145, 151
webcams, profile pictures with, 70
WiFi hotspots
  connecting to, 140-141
  definition of, 140

Wi-Fi Protected Setup technology, 34

windows
    closing, 104
    maximizing, 104
    minimizing, 104
    restoring, 104
    scrolling, 103
    snapping, 105

Windows 8
    desktop. See desktop
    File Explorer, 121
    help, 50-51
    Lock Screen, 17, 25, 53
        alarms, displaying, 59
        apps, adding, 58-59
        picture, 54-55, 235
        slide show, displaying, 56-57
    logging on to, 25
    settings, configuring, 72-73
    user accounts
        configuring, 74-76
        logging out, 77
        switching between, 77

Windows Action Center, 244

Windows Control Panel, 244

Windows Defender, 245

Windows Explorer. See File Explorer

Windows Favorites, 123

Windows key, 10

Windows Media Player, 218

Windows SkyDrive. See SkyDrive

Windows Store, 94-95

wireless adapters, 30-32

wireless home networks, 28
    accessing computers in, 39
    additional PCs, connecting, 32-34
    HomeGroups
        accessing computers in, 38
        adding computers to, 35-37
    how they work, 29
    main PC, setting up, 30-31
    security, 31, 34
    wireless routers, 30

wireless keyboards, 10

wireless routers, 30

Word (Microsoft), 108
    desktop app, launching, 112
    documents
        creating, 114
        naming, 118
        printing, 119
        saving, 118
    keyboard shortcuts, 115
    paragraph formatting, 117
    text editing, 115
    text entry, 114
    text formatting, 116
    versions of, 109
    Word Web App
        launching, 110-111
        navigating, 113

word processor. See Word

X

Xbox Music app
    downloading music, 220-221
    navigating, 217
    playing music, 218-219
    streaming music, 222-223

Xbox Music Pass service, 222

Xbox Video app
    downloading movies with, 212-213
    watching movies with, 214-215

Y

Yahoo! Mail, 172-175

YouTube
    uploading video to, 211
    watching videos on, 210-211

Z

zip files, 134

Zoom (-) button, 62

zooming in/out, 45

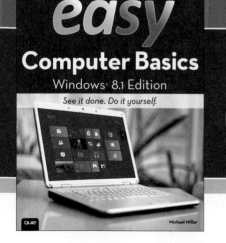

FREE
Online Edition

Safari
Books Online

DISCARD

Your purchase of *Easy Computer Basics, Windows 8.1 Edition* includes access to a free online edition for 45 days through the **Safari Books Online** subscription service. Nearly every Que book is available online through **Safari Books Online**, along with thousands of books and videos from publishers such as Addison-Wesley Professional, Cisco Press, Exam Cram, IBM Press, O'Reilly Media, Prentice Hall, Sams, and VMware Press.

Safari Books Onland access to thousands of technology, digieos from leading publishers. With ited access to learning tools and informatopment, tips and tricks on using your favodesign, and much more.

at

STEP 1:

STEP 2:

ation form.

ion,

Addison Wesley   Adobe   New Riders   O'REILLY

Peachpit Press   PRENTICE HALL   WILEY   wrox